COLLINGWOOD STUDIES
VOLUME 6

COLLINGWOOD STUDIES

Volume Six
1999

Idealist Contexts

Edited by
DAVID BOUCHER
and
BRUCE HADDOCK

R. G. Collingwood
Society

Published by the R. G. Collingwood Society
Registered Charity No. 1037636
Department of Political Theory and Government,
University of Wales, Swansea SA2 8PP

ISSN 1356-0670
ISBN 0 9524393 6 0

British Library Cataloguing in Publication Data.
A catalogue record of this book is available from the British Library.

Printed in Wales, UK, by Dinefwr Press, Llandybïe

THE R. G. COLLINGWOOD SOCIETY

Officers of the Society

COLLINGWOOD STUDIES
VOLUME SIX

TABLE OF CONTENTS

Collingwood's Logic of Question and Answer, its Relation to Absolute Presuppositions: another Brief History[1]

RIK PETERS

University of Groningen, The Netherlands

In *Collingwood Studies* volume five (CS, V) and in his Introduction to the revised edition of *An Essay of Metaphysics*, Professor Martin makes two thought-provoking claims.[2] First, he claims that 'there is no essential connection between fundamental presuppositions and any so-called logic of question and answer' (CS, V, 130). Secondly, he claims that until *An Essay on Metaphysics* was written, Collingwood himself 'did not commit implicitly or explicitly to the notion that there was, let alone that there had to be, such a connection' (CS, V, 130). On the basis of these two claims Martin concludes that for Collingwood, there is only an essential connection between the *term* absolute in the *name* absolute presuppositions and the *logic* of question and answer (CS, V, 130).

In a note Martin specifies these two claims. By *logic* of question and answer he means 'the idea that the truth of a proposition or its very meaning is logically tied to a specific and prior question' (CS, V, 131n6). In Martin's view, the logic of question and answer is dubious in many respects, and not helpful as an explanation of the notion of fundamental presuppositions in *An Essay on Metaphysics* (CS, V, 125). Though he recognizes that the logic provided a 'handy way' for removing truth value from the absolute presuppositions, he points out that it also had the unfortunate effect of removing meaning from them. According to Martin, in the logic of question and answer, only propositions that stand as answers to questions have a meaning. Therefore, absolute presuppositions, defined as presuppositions that never stand as answers to questions, have no meaning in the logic of question and answer (EM, xxii). Being meaningless, Martin remarks, they cannot be supposed or presupposed so that the logic of question and answer is too neat a basis for metaphysical inquiry (EM, xxii-iii).

Martin gives two reasons for his second claim that Collingwood himself did not commit to the notion that there was a connection between the logic of question and answer and fundamental presup-positions. In the first place, he holds that there is no evidence that Collingwood developed a logic of question and answer early in his career; it was not, as Collingwood says in his *Autobiography*, expounded in *Truth and Contradiction* of 1917, nor, as many interpreters hold, in *Speculum Mentis* of 1924 (CS, V, 127-9). Secondly, Martin holds that though Collingwood had dealt with fundamental presuppositions from his early career, the term 'absolute presuppositions' appears only in *An Essay on Metaphysics*. (CS, V, 125).

Martin's two major claims have far-reaching consequences for both Collingwood's reform of metaphysics and for the interpretation of his intellectual development. His first claim makes a large part of Colling-wood's metaphysical project redundant. Henceforth, the metaphysician should dispense with the paraphernalia of the logic of question and answer and deal with the presuppositions directly. In this context, Martin suggests that he should approach the presuppositions as 'recur-ring features of a scientific practice', seeing them not as 'statements' but as 'proto-statements', which are meaningful in spite of the fact that they do not have truth value (EM, xxvii). In short, Martin thus proposes nothing less than a reform of Collingwood's reform of metaphysics.

Martin's second claim throws considerable doubt on the trust-worthiness of Collingwood's *Autobiography* as a *livre de bonne foi*. In fact, he rejects most of what Collingwood had to say on the develop-ment of his logic of question and answer in connection with his clash with his Realist teachers, his archeological practice, and the history of philosophy. Finally, Martin's view that Collingwood stated his *logic* of question and answer only to give the name 'absolute' to absolute presuppositions in *An Essay on Metaphysics* suggests that Collingwood changed his mind on the relation between the logic and presuppositions overnight, and this amounts to a 'conversion-hypothesis' that is even more radical than Knox's or Donagan's.

Martin's proposal for a reform of Collingwood's reform of metaphysics would be most welcome, if both his analysis of the relation between the logic of question and answer and presuppositions on the one hand, and his interpretation of Collingwood's philosophical development on the other, were correct. However, I think that this is not the case.

Martin's first claim is an *argumentum ad consequentiam*; he does not directly challenge the necessary connection between question and answer logic and fundamental presuppositions, but rejects it on the ground that it leads to the not so 'handy' consequence of making the absolute presuppositions meaningless. This view in itself is based on the unwarranted singular assumption that there is only one kind of meaning, namely the meaning of propositions as answers to questions, whereas Collingwood clearly distinguishes many kinds of meaning ranging from the meaning of artistic expressions, to the meaning of presuppositions. This is clearly shown by part III of *An Essay of Metaphysics,* where Collingwood explicitly discusses the meaning of absolute presuppositions like the existence of God, Kant's *a priori* concepts, and the notion of causality. Moreover, in order to make his first claim Martin is required to restrict the notion of Collingwood's *logic* to two 'earmarks': the dependence of meaning and truth on prior questions. However, Collingwood himself attributed many more 'earmarks' to his logic, and, more importantly, also saw a logical connection between them.

Martin's second claim is an argument from silence. From the fact that there is no evidence to prove Collingwood's claim that he developed his logic of question and answer early in his career, he concludes that he did not have such a logic completed. This argument might be valid if Martin had weighed all the evidence for and against Collingwood's claims, but in fact he only considers some minor evidence against.

In this paper I will follow an alternative route and consider what evidence there is for Collingwood's claims in his *Autobiography*. On the basis of a chronological review of his published and unpublished works I will show that most of his claims concerning the development of his logic of question and answer early in his career can be corroborated, or else reconstructed on the basis of factual circumstantial evidence. Since I do not believe that this would cut Martin's claims off at the root, as he himself maintains (CS, V, 126), I will also show that Collingwood always saw a close connection between his logic of question and answer and fundamental presuppositions.

AN AUTOBIOGRAPHY

Collingwood's own account of the development of his logic of question and answer in his *Autobiography* is straightforward and to the point. He states that he is not writing a treatise on logic, but an autobiography, so that brevity is his first aim (A, 31). For this reason, he does not go deeply into the relation between his own logic and other contemporary logics. Basically, he presents his logic as a further elaboration of the insights of Bacon, Descartes and Kant, which he developed with the help of 'others' (A, 37). In spite of these strictures, Collingwood's account is detailed enough to form a clear picture of the development of his logic of question and answer. He remarks that already as a young boy he saw 'that the only way to tackle any historical question, such as the tactics of Trafalgar, was to see what the different people concerned were *trying* to do' (A, 58). The word 'trying' is central here; it indicates that he took purposeful action in terms of trial and error, or attempts and failures, as the key to understand human action. In archeology, where a Baconian revolution was well under way, Collingwood further developed this habit, and learned that all knowledge consists of two halves: questions and answers (A, 26). It was this basic insight that caused his first vague feelings of dissatisfaction with the positive doctrines and critical methods of his Realist teachers around 1910, when he began to read philosophy. In their positive doctrines, the Realists tended to pass over the questioning activity in knowledge; to know something meant for them to 'apprehend' an object (A, 25-6). In their critical methods the Realists also passed over the questioning activity. They refuted Idealism without taking pains to retrieve the questions Idealists were addressing, and they tended to see the history of philosophy as a series of solutions to eternal problems (A, 22, 27, 59). However, out of a 'diffidence of youth', Collingwood did not venture to reject the teachings of his masters because he did not see a connection between their positive doctrines and their critical methods (A, 22-3). Meanwhile, after taking his degree in 1912, Collingwood undertook a 'flank attack', consisting of two 'lines' (A, 28). First, he learned how to test epistemological doctrines in his archeological 'laboratory', and in his teaching he stressed that one must first find out what a philosopher says and means, before passing judgement on the truth of his doctrines (A, 24, 27). However, in spite of this flank attack Collingwood could not throw off his diffidence of youth until the first World War. This happened around 1916, when he began to meditate on the ugliness of the Albert Memorial on his daily walks to the Admiralty Intelligence Division, where he was serving (A, 29). These meditations enabled him to elaborate his logic of question and answer completely, and in his spare time he wrote 'all this' down in a book *Truth and Contradiction*, which he offered to Macmillan in 1917. In spite of Henry Jones's positive reader's report, this book was not published, because the times were hopelessly bad for such books (A, 42).

Let me try to flesh this out a little bit. The first thing that must be stressed is that Collingwood does not claim any originality for his logic. Despite his battle cry 'In logic I am a revolutionary' (A, 52), he does not fail to mention the 'founding fathers' of that revolution, nor his 'fellow revolutionaries'. Among the first are Plato, Descartes, Bacon and Kant. Collingwood was consistent in this; we find the same names in *Speculum Mentis* and in *The Principles of History*, where he adds Socrates to the list (A, 35, 37; SM, 77; PH, 29). Among Collingwood's fellow revolutionaries were the British Idealists, whose logic was in his view partly a logic of question and answer (A, 52).[3] But the British Idealists were not the only revolutionaries. In *Speculum Mentis* Collingwood also mentions that the importance of the questioning activity 'has dawned on the astonished gaze of the pragmatists' (SM, 78), and in *The Principles of Art* he even quotes his Realist teacher Cook Wilson's views on the relation between questioning and the meaning of propositions (PA, 265n). All these names show that Collingwood knew that he was not fighting a revolution on his own. This is corroborated by Passmore who mentions Bradley, Bosanquet, Sidgwick, Cook Wilson, F.C.S. Schiller, and Dewey as critics of formal logic who tried to replace that logic by a theory of inquiry.[4] However, Collingwood cannot be put into the same group with these philosophers because their reforms were oriented towards science, whereas his was oriented towards history. In this, he was at one with the Italian Idealists, to whom we turn now.

COLLINGWOOD'S FIRST CRITICISMS OF CROCE

Croce's *Logica come scienza del concetto puro* of 1909 was one of the first attempts to do justice to the logic of history, and the same can be said of Gentile's first actualist papers. Collingwood knew Croce's work from 1909, and he must have heard of Gentile through the lectures of J. A. Smith. Most importantly, Smith also directed him to the work of 'another independent ally of Croce's and a collaborator with him and Gentile in the journal *La Critica*': Guido de Ruggiero.[5] This young Italian philosopher, who was to become Collingwood's friend in 1920, described his own philosophy as absolute empiricism. This was his name for a philosophy which tries to account for both the empirical and the *a priori* side of thought by describing it as an 'eternal problem which is at the same time an eternal solution'.[6] In *La scienza come esperienza assoluta* of 1912, de Ruggiero offers an absolute empiricist view of science by describing it as a 'dialectic of problem and solution'. This work was on Smith's shelves, and Collingwood would translate it for private use in 1920.[7] But before the first World War, he translated parts of de Ruggiero's *La filosofia contemporanea*, in which the absolute empiricist point of view was clearly expounded.[8]

Fortunately, we have some independent evidence for the way in which Collingwood tested works like these in the form of his comments in the margins of his copies of Croce's *Filosofia dello spirito* of 1912.[9] These comments are, to say the least, astonishing. Collingwood continually compares Croce's doctrines on art, history, and practice with his own experience in these fields. He describes this experience explicitly in terms of processes, and confronts this with Croce's view, which concentrates on the finished products of the mind. Moreover, the comments show that Collingwood was especially interested in the relation between Croce's philosophy of mind, that is, his positive doctrines, and his logic, or his critical methods. Unfortunately, Collingwood's copy of Croce's *Logica*, which contains full-scale logic of question and answer, is missing from the shelves, but on the basis of the other comments it is perfectly possible to reconstruct Collingwood's opinion. But first, we must turn to Croce's famous and notorious identity of philosophy and history, which lies at the basis of his logic of question and answer.

In his *Logica*, Croce indicates that he developed his identity of philosophy and history in analogy to the identities of intuition and expression in his *Estetica* and the identity of will and action in his *Pratica*. The identity of intuition and expression expresses his view that we never first intuit something, and then express it, but we always do both things at once; to intuit something is simply to express it. Next, Croce observes that will and action are identical; we do not first will to move our legs and then do it, but we do both things at once. Finally, Croce holds that philosophy and history are identical; we do not first think out the meaning of our philosophical concepts and then apply them to history, but we always do both things simultaneously. In other words, we cannot grasp the meaning of our pure concepts *in vacuo*, but only by applying them to history. For example, the historian attributes meaning to the philosophical concept 'bad' by predicating it to his intuition of Napoleon in the historical judgement that Napoleon was a bad man.[10]

On this basis, Croce draws the startling conclusion that there is no distinction between philosophy and history, or between *a priori* thought and empirical thought; the necessary and universal truth of philosophy and the contingent or individual truth of history are not different kinds of knowledge but inseparable elements in every cognition. More than forty years before Quine, Croce expressed his rejection of the analytic-synthetic distinction by saying that *verités de raison* and *vérités de fait* are 'identical'.[11]

Croce offers a 'double proof' of this thesis. First, he shows that every individual judgement contains the definitive judgement within itself in the form of a predicate.[12] Secondly, he shows that every definitive judgement presupposes an individual judgement. Collingwood, in his discussion of Croce in *The Idea of History*, refers to this second proof with his example of the historicity of Mill's definition of happiness (IH, 195), but he leaves out Croce's own argument, which is the most interesting part of his theory:

> Every definition is an answer to a question, the solution of a problem; and there would not be a reason to pronounce one, if we did not ask questions or formulate problems . . . But the question, the problem, or the doubt, is always conditioned by particular circumstances, the doubt of a child is not the doubt of an adult, the doubt of an uneducated man is not the doubt of an educated man, the doubt of the novice is not the doubt of the learned, the doubt of an Italian is not that of a German, and the doubt of a German of 1800 is not that of a German of 1900; thus the doubt formulated by an individual at a certain moment is not that which the same individual formulates a moment later . . . In reality, every question is different from another, and each definition, no matter how constant it sounds and how circumscribed it is by certain words, is different from another definition because the words, even when they seem materially the same, are in fact different according to the spiritual diversity of those who pronounce them, and these are always individuals who find themselves always in new and particular circumstances.[13]

In the above passage, Croce clearly expresses a *logic* of question and answer, even in the narrow sense of the word logic; he explicitly ties the meaning of a philosophical definition to a specific, historically conditioned prior question. Moreover, Croce sees an important connection between the logic of question and answer and presuppositions; as answers to questions that arise in a particular historical situation, philosophical judgements presuppose the individual judgements of history. Conversely, individual judgements themselves are answers to questions which presuppose philosophical judgements. In short, philosophy and history mutually presuppose each other through the logic of question and answer. But the most interesting thing is that all this is logically connected to Croce's rejection of the analytic-synthetic distinction.

From 1912, when Collingwood read Croce's *Logica*, he never failed to acknowledge the importance of Croce's doctrine. In the lectures on the philosophy of history of 1929 he calls it 'revolutionary'.[14] However, from the beginning he also held that Croce had not entirely understood the nature of historical thought. Typically, he found the reason for this not in Croce's logic, but in his aesthetics. In his 1912 marginal comments, Collingwood rejects the identity of intuition and expression by pointing out that an artist does not express himself in a single blow, but begins with a primitive expression which he gradually develops into a fuller expression.[15] Given Croce's own analogy between the identity of intuition and expression with the identity of philosophy and history, we may safely assume that Collingwood also rejected Croce's theory of the formation of philosophical concepts. In contrast to the latter's view that philosophical concepts are formed *simultaneously* with the historical judgement, Collingwood must have defended a theory which accounts for the *gradual* development of concepts in a question and answer process. Just as the artist develops his primitive intuitions into 'fuller views', the historian first makes a provisional judgement which he gradually develops into a fuller judgement by asking questions and answering them. That Collingwood held such a view in 1912 becomes clear from one of the marginal comments, in which he criticizes Croce for not understanding the dialectic of meaning that leads from astrology to astronomy.[16] Clearly, these comments are consistent with his later statements in the *Autobiography* on the *gradual* development of question and answer, which he developed in his 'archaeological laboratory':

> At the same time I found myself experimenting in a laboratory of knowledge; at first asking myself a quite vague question, such as: 'was there a Flavian occupation on this site?' Then dividing that question into various heads and putting the first in some such form as this: 'are these Flavian sherds and coins mere strays, or were they deposited in the period to which they belong?' and then considering all the possible ways in which light could be thrown on this new question, and putting them into practice

one by one, until at last I could say, 'There was a Flavian occupation; an earth and timber fort of such and such plan was built here in the year a±b and abandoned for such and such reasons in the year x±y'. Experience soon taught me that under these laboratory conditions one found out nothing at all except in answer to a question; and not a vague question either, but a definite one (A, 24).

This idea of *gradual* question and answer process entails an important modification of Croce's theory of the formation of philosophical concepts. With Croce, Collingwood held that philosophical concepts are formed as answers to questions, which are conditioned by the historical judgement of reality. But unlike Croce, Collingwood stressed the gradual development of historical judgements in a question and answer process, which also entails a gradual development of philosophical concepts. Here lies one of the most important reasons why Collingwood saw his life's work not in Croce's terms of an *identity* of philosophy and history, but in terms of a *rapprochement* between philosophy and history. Moreover, this view of the relation between philosophy and history has important implications for Collingwood's notion of truth; truth does not come in a single blow, but develops gradually in a question and answer process, beginning from vaguer truths leading to preciser truths. It is this view of truth that Collingwood would elaborate in his first book *Religion and Philosophy*.

RELIGION AND PHILOSOPHY (WRITTEN 1912-15)

In his first book, Collingwood seems to be obsessed with questions and answers, or problems and solutions. In the very first line he presents the book as 'an *attempt* to treat the Christian creed not as dogma but as a critical *solution* of a philosophical *problem*' (RP, xiii, emphasis added). Furthermore, he organizes most chapters as question and answer sequences, in particular the last chapter on miracle, which may serve as a practical exercise in question and answer logic. Typically, with Croce, Collingwood rejects the analytic-synthetic distinction; he holds that history is identical with philosophy because both presuppose each other (RP, 49). From this he draws the conclusion that 'the difference between a temporal event and a timeless truth is a difference not between two different classes of thing, but between two aspects of the same thing' (RP, 50). On this basis he concludes, just as Croce had done before him, that 'a single truth never means quite the same thing to different minds; each person invests it with an emphasis, an application, peculiar to himself' (RP, 106).

In Part II, Chapter I, Collingwood applies this view of meaning and truth to the metaphysical concepts 'God' and 'matter'. He first points out that 'To attach meaning to a word, is to claim that this meaning is a right one: that is, that the thing whose name it is really exists, and that this is its actual nature' (RP, 62). Next, he says that it is impossible to distinguish between the question, 'What do I mean by God?' and the question 'Does God exist, and if so what is he like?'. In Collingwood's view, the expression of what we mean by God is not 'the mere expression of a subjective idea or of the meaning of a word' because 'it presupposes that we have reasons for believing that idea, that meaning to be the right one' (RP, 62). On the same lines, Collingwood points out that the task of the scientist is 'to ask whether the matter conceived by his predecessors exists at all', but this very question commits him to the 'assumption' that matter really exists. Moreover, 'there is no limit to the degree of change which the meaning of the word 'matter' will undergo in his hands' (RP, 63). Passages like these, which can be found in almost every chapter of *Religion and Philosophy*, establish beyond doubt that Collingwood not only thought in terms of question and answer processes which give meaning to concepts, but also that he had a firm grasp of the relation between these processes and 'assumptions', or fundamental presuppositions.[17]

In the chapter on 'Evil', which was added in 1915, Collingwood elaborates this theory of meaning and truth into what he later called 'a much more mature point of view'.[18] He first rejects all theories which deny the existence of error in one way or another. Among these theories we find Descartes' and Croce's interpretation of error as an act of the will (RP, 128). Contrary to these views Collingwood holds that error really exists as thought, and that evil is a real form of action. This recognition of the reality of error and evil raises the question 'how evil and error can co-exist in the same universe side by side with truth and goodness, and how a universe so composed can be described' (RP, 137). Collingwood answers that 'every truth takes its form by correcting some error' (RP, 138). On this basis, he points out that truth and error cannot co-exist in relation with one another, because if they are brought into contact, the error is abolished by truth. But, Collingwood avers, this process of correction is never completed, because 'the life of the world, like the life of man, consists in perpetual activity' (RP, 141). Finally, he concludes that error is an 'unfinished thought-process' (RP, 140). As we will see, this theory of error is central to Collingwood's logic of question and answer. In spite of this more mature point of view, *Religion and Philosophy* still shows Collingwood's diffidence of youth; Collingwood does not explicitly attack the Realist positive doctrines and critical methods, and on one point he even remarks that he has tried to express a doctrine that 'contains little if anything which contradicts the principles of either Realism or Idealism in their more satisfactory forms' (RP, 101n1). As stated in his *Autobiography* Collingwood overcame this diffidence when meditating on the Albert Memorial.

THE ALBERT MEMORIAL MEDITATIONS 1916

At the outbreak of the war, Collingwood joined the service of the Admiralty Intelligence in London. And there, while relatively isolated from Oxford, he would turn away definitely from his Realist teachers. Later, in his personal copy of *Religion and Philosophy*, he wrote that 1916 was the year of 'negative criticism'.[19] Collingwood's criticism of the Realists began with his meditations on the ugliness of the Albert Memorial which he passed every day. In his autobiography Collingwood writes:

> Everything about it was visibly misshapen, corrupt, crawling, verminous, for a time I could not bear to look at it, and passed with averted eyes; recovering from this weakness, I forced myself to look, and to face day by day the question: a thing so obviously,

so incontrovertibly, so indefensibly bad, why had Scott done it (A, 29)?

To this question Collingwood considered several answers, but none of them could satisfy him:

> To say that Scott was a bad architect was to burke the problem with a tautology; to say that there was no accounting for tastes was to evade it by *suggestio falsi*. 'What relation was there, I began to ask myself, between what he had done and what he had tried to do (A, 29)?'

Again, as in the 1912 comments and in *Religion and Philosophy* we see that Collingwood takes purposeful action in terms of trial and error. This time, however, we find it on two sides; *a parte subiecti* Collingwood *tries* to understand the Albert Memorial, *a parte obiecti* there is Scott who *tried* to achieve something. In his *Autobiography*, Collingwood does not tell how he solved the problem of the ugliness of the Albert Memorial. Instead, he says that his solution led to the further development of a thought already familiar to him, namely the questioning activity of knowledge. Collingwood gives a detailed sequence of this development. He begins by observing that you cannot find out the meaning of something unless you find out the question to which the thing said or written was meant as an answer (A, 31). This observation was based on the 'principle of correlativity', by which Collingwood meant that a particular answer inseparably belongs to a particular question (A, 31-2). The next step was to apply this principle of correlativity to the idea of contradiction, showing that two propositions cannot contradict each other unless they are answers to the same question (A, 33). Next, he applied the principle of correlativity to the idea of truth by pointing out that 'if the meaning of a proposition is relative to the question it answers, its truth must be relative to the same thing' (A, 33). Finally, and this was crucial, he discovered that both the Realist doctrines and their critical methods were based on the propositional principle, and this finally enabled him to throw off his diffidence of youth and reject the Realist teachings as a whole.

This short autobiographical account makes three things clear. First, Collingwood, like Croce, saw a close analogy between artistic and logical activities of the mind. Second, he distinguished not two but at least four characteristics of the logic of question and answer: the dependence of meaning on questions, or correlativity principle, the principle of contradiction, the notion of truth, and the propositional principle. Third, he saw a logical connection between all these characteristics, which shows that he took the logic of question and answer as a coherent whole. But before we can understand this whole, we must come to grips with Collingwood's first step, which is the most difficult to understand; how could Collingwood's attempts to understand the ugliness of the Albert Memorial lead to the notion that you cannot find out the meaning of a statement unless you consider it as an answer to a question?

On the basis of the foregoing it is possible to reconstruct Collingwood's steps.[20] Facing the ugliness of the Albert Memorial, Collingwood most probably started from the view, expounded in *Religion and Philosophy*, that absolute ugliness cannot exist; Scott, the artist, had attempted to create a work of beauty and *ex hypothesi* there had to be some beauty in the Albert Memorial. On the other hand, Scott's attempt to create beauty had lead to an example of ugliness. The only way of explaining this co-existence of beauty and ugliness in the Albert Memorial was to understand what Scott had *tried* to do, as Collingwood says. Again, the word *tried* is crucial; it indicates that Collingwood saw a work of art as a product of a process of attempts and failures, or problems and solutions. This was Collingwood's view of mental processes until his last book (NL, 34.58), and we also find it in the 'Preliminary Discussion' of 1927. His analysis there differs on only two points from the one offered in his *Autobiography*. First, his example of ugliness is not the Albert Memorial but the Randolph Hotel, and secondly, and more importantly, he gives the philosophical import of his analysis which is the difference between the empirical and philosophical concept of art. For the artist, Collingwood says, art is an empirical concept which is present in some works and absent in other works. The empirical concept art is applied to some objects and not to others. The artist thus makes clear-cut distinctions between art and not-art. From this it follows that a work of art is always good art and that a bad work of art is simply not art (IH, 353). To this the philosopher 'has to reply that the Randolph Hotel is at least *trying* to be a work of art, and that such an attempt cannot conceivably be an unmitigated failure' (IH, 353). For the philosopher, art is a philosophical concept which means that art is universally and necessary present in every operation of the human mind. This does not mean that it is 'indifferently exemplified in every operation or creation of the mind' but that it 'is differentiated in the different particulars: different works of art represent not different embodiments of one and the same beauty but different beauties, different ways of being beautiful' (IH, 354).

An analysis like this must have provided Collingwood with the key to draw a very close parallel between artistic and logical activities. Just as the artist tries to express himself, the thinker tries to answer a question, and just as beauty and ugliness can be explained as the artist's success or failure to express himself, truth and error can be explained as a thinker's success or failure to answer his question. Moreover, just as each work of art represents a different way of being beautiful, a work of thought, or theory represents a different kind of truth. On this basis Collingwood would further modify Croce's account of the question and answer process. Croce had always sharply distinguished that question and answer process from the process of intuitions and expressions of art. Meditating on the ugliness of the Albert Memorial, Collingwood began to understand that such a distinction is untenable, and that what is required is a description of a continuous process, or 'overlap', beginning from the intuition in art and ending with the formation of concepts in philosophy. Not surprisingly this is exactly the theory that Collingwood expounded in *Speculum Mentis* (SM, 76-80) and elaborated in *The Principles of Art*.[21]

The identification of art and logic also yielded the 'principle of correlativity' which Collingwood mentions in his *Autobiography*. The meaning of the Albert Memorial is not identical with the Albert Memorial itself, yet it cannot be separated from it; intuition and expression are distinct from each other and at the same time inseparable; every work of art expresses a highly individual meaning. The Albert Memorial is Scott's expression of his particular aesthetic problem; it is his way of realizing his particular ideal of beauty. In the same way every answer is distinct and yet inseparable from the question which leads to it; every answer is the 'expression' of a particular meaning to a particular question. In other words, question and answer are 'correlative' (A, 31-2).

Having found the principle of correlativity, Collingwood could reject the principle of contradiction. Current logic held that two propositions in themselves can contradict each other, and that this is found out by examining them as propositions in themselves. Against this view Collingwood held that two propositions can only contradict each other, if they are answers to the same question (A, 33). This is also a translation of the view that beauty and ugliness coexist in one object of art; two elements in a work of art can only be seen as 'contradictory' when they are intended as solutions to the same artistic problem. It is important to note that Collingwood did not reject the principle of contradiction itself; he admits that two propositions can contradict each other, but he stresses that we have to find out their meaning before we reach that conclusion. And since meaning is formed in the question and answer process, we must recreate this process in order to understand it.

The last and most important step was to apply the principle of correlativity to the notion of truth by observing that if the meaning of a proposition is relative to the question it answers, its truth must be relative to the same thing. On this point Collingwood writes in his *Autobiography*:

> Meaning, agreement, and contradiction, truth and falsehood, none of these belonged to propositions in their own right, propositions by themselves, they belonged only to propositions as the answers to questions: each proposition answering a question strictly correlative to itself. (A, 33).

This principle also follows from the observation that the coexistence of beauty and ugliness in the Albert Memorial can only be understood by re-constructing the process in which Scott solved his artistic problem.

Given the principle that this artistic process is only an aspect of the general self-conscious activity of the mind, it can easily be translated into logical terms. This leads to the startling conclusion that truth and error co-exist in each proposition; no proposition is completely true or false in itself, but its truth or falsity is dependent on the process in which it is formed. This process is the question and answer activity of thought. On this point Collingwood made his crucial discovery; truth and falsehood do not belong to propositions as such, but to the entire complex of question and answers of which these propositions belong. In short, Collingwood discovered that the true unit of thought is not the proposition, but the entire question and answer complex (A, 37).

Typically, it is for this discovery and *not* for the logic of question and answer that Collingwood claims originality (A, 36). I think his claim is justified; several thinkers were working on the logic of question and answer, but they all still saw the proposition as the unit of thought. Even Croce, who was one of the first to reject the analytic-synthetic distinction and to elaborate a logic of history and philosophy in terms of questions and answers still gave propositions an independent status. Collingwood was the first to draw the full consequence of the rejection of the analytic-synthetic distinction and to conclude that propositions never stand alone but form a complex network together with the questions to which they are the answers.

This discovery enabled him to answer the question regarding the necessary connection between the Realist positive doctrines and their critical methods. In their positive doctrines, that is the theory of apprehension, they assumed the propositional principle; they regarded propositions as 'this is a red rose' as a unit of thought without taking the questioning activity into account (A, 26). Likewise, they assumed the propositional principle in their critical methods; by dealing with the history of philosophy as a series of answers to some 'eternal problems' with the result that they compared Plato's *polis* to the modern State as the similar answers to the same question (A, 61-4). On this point Collingwood threw off his diffidence of youth, and rejected the Realist doctrine as a whole. But soon he began to understand that the propositional principle underlay all current theories of truth as he would expound in *Truth and Contradiction*.

Truth and Contradiction 1917

On the authority of Connelly and Jones's reader's report Martin claims that the only surviving chapter of *Truth and Contradiction* contains no direct discussion of the logic of question and answer, although what is said may have 'some affinities' with that logic (CS, V, 125). However, a closer look at the manuscript itself reveals considerably more than mere 'affinities' with the logic of question and answer; in fact it contains all of the characteristics of that logic. First, Collingwood attacks the principles of the coherence theory of truth, which is in his view based on the distinction between analytic and synthetic judgements. Collingwood points out that analytic judgements are based on the law of identity. He does not reject that law but points out that it cannot be the basis of thought which is in his view always an answer to a question:

> A *is* A; a thing *is* what it is. But *what* is it? All our judgments are concerned with answering this question' (TC, 5).

This passage, which is the conclusion of a long argument, shows beyond doubt that Collingwood identified thought with a question and answer process in which judgements, or propositions stand as answers to questions. In the remainder of the chapter Collingwood tries to show how this question is answered in a process of thought which he typically illustrates with a debate between two parties. For the sake of brevity, I will not go into this, but focus on Collingwood's conclusions. The first is that coherence-theorists of truth tend to 'dissect' theories into true and false statements. Against this view Collingwood holds that:

> Truth and falsehood are attributes not of single isolated judgments but of systems of thought, systems in which every judgment is coloured by all the others (TC, 11).

In this passage we recognize Collingwood's criticism of the 'propositional principle', or the view that truth belongs to a single proposition (A, 36-7). In *Truth and Contradiction* Collingwood rejects this principle by giving an interesting example which clearly shows how his theory of knowledge is related to his theory of history:

> Let us take any 'perfectly simple judgment, as that William the Conqueror won the battle of Hastings'. Here we have a fragment of European history detached absolutely from its context; and yet surely, a critic may reply, it is still absolutely true. Yes, doubtless it is still true, but *only* because it has refused to be severed entirely from its context. To separate it successfully, we must forget all we know of William and of the battle of Hastings; we must force out of our mind everything about William except that he won the battle of Hastings, and everything about the battle of Hastings except that it was won by William. And so treated, it is surely clear that all meaning and therefore all truth has been removed from the judgment. If a person were absolutely ignorant of English history, and, wishing to instruct him, you began by saying William the Conqueror won the battle of Hastings, the statement would be mere noise to him until you had sketched the general situation of the time, and the significance of the battle; till, that is, you had expanded your unitary judgment into a system of judgments which for the first time gave it significance – and therefore the possibility of truth or falsehood – by defining the meaning of its terms. But for the future your pupil may carry the whole system – the whole history-lesson – in his head so far as he remembers it at all, of course) in the form of meaning attached to the one judgment 'William won the battle of Hastings', and so that one judgment may, to a person who knows, summarize and express in itself a whole period of English history. It is in this sense that a single judgment may be true; true not by being isolated from others, but by absorbing other into itself and acquiring in the process its significance; by becoming the concentrated vehicle of a whole system of thought (TC, 10 verso).

The above passage shows the true reason for Collingwood's rejection of the 'propositional principle'; every judgement, even the simplest, is the result of a long process which gives it its meaning. Collingwood accordingly describes the judgement as a 'concentrated vehicle of a whole system of thought' (TC, 10 verso). But given the fact that Collingwood saw judgements as answers to questions, we may infer that the truth and meaning of a judgement is dependent on the question and answer process of which it is the finished product. In *Truth and Contradiction* Collingwood draws the conclusion that we cannot interpret truth and error as mutually exclusive species of a common genus. He regards error as incomplete truth, truth that has not yet resolved all contradiction. On the other hand he remarks that truth is never complete. From this follows that every error is a partial truth, and that every truth is a partial error. All judgements are therefore capable of improvement, we can always make them more comprehensive. In a later insertion Collingwood formulates the nature of truth as follows:

> We seem forced to the conclusion that the truth of a judgment is shown not by its power of resisting contradiction and of preserving itself unchanged in the face of opposition, but precisely by the ease with which it accepts contradiction and undergoes modification in order to include points of view which once it had excluded. Not self-preservation but self-criticism is the mark of a truth (TC, 12 inserted page).

In this passage Collingwood draws the ultimate consequence from his criticism of the 'propositional principle'; the aim of thought is truth, but truth is not contained in propositions in themselves, but in complexes of propositions. Thought does not aim at producing singular propositions by brushing contradictory propositions away, but by trying to bring contradictory statements into a coherent whole. *Truth and Contradiction* is therefore not so much an exposition of the logic of question and answer, but an application of it, or more precisely it is an application of the 'propositional principle' which Collingwood had discovered a year before. The above discussion solves the puzzle of what Collingwood meant in his *Autobiography* with 'all this, during my spare time in 1917, I wrote out at considerable length . . . in *Truth and Contradiction*' (A, 42). 'All this' refers not to the question and answer logic, but to its most significant result, the rejection of the propositional principle, which he applied to all contemporary theories of truth. Apparently, he did so successfully, because Jones wrote in his reader's report that Collingwood's dialectic is a version of Plato's and Hegel's 'but done in a fresh way: clear, frank, interesting, and somehow very taking'.[22] Not surprisingly, Jones advised Macmillan to publish the book, but the publisher turned it down because 'the times were hopelessly bad for a book of that kind' (A, 42). *Truth and Contradiction* thus remained one of Collingwood's many unfinished works and that was the reason why he dedicated a long chapter to it in his *Autobiography*, 'whose purpose is to put on record some brief account of the work I have not yet been able to publish, in case I am not able to publish it in full' (A, 118).

THE FURTHER DEVELOPMENT OF THE LOGIC OF QUESTION AND ANSWER

With *Truth and Contradiction* Collingwood did not conclude his logical inquiries. In the Spring of 1920, Collingwood translated both de Ruggiero's *La filosofia contemporanea* and *La scienza come esperienza assoluta*. In the latter book de Ruggiero describes the dialectic of science in three long chapters: 'Science as a Problem', 'Science as a Solution', 'Science as an Absolute Problem'. After finishing his translation Collingwood wrote a letter to de Ruggiero on the 1st of July 1920:

> My translation of your *Scienza*, just finished, was undertaken only to help myself to a fuller understanding of the thesis: I would most willingly publish it, for I have seen nothing that seems to me so good or so useful on this problem, which is, I think the central problem in philosophy today . . . To me your book has been a new inspiration; it has confirmed and defined ideas towards which I have long been travelling, and if I dared be so bold I should say that in you I for the first time find and possess myself.[23]

Collingwood was certainly sincere when he wrote this. As we have seen he spent his whole early development in laying down the principles of thought as a question and answer process. Three weeks later Collingwood elaborated his views on logic and metaphysics in *Libellus de Generatione*, which he dedicated to de Ruggiero, with the subtitle 'An Essay in Absolute Empiricism'. Not surprisingly, Collingwood's 'booklet' contains a long passages in which he applies the logic of question and answer to the history of philosophy. In the Autumn of 1920, Collingwood lectured on de Ruggiero's *Scienza* and began to prepare 'a possible work on logic'.[24] This work was never published but we find its main results scattered through Collingwood's half a dozen manuscripts on logic, his early papers on science and history, his Moral Philosophy Lectures and finally in *Speculum Mentis*.[25] Contrary to Martin, I hold that the latter work does contain a logic of question and answer. On p. 78 for example, we read 'People who are acquainted with knowledge at first hand have always known that assertions are only answers to questions'. More significant is Collingwood's analysis of the relation between science and history as question and answer which has already been analysed by James Somerville.[26] After *Speculum Mentis* Collingwood continued to refine his logic on many points, but there is no space here to describe all that. I only mention the predominant role of questioning in *An Essay on Philosophical Method*, *The Idea of Nature* and *The Idea of History*. Finally, the first chapter of the work that was to become his final report on his life's work, *The Principles of History*, is entirely dedicated to the logic of question and answer; clear proof that Collingwood saw the logic of question and answer as an important part of his life's work.

In the following section I will deal with its relation to fundamental presuppositions.

THE LOGIC OF QUESTION AND ANSWER AND FUNDAMENTAL PRESUPPOSITIONS

Above we have seen that from his early career Collingwood discussed fundamental assumptions, presuppositions, or principles in connection with his logic of question and answer. In *Religion and Philosophy* he related questions to 'assumptions'. The problem of Albert Memorial could only be solved when the artistic principles embodied in it were fully understood. In *Truth and Contradiction* Collingwood remarks in several places that contradiction between opponents can only be overcome if the point of view of the opponent is understood.[27] A year later in *Ruskin's Philosophy* Collingwood would identify this notion of 'point of view' with 'a solid ring of thought' which has often been interpreted as a first statement of the notion of absolute presuppositions.[28] I fully agree therefore with Martin when he says that the notion of fundamental presuppositions has a long and important history in Collingwood's thought (CS, V, 125-6). However, I disagree with his view that that there is 'no history of absolute presuppositions at all' and that these appeared only in *An Essay on Metaphysics* 'fully formed like Athena from Zeus's brow' (CS, V, 125). The history of absolute presuppositions is considerably longer. In fact it was 65 years old. The term appears for the first time in Bradley's *Presuppositions of Critical History* of 1874, and most importantly, with almost the same connotations as Collingwood later gave to it. First, he claims that scientific practice necessarily involves presuppositions:

> The fact of the existence of scientific experiment proves the existence of an absolute presupposition, which it can be said to found, only because upon that itself is already founded.[29]

Secondly, Bradley holds the truth or falsity of absolute presuppositions cannot be verified because the very proof would involve the absolute presupposition itself:

> Can science testify to a breach of the law which forms its presupposition? This would amount to a contradiction in terms; it would be an observation based upon a rule to prove the nonexistence of the rule.[30]

Thirdly, all scientific hypotheses start from absolute presuppositions:

> We find then that, as starting from a conception which it cannot

prove, natural science is, in this sense hypothetical, and exhibits in detail the truth of its hypotheses.[31]

Collingwood read Bradley's *Presuppositions of Critical History* in 1932 and it seems to have had a great impact on his development.[32] In 'The Historical Imagination', notably his inaugural lecture as a Waynflete Professor of Metaphysics, Collingwood hails Bradley's essay as a 'Copernican Revolution in the theory of historical knowledge' (IH, 240). In 'The Historical Imagination' we find Bradley's theory in company of now very familiar themes: the rejection of the analytic-synthetic distinction, historical imagination, that is, Croce's 'intuition', the detective-story as illustration of the logic of question and answer, and last but not least: the innate, or *a priori* idea of history. It was Mink who first recognized in this the first formulation of an absolute presupposition, and other interpreters, notably Flanigan, and Vanhees-wijck, have traced the development of this notion of the a priori ideas to the absolute presuppositions in *An Essay on Metaphysics*.[33]

All in all, we may conclude that it was not the logic of question and answer that gave the term 'absolute' to absolute presuppositions because Collingwood took the term from Bradley. But at the same time, he integrated the term into his earlier developed logic of question and answer replacing Bradley's inferences from absolute presupposition to hypotheses, with inferences from absolute presuppositions to questions.[34] For this reason I do not think that Collingwood used the logic of question and answer as a 'handy way' to remove truth value from fundamental principles as Martin holds. Bradley had already shown that the truth or falsity of absolute presuppositions cannot be proven. Morever, early in his career Collingwood recognized that fundamental presuppositions have no truth value. In 1920, for example, he remarks that Croce's pure concept cannot be verified because 'their existence or validity is not vouched for by external evidence but by its own inherent characteristic' which it derives from a 'positive metaphysical system'.[35] Even less did Collingwood think that the connection of absolute presuppositions to his logic of question and answer would remove all meaning from them. In Part III of *An Essay on Metaphysics* he explicitly discusses the meaning of the absolute presuppositions as 'God exists',

Kant's transcendental concepts, and the notion of causality. These discussions show that absolute presuppositions do have a meaning, but not as answers to questions. Absolute presuppositions derive their meaning from their function as presuppositions of an entire question and answer complex of a given science. For example, the absolute presupposition 'cause' has a specific meaning in the question and answer complexes of historians and another meaning in the question and answer complexes of scientists (EM, Part III).

In my view, Collingwood only connected the logic of question and answer to absolute presuppositions because he identified 'high grade thinking', like history, science and philosophy, with the asking of questions, the asking of questions with the positing of presuppositions. For Collingwood these were *necessary* connections; to ask a question is to presuppose something. On this point he never changed his mind; from *Religion and Philosophy* to his very last work *The New Leviathan* Collingwood saw all thought as a process of questions and answers based on presuppositions (NL, Chapter XIV). However, the necessary connection between questioning and presuppositions does not entail that both notions must always be discussed together. In fact, occasionally Collingwood discusses the logic of question, or parts of it, and answer separately from the notion of presuppositions, as for example in the chapter on the logic of question and answer in *Speculum Mentis*.[36] He also discusses fundamental presuppositions without invoking the logic of question and answer as for example in 'Ruskin's Philosophy' or in 'The Function of Metaphysics in Civilization'.[37] But when it came to a full-scale account of fundamental presuppositions, as in *An Essay on Metaphysics*, Collingwood could not do but what he had done all his life and discuss the fundamental presuppositions in the context of his logic of question and answer.

CONCLUSION

On the basis of the foregoing, I mean two claims to stand. First, Collingwood was committed, both explicitly and implicitly, to the notion that there is a connection between the logic of question and answer and fundamental presuppositions. This connection follows from the identification of high-grade thinking, as in science, history and philosophy, with the asking and answering of questions combined with the view that questions logically involve presuppositions.

Secondly, from his early days as a college student, Collingwood stood explicitly and implicitly committed to this view. I have corroborated most of Collingwood's claims with respect to his development of the logic of question and answer and its connection to fundamental presuppositions. Moreover, I have shown how this view was related to his rejection of the analytic-synthetic distinction which enabled him to reject all current theories of truth early in his career. Finally, I have shown how Collingwood derived the notion absolute presuppositions from Bradley, to incorporate it in *An Essay on Metaphysics* in his logic of question and answer, which he had completed years before.

The history of the relation between the logic of question and answer and fundamental presuppositions was a brief history; it was indeed as brief as Collingwood's life.

NOTES

1 This paper is the first half of 'Collingwood's Logic of Question and Answer Revisited', delivered at the R. G. Collingwood Conference, St. Catherine's College, Oxford, July 1997. The second half of that paper, which deals with the relation between the logic of question and answer and Collingwood's philosophical method and his notion of the living past, will be published later. Both halves are based on chapters 5, 7 and 9 of my dissertation *The Living Past, Philosophy, History and Action in the Thought of Croce, Gentile, de Ruggiero and Collingwood* (Nijmegen, 1998). I thank my friends Herman Simissen and Willem de Zwijger for their critical comments on this paper. I dedicate this paper to Jan van der Dussen, who never failed to remind me of the trustworthiness of Collingwood's *Autobiography.*

2 For the convenience of the readers of this journal, I will refer to *Collingwood Studies V.*

3 Probably Collingwood had F. H. Bradley and H. H. Joachim in view since he praised the logic of the former in *The Idea of History* (IH, 140) and the logic of the latter in the *Autobiography* (A, 18, 36).

4 John Passmore, *A Hundred Years of Philosophy* (Harmondsworth, Penguin Books, 1984) 156-73.

5 J. A. Smith, 'Lectures on Gentile', Manuscript of about 1916 or 1917, Magdalen Ms 1026/XI/13, no page numbers. Smith lectured on the Italians from 1910.

6 Guido de Ruggiero, *Modern Philosophy*, English translation of *La filosofia contemporanea*, 1912, by A. H. Hannay and R. G. Collingwood (London and New York, Allen and Unwin, 1921), 340.

7 J. A. Smith, 'Lectures on Gentile', no page numbers.

8 David Boucher, ed., *R. G. Collingwood: Essays in Political Philosophy* (Oxford, Oxford University Press, 1989), 8, n24.

9 I thank Mrs. Smith for allowing me to consult her father's copies of Croce's *La filosofia dello spirito*.

10 Benedetto Croce, *Contributo alla critica di me stesso, Edizione di 100 esemplari fuori commercio*, reprinted in *Etica e politica* (Bari, Laterza, 1931), cited from *Etica e politica* (Bari, Laterza, terza edizione economica, 1981) 349; Benedetto Croce, *Logica come scienza del concetto puro* (Bari, Laterza, 1909), cited from 5th edn. 1928., 142.

11 Benedetto Croce, *Logica*, 128. This clarifies Martin's 'wrinkle' concerning the relation between Quine's and Collingwood's logic (CS, V, 132n6).

12 Croce, *Logica*, 129-30.

13 Croce, *Logica*, 133-4.

14 R. G. Collingwood, 'Lectures on the Philosophy of History – II Trinity Term 1929', Dep. 12/6, 35.

15 R. G. Collingwood, 'Marginal Comments in Croce, *Estetica*', 1912, 121.

16 Collingwood, 'Marginal Comments in Croce, *Estetica*', after *Capitolo XIV*.

17 See for example, R. G. Collingwood, *Religion and Philosophy* (London, Macmillan, 1916), 68, 71, 74, 83-4, 86, 118, 121, 124, 127, 140, 161, 166 and especially the last chapter 'Miracle', 194ff.

18 Donald S. Taylor, *R. G. Collingwood, A Bibliography* (New York and London, Garland Publishing, 1988), 90.

19 Cited by Taylor, *R. G. Collingwood, A Bibliography*, 90.

20 This paragraph is based on Rik Peters, 'Collingwood on Hegel's Dialectic', in *Collingwood Studies*, 2 (1995), 107-125.

21 In a letter to Samuel Alexander of the 24th of May 1925 Collingwood writes that he rejected Croce's aesthetics 'on first reading', letter cited by Taylor, *R. G. Collingwood, A Bibliography*, 55.

22 Boucher, *Collingwood: Essays in Political Philosophy*, 231.

23 Collingwood, 'Letters to Guido de Ruggiero', 1920-38, Dep. 27, letter of 1 July 1920.

24 Collingwood, letter of November 22, 1921.

25 Collingwood laid the foundations for that logic in 'Notes on Hegel's Logic', 19 September 1920, Dep. 16/2; 'Sketch of A Logic of Becoming', 19 September 1920, Dep. 16/3; 'Notes on Formal Logic', 1920, Dep. 16/4 and in 'Draft of Opening Chapters of a " 16/6. Applications of the logic are found in Lectures on Moral Philosophy for MT 1921, written at various times 'Prolegomena to Logic' or the like, 1920, Dep. 16/5 and 'An Illustration from Historical Thought', 1920, Dep., May-October 1921', Dep.4 and 'Action. A Course of Lectures on Moral Philosophy', written in September 1923 and rewritten in M.T. 1926, Dep. 3/1.

26 James Somerville, 'Collingwood's Logic of Question and Answer', in *The Monist*, 72 (1989), 531.

27 'We do not simply aim at showing him that he is wrong, and thereby drive him to adopt our view as the only alternative. We aim rather at understanding with his view and sympathising with it: we admit freely that within limits it is true and sound; and only when that is accomplished do we go on to show that it falls short of being as satisfactory as it might be, and that it is capable of certain more or less definable improvements' (TC, 19).

28 R. G. Collingwood, *Ruskin's Philosophy, An Address delivered at the Ruskin Centenary Conference, Coniston, August 8th, 1919* (Titus Wilson, Kendal, 1922), cited from

A. Donagan, ed., *Essays in the Philosophy of Art by R. G. Collingwood* (Bloomington, Indiana University Press, 1964), 9-10.

29 F. H. Bradley, *The Presuppositions of Critical History* (Bristol, Thoemess Press, 1993), 16; first edition 1874.

30 Bradley, *Presuppositions of Critical History*.

31 Bradley, *Presuppositions of Critical History*, 17.

32 Collingwood, IH, 437n.

33 Louis O. Mink, *Mind, History, and Dialectic, The Philosophy of R. G. Collingwood,* (Middletown, Wesleyan University Press, 1969), 185. Rosemary Flanigan, 'Metaphysics as a Science of Absolute Presuppositions. Another Look at R. G. Collingwood, in *The Modern Schoolman*, 64 (1987), 161-185. Guido Vanheeswijck, *Metafysica als een Historische Discipline. De Actualiteit van R. G. Collingwoods 'Hervormde Metafysica'* (Assen and Maastricht, Van Gorcum, 1993).

34 In this context it is interesting to note that in *Speculum Mentis* Collingwood did not clearly distinguish between intuition, hypothesis, supposal and questioning.

35 Collingwood, 'Lectures on the Ontological Proof of the Existence of God', Dep. 2, 87.

36 This is not Collingwood's final view of the matter as the rest of *Speculum Mentis* shows. The gist of that book is that all forms of experience, and *ipso facto* their question and answer processes *presuppose* each other: science presupposes history, and history presupposes science (SM, p. 186-7). Science and history presuppose philosophy, or 'absolute knowledge', the knowledge of 'absolute fact', 'one of which there can never in anybody's mind be any doubt' (SM, 298). This connection between question and answer processes and 'absolute fact' is the Alpha and Omega of *Speculum Mentis* as the very last lines of that book show: 'For the life of the mind consists of raising and solving problems, problems in art, religion, science, commerce, politics, and so forth . . . Philosophy is . . . the self-recognition of the mind in its own mirror' (SM, 317).

37 Contrary to Martin I do not think that the latter manuscript shows that there is no connection between the logic of question and answer and fundamental presuppositions because, as Martin himself says, the manuscript begins in mid-paragraph and it has not functioned as a draft for Part I of *An Essay on Metaphysics* (CS, V, 122).

How Kantian is Collingwood's Metaphysics of Experience?[1]

GIUSEPPINA D'ORO
University of Keele

Collingwood's name is usually associated with his work in the philosophy of history: most professional philosophers are likely to be acquainted with Collingwood's defence of history as an autonomous discipline with a distinct method and subject matter, either through first hand acquaintance with *The Idea of History*,[2] or via Collingwood-inspired clarifications of the distinction between understanding and explanation.[3] However, in spite of the fact that a great part of Collingwood's work was meant as a reflection on the method and task of philosophy and explicitly presented as an attempt to re-think what metaphysics is,[4] Collingwood's name rarely features in discussions of the fate of metaphysics in twentieth century thought and, in particular, in European philosophy after Kant. When Collingwood's name appears in histories of philosophy it is usually under the heading of 'The British Idealists' a heading which, although not inappropriate, tends, more often than not, to suggest that he is a relatively minor figure, a member of a school, whose group membership is more important than his individual contribution. There has, in other words, been relatively little interest in Collingwood's work as a valuable addition to that ongoing dialogue that is the history of philosophy. It is not easy to surmise the reasons for this neglect. It could be because Collingwood was writing at the tail end of an idealist tradition which came to be viewed as largely anachronistic. Or it could be because Collingwood chose to describe his project as an attempt to reform metaphysics, rather than critique it, at a time when both the emerging traditions of the philosophy of language in the Anglo-American world and that of phenomenology in continental Europe preferred to describe themselves in opposition to, rather than on a continuum with, the metaphysics of the past. In this paper I attempt to do two things. My immediate goal is to explore the reform of metaphysics in Collingwood's work with an eye to highlighting the Kantian heritage within it. My mediate, but more crucial goal, is to highlight how central some of Collingwood's concerns are to that very history of philosophy which has often neglected him. I am aware that comparative analyses are often treacherous[5] and always at risk of being shallow; yet it is only in relation to an ongoing dialogue in the history of philosophy that a thinker's achievements can be understood. The paper is divided in two sections. In the first I will highlight the main Kantian themes and Kantian inspired arguments in Collingwood's reform of metaphysics.[6] In the second I will focus on the differences between Kant's and Collingwood's reform of metaphysics with an eye to explaining why Collingwood's reform of metaphysics may be understood as a radicalisation of Kant's transcendental philosophy.

I

Let's begin by outlining four Kantian themes in Collingwood.[7]

First, both Kant and Collingwood saw themselves not only as critics but also as reformers of metaphysics. On the one hand Kant's transcendental philosophy was put forward as an explicit critique of the rationalist metaphysics of Leibniz and Wolff. Kant thought that rationalist metaphysicians had failed to clearly distinguish between concepts and intuitions and, as a result, held that an analysis of our concepts would yield knowledge of things-in-themselves. On the other hand, in the *Critique of Pure Reason*, when introducing the idea of a Copernican turn, Kant claimed that we should "make trial whether we may not have more success in the tasks of metaphysics, if we suppose that objects must conform to our knowledge".[8] Within the terms of reference of the Copernican revolution the task of metaphysics is to analyse, not the structure of reality but the structure of experience: unlike rationalist metaphysics, the new metaphysics did not seek to uncover the ultimate structure of reality or of things-in-themselves by an analysis of concepts. Kant believed nonetheless that this new project still deserved the name of metaphysics. Collingwood too thought that metaphysics stood in need of both critique and reform: metaphysics, he argued, cannot take the form of a study of pure Being, it must rather be a study of the absolute presuppositions which govern different domains of enquiry, such as religion, natural science, history or art. Kant and Collingwood appear to have similar reasons for holding that what appears to be an epistemological enquiry into either the structure of cognition in general, or into the absolute presuppositions which govern different disciplines, still deserves to be named metaphysics. The need for metaphysics, for both Kant and Collingwood, arises out of the realisation that there is an element in knowledge or experience that is non empirical. The recognition of this non-empirical element in knowledge can give rise to two very distinct conceptions of the task of metaphysics. On the one hand metaphysics can take the form of a study of a supra-sensory realm of real entities. So conceived metaphysics takes the form of a study of the ultimate components of reality. On the other hand, metaphysics can seek the non-empirical element within knowledge in a set of a priori concepts or principles which cannot be justified empirically but which nonetheless explain how knowledge or experience is possible. So conceived metaphysics takes the form of an enquiry into the a priori element within knowledge or experience and it is in this sense that both Kant and Collingwood thought themselves to be justified in naming what appears to be primarily an epistemological enquiry, 'metaphysics'. It goes without saying that whereas Kant had to defend the need for metaphysics against the early empiricism of Locke, who described the empiricist thesis primarily in genetic rather than verificationist terms, as a theory concerning the origin of knowledge rather than its mode of justification, Collingwood, on the other hand, had to defend metaphysics against logical positivism which presented itself as a thesis concerned not with the origin of knowledge but with its mode of justification. It was primarily in an attempt to awake the logical positivists to the need for metaphysics that Collingwood developed his account of absolute presuppositions and insisted on the claim that such presuppositions are meaningful but neither true nor false, i.e., incapable of being empirically verifiable, thereby attacking the logical positivists' tenet that all propositions are either empirically verifiable or meaningless. Collingwood's account of absolute presuppositions is developed in *An Essay on Metaphysics*, where he illustrates what is meant by an absolute presupposition by considering the different explanatory principles employed in the historical sciences and in the practical and theoretical sciences of nature. For Collingwood, the historical sciences, the practical and the theoretical sciences of nature, employ different explanatory principles because they each make use of a different notion of causation. In the historical sciences, Collingwood claims "that which is caused is the free and deliberate act of a conscious and responsible agent, and causing him to do it means affording him a motive for so doing (EM, 285). In this first sense of the word cause, the term is used in expressions such as "Mr Baldwin's speech compelled the speaker to adjourn the house" or "a solicitor's letter caused a man to pay his debt". By contrast, in the practical sciences of nature (such as medicine and engineering) "that which is caused is an event in nature and its cause is an event or state of things by producing or preventing which we can produce or prevent that whose cause it is said to be" (EM, 296-97). This is the sense in which the term cause is employed in expressions such as "the cause of malaria is the bite of a mosquito" or "the cause of books going mouldy is their being in a dark room". Finally, Collingwood says, the term 'cause' is also employed in the theoretical sciences of nature (such as physics) where "that which is caused is an event or state of things and its cause is another event or state of things such that (a) if the cause happens or exists, the effect must happen or exist even if no further conditions are fulfilled and (b) the effect cannot happen or exist unless the cause happens or exists".[9] Collingwood, like Kant, thought that the absolute presuppositions which govern the historical and the natural sciences cannot be empirically verified. Kant had claimed that the categories of the understanding stood in need of a transcendental deduction, as an empirical deduction would not be available in their case.[10] Analogously Collingwood thought that the absolute presuppositions which govern certain domains of enquiry cannot be verified empirically as they are the pre-condition for making empirically true or false statements and identified the study of this a priori element within knowledge with metaphysics.

Secondly, both Kant and Collingwood saw their work as standing in a complex relationship to the idealist tradition. Kant referred to his idealism as 'transcendental', to distinguish it from the ontological or metaphysical idealism of Berkeley and Collingwood went so far as refusing the label 'idealist' altogether. In both Kant's and Collingwood's case, what makes their relationship to idealism complex is that they both wished to distinguish between epistemological issues, or issues pertaining to the order of knowledge and ontological issues, or issues pertaining to the order of existence. Whereas Kant signalled that his idealism was of an epistemic rather than an ontological nature by naming his idealism transcendental, Collingwood preferred to express the epistemological nature of his project by saying that a metaphysics of absolute presuppositions is effectively a metaphysics without ontology.[11] In *An Essay on Philosophical Method* Collingwood illustrated the purely epistemological nature of the principles which lie at the basis of certain domains of experience through the doctrine of the overlap of classes. He illustrates this doctrine by considering the internal subdivision of the concept of the good into the specific concepts of the pleasant, the expedient and the right (EPM, 41). One and the same action, Collingwood says, can be both expedient, pleasant and right: the classification of action into expedient, pleasant and right, according to Collingwood, is not an empirical classification and therefore, the class of objects which, under one possible description could be an instance of the specific concept of the right could, under a different description, be an instance of the pleasant. Equally, the subdivision of experience into religious, artistic, scientific, historical, does not cut nature at the joints because such a subdivision serves a merely epistemological purpose. One important implication of Collingwood's doctrine of the overlap of classes is that the distinction between the various areas of knowledge or experience is purely conceptual: whereas the metaphysics of the past sought to map conceptual distinctions onto real distinctions, Collingwood's metaphysics of absolute presuppositions, understood as a metaphysics without ontology provides a purely conceptual map of reality.

The task of philosophy, Collingwood says explicitly, is the "distinguishing of concepts . . . coinciding in their instances" (EPM, 51). If the distinction between the presuppositions which govern say, the natural sciences and history[12] or the social sciences at large were an empirical rather than a purely conceptual distinction, there could be no overlap in the class of objects studied by natural scientists and the class of objects studied by historians or by social scientists. This is a conclusion that Collingwood would not accept because his claim that a metaphysics of absolute presuppositions is a metaphysics without ontology entails precisely the possibility of full extensional equivalence.

Thirdly, both Kant and Collingwood saw the project of enquiring into the structure of experience as that of uncovering the logical rather than the psychological conditions of knowledge. Like his empiricist predecessor, Locke, Kant thought that to find out the extent and limits of knowledge it was necessary to carry out an enquiry into the cognitive faculties[13] but, unlike Locke he did not offer an empirical psychology: whereas Locke defined ideas as whatever is present to the mind when a man thinks, Kant did not identify concepts with consciously entertained thought processes. Secondly, Kant did not offer an account of how knowledge is acquired: his interest was in providing a validation or justification of knowledge, not a genetic account of how it is arrived at. Collingwood shared Kant's critique of psychologism: he clearly distinguished, for instance, between presuppositions and assumptions. 'Presuppositions' is the name Collingwood gives to logical, 'assumptions' the name he gives to psychological presumptions. He illustrated the distinction between (logical) presuppositions and (psychological) assumptions through the following example:

> A man (or at any rate an intelligent man) need not regard himself as insulted if someone who has paid him a sum of money asks him for a receipt, or if the family of a lady whom he is about to marry proposes that a marriage settlement should be drawn up. He knows that the request or proposal is based on the assumption that he is capable, or will one day become capable, of acting dishonourably; but though he knows people assume this he does not necessarily think they believe it. He finds no

difficulty in distinguishing their supposing him a rascal and their believing him one, and he does not regard the former as evidence of the latter (EM, 28-29).

According to Collingwood (logical) presuppositions need not be self-consciously entertained; the practitioners of a given discipline need not be aware of the principles which underpin their activities. Consequently, (logical) presuppositions do not entail the presence of true beliefs: an accomplished artist invited to provide some reflections on the nature of artistic production may reveal himself to be a poor art critic; it is because presuppositions are of a logical rather than psychological nature that it is possible for there to be a mismatch between what the practitioners of a particular discipline believe themselves to be doing and what they ought to believe about the nature of their subject matter.

Fourthly, Collingwood's notion of philosophical method may be said to bear many similarities to Kant's transcendental philosophy. Kant's method, in the *Critique of Pure Reason*, is to proceed from a fact of experience to the conditions of its possibility. Hence, for instance, in the Transcendental Aesthetics Kant argues that space is a necessary epistemic condition for representing objects as distinct from the subject as well as numerically distinguishable from other objects: if the representation of space were not presupposed, Kant argues, it would not be possible to distinguish numerically between qualitatively identical objects.[14] The same argumentative strategy is employed by Kant in the Transcendental Analytic in the context of his discussion of causality in the second analogy.[15] Here Kant argues that we are justified in employing the concept of cause, or that the employment of the concept of cause is legitimate, in so far as the category of causality is to be presupposed if we are to be capable of distinguishing between changes in our representations (subjective changes) and representation of change (objective changes). The method of proceeding from a fact of experience to its logical ground has been described by Ameriks as regressive,[16] and it is to be contrasted with the progressive method which is employed in deductive arguments which proceed from independently established premises to the conclusions. Whereas the progressive method is not circular, (in a deductive argument the truth of the premises is established independently of the truth of the conclusion) the regressive method is circular in that the truth of the premises is not established independently of the conclusion of the argument: regressive arguments begin, so to speak, from the conclusion (e.g. the experience of objects which are qualitatively identical and yet numerically distinct) and show the premises (e.g. the representation of space) to be true if the conclusion is true. Collingwood's notion of philosophical method may be said to be Kantian in its parentage because Collingwood, like Kant, thought that the absolute presuppositions which structure certain domains of enquiry must be defended by their success in explaining our experience (EPM, 174). He claims that philosophy does not "bring us to know things of which we were simply ignorant, but brings us to know in a different way things which we already knew in some way" (EPM, 161). The method by which the philosopher uncovers the basic principles which structure certain areas of experience or domains of enquiry, for Collingwood, is neither deductive nor inductive. It is not deductive because the absolute presuppositions which structure a given domain of enquiry do not have the status of intuitively true Cartesian first principles which are known through the light of reason and from which the edifice of knowledge can be built through careful step by step deductive inferences. The geometrical method which inspired Cartesian rationalism is unsuitable to uncovering absolute presuppositions because for Collingwood, such principles must, as we have seen, be defended by their success in explaining our experience, rather than being independently established by means of intellectual intuition. The method by which absolute presuppositions are brought to light is also unlike the inductive method employed in the sciences of observation and experiment. This is because the principles which lie at the basis of any given form of knowledge need to be already implicitly possessed by the practitioners of those disciplines in order for any particular form of experience to be possible. Given that such principles make a particular form of experience possible, they cannot be derived empirically or known inductively. The philosopher must consequently begin from certain disciplines, and regressively ascend to the conditions of their possibility. In this way philosophy uncovers principles which are a priori, not in the sense that they are necessarily true or cannot be denied without contradiction but in the sense that they underpin, structure and make possible a particular area of knowledge or experience. The method that philosophy employs is therefore not a priori in the sense that the philosopher establishes certain principles either intuitively or deductively. It is a priori in the much weaker sense that philosophy uncovers or brings to light certain principles by reflecting on the nature of experience. Unlike the deductive sciences, philosophical method, according to Collingwood, cannot merely presuppose the principles which lie at the basis of the various areas of knowledge or experience; it must "verify" them by checking or comparing them with the kind of experience or knowledge which they make possible. Collingwood's understanding of philosophical method resembles Kant because Collingwood, like Kant, sought for a mode of justification which was neither narrowly analytic (e.g. the principle of non-contradiction) nor purely empirical (the checking of a concept against its alleged instance). Where Kant spoke of the need for a transcendental deduction of the forms of thought or the categories of the understanding, in contrast with a merely empirical or a posteriori justification for the legitimate employment of such concepts, Collingwood, on his part, claimed that philosophical method follows the Socratic principle "that philosophical reasoning leads to no conclusions that we did not in some sense know already" (EPM, 161) and that the principles which are advanced in explanation of certain areas of knowledge or experience are answerable to the kind of experience that they attempt to explain. Collingwood believed that whereas the principles which lie at the basis of experience or knowledge are not analytically true or necessary in the sense that their denial involves a contradiction, they are necessary to the extent that they must be appealed to in any attempt to account for how a certain kind or knowledge or experience is possible. Both Kant and Collingwood, therefore, looked for a notion of non-analytic necessity which found its expression respectively in Kant's attempt to provide a non-empirical or transcendental justification for the a priori forms of knowledge and in Collingwood's claim that the absolute presuppositions which lie at the basis of different areas of knowledge or experience are to be validated not empirically but by assessing their ability to clarify, explain and account for the possibility of religion, art, natural science and history.

Collingwood's work, therefore, may be said to be Kantian in four important respects: both Kant and Collingwood articulated their project as one of reform rather than mere critique of metaphysics; unlike dogmatic rationalist metaphysicians they both distinguished between epistemological and existential issues; they shared a critique of psychologism and they both looked for a notion of "verification" which was neither empiricist, nor narrowly analytic. As mentioned earlier, however, Collingwood's work is best understood as a radicalisation of Kant's transcendental philosophy. To explain why this is the case we must turn to consider a number of aspects in which Collingwood's thought appears to depart from Kant's.

II

Kant's influence on Collingwood is not always straightforward. In the following I will outline four main differences between Kant's and Collingwood's reform of metaphysics. There is first of all the issue of the relationship in which their respective philosophical systems stand to the question of scepticism: are they meant as straightforward refutations of scepticism? If so, are they successful? Kant did, at least at times, suggest that transcendental idealism was advanced as a solution to the kind of sceptical questions raised in the first of the Cartesian *Meditations*. In the preface to the *Critique*, for instance, Kant stated that "it still remains a scandal to philosophy and to human reason in general that the existence of things outside us (from which we derive the whole material of knowledge, even for our inner sense) must be accepted merely on *faith*, and that if anyone merely thinks good to doubt their existence, we are unable to counter his doubts by any satisfactory proof" (CPR, Bxl). Statements such as these suggest that a proof for the existence of the external world is forthcoming in transcendental idealism or, at the very least, that attempting to provide such a proof is a worthwhile philosophical undertaking. On the other hand Kant also seemed to suggest that transcendental idealism was devised in answer to a rather different concern, that of explaining the possible and peaceful co-existence of theoretical and practical reason: he claimed therefore that he had "found it necessary to deny knowledge in order to make room for faith" (CPR, Bxxxi, p. 29). It is when conceived as an answer to the antinomies of pure reason or contradictions inherent in the claim that things-in-themselves are both causally determined and free, that transcendental idealism seems to have exercised a more direct influence on Collingwood. Collingwood believed the various forms of knowledge or experience to be attitudes of mind which provide not mutually exclusive accounts of what exists but complementary explanatory principles on the basis of which what is or exists can be described. According to Collingwood the artist looks at the world as an artistic creation, the natural scientist as a series of events governed by deterministic causal laws, the historian as a product of human activity. This is so because the absolute presuppositions which underpin art, natural science and history disclose the world respectively as artistic creation, a system of natural laws, the product of human activity. Collingwood saw the major threat to the complementarity thesis to arise from the endorsement of realism which he disparagingly described as the thesis that "knowing makes no difference to what is known"[17] and believed that the attempt to define the domain of enquiry of each area of knowledge or experience by reference to a realist criterion of truth rather than by appeal to the absolute presuppositions which govern these different domains of enquiry would constitute a hindrance to their peaceful coexistence because it would inevitably result in the view that each area of knowledge puts forward competing claims about the same objects rather than complementary explanatory principles. Collingwood's main concern was to account for the possible coexistence of the various areas of knowledge or experience rather than provide a refutation of sceptical doubts concerning the existence of the external world.

A second aspect in which Kant's influence on Collingwood is ambivalent concerns the very nature of transcendental arguments. Kant's scholarship is divided on this issue. It may not be an unfair generalisation to say that whereas those who do not see Kant's transcendental philosophy to have been devised as an answer to scepticism are much more willing to accept the thesis that Kant's transcendental idealism offers, in Gardner's words, "metaphysically neutral but epistemologic-ally forceful arguments",[18] those who do believe transcendental idealism to be devised as an answer to external world scepticism tend to regard transcendental arguments as attempting (but not necessarily succeed-ing) to establish ontological conclusions on the basis of purely epistemic premises. Barry Stroud is perhaps the best representative of the view that Kant sought to defeat external world scepticism but also failed to do so because the kind of transcendental arguments which are often attributed to Kant are powerless against the sceptic. External world scepticism, according to Stroud, is not affected by the consideration that there are criteria to distinguish between merely subjective repre-sentations, such as dreams or hallucinations, and objective representa-tions, i.e. representations of objects that exist independently of the self. The sceptic is not affected by such considerations because what he questions is not the existence of any such criteria but knowledge of whether they are correctly applied. It is precisely this knowledge that the sceptic claims is lacking (as is well illustrated by the introduction of the dream argument in the First Cartesian Meditation).[19] To under-stand how the kind of arguments which are at times attributed to Kant may fail to deliver weightier ontological conclusions, one may consider, once again, Kant's anti-Leibnizian point in the Transcendental Aesthetics. Kant's first argument for the necessity of the representation of space, as we have seen,[20] is that space is the condition of the possibility for experiencing qualitatively identical objects as numerically distinct. It would be invalid to argue from such an epistemological premise to the ontological conclusion that there are objects which exist independently of the self, even if this is the very conclusion needed to defeat external world scepticism. To argue from the epistemological consideration that space must be presupposed in order to represent objects as numerically distinct, to the ontological conclusion that there are objects which exist independently of the self (and that external world scepticism is, con-sequently, false), would be tantamount to arguing, by analogy, that (i) since we regard agents to be morally responsible and that (ii) since freedom of will is the condition of the possibility for ascribing moral responsibility to agents, metaphysical determinism is false. To establish the latter claim one would have to know not only what an agent is (i.e.

have conceptual knowledge or knowledge of the conceptual distinction between agents and things) but to have correctly identified one. It is not my desire, in this context, to settle the question whether Kant's concern was purely conceptual, whether he was, say, concerned purely with the question of establishing what are the criteria for distinguishing between inner and outer representations, or whether it was also his intention to provide a theory of knowledge which would refute external world scepticism. Whatever stance one might take on the issue of the relationship between transcendental idealism and scepticism it is clear that Collingwood's metaphysics of absolute presuppositions is quite explicitly a purely conceptual enquiry. Collingwood's defence of metaphysics, as we have seen, consisted primarily in showing that the kind of propositions which the logical positivists would have regarded as meaningless are the conditions of the possibility for making empirically true and false claims, i.e. for applying the verificationist principle. Collingwood's question is "What is art?; What is science?; What is history?" not whether there exist, metaphysically speaking (in the non-Collingwoodian sense of the word) art products, events or actions. Such a conceptual enterprise, which consists in outlining the absolute presuppositions which lie at the basis of the various areas of knowledge is not, and arguably is not meant, to provide an answer to scepticism. Collingwood's interest was in uncovering the criteria for making the kind of statements which are made by, e.g. historians and natural scientists, rather than showing that absolute presuppositions have validity beyond the experience whose possibility they account for. If demonstrating the validity of absolute presuppositions beyond the limits of the form of experience or knowledge which they make possible is what it takes to satisfy external world scepticism then Collingwood's metaphysics of absolute presuppositions does not constitute a reply to it; at best Collingwood shows that doubt makes sense only against the background of certain presuppositions.

A third aspect in which Kant's influence on Collingwood is unclear concerns their understanding of conceptual knowledge. In the *Critique* Kant saw his task as that of defending the possibility of synthetic a priori knowledge. The meaning of Kant's notion of the synthetic a priori, however, is as ambiguous as his notion of transcendental arguments. It is not completely clear whether by synthetic a priori judgements Kant meant judgements which are existential and necessary in some non logical (metaphysical) sense or whether by synthetic a priori claims Kant meant judgements which are necessary in a much weaker (purely explanatory) sense. In other words, it is unclear whether the notion of non-analytic necessity that Kant was looking for was metaphysical or epistemic. Kant defined synthetic judgements as judgements which are ampliative, i.e. as judgements in which the predicate is not contained in the concept of the subject.[21] Such a negative definition, however, leaves open at least two possibilities. The first is that synthetic judgements are ampliative in the rather weak sense that they are not judgements of identity such as "a bachelor is an unmarried man". In this rather weak sense of the term ampliative, synthetic a priori judgements could still be clarificatory, that is, conceptual judgements. The second possibility is that what makes a judgement synthetic is the fact that it predicates a concept not of another concept but of an extra-conceptual, intuitive element. According to this second possibility synthetic a priori judgements are ampliative in the much stronger sense that they are not explicative or clarificatory and consequently they 'expand' the concept of the subject in virtue of the fact that they are existential.[22] Kant's second definition of analyticity does not dispel the ambiguity of his understanding of the synthetic a priori. This second definition, according to which analytic judgements are judgements which are made true by the principle of non-contradiction,[23] identifies analytic knowledge with self-evident truths thereby leaving open the possibility that synthetic a priori judgements may "expand" the concept of the subject not because they are existential (i.e. relate a predicate to an object rather than to another concept) but simply because they are not judgements of identity.[24] In contrast with Kant, Collingwood is clear on the claim that philosophy does not, in any way enlarge or expand our knowledge.[25.] Philosophy, Collingwood claims, "does not . . . bring us to know things of which we were simply ignorant, but brings us to know in a different way things which we already knew in some way (EPM, 161). Philosophy is therefore a reflective activity whose task is to bring to light or render explicit what was already implicitly known. The subject matter of philosophy, as we have seen, is the key principles which structure certain areas of knowledge and which are implicitly known to the practitioners of those disciplines. Therefore, whereas on the one hand Collingwood, like Kant, thought that knowledge of the absolute presuppositions which structure the various areas of experience is not analytic, on the other, unlike Kant, he did not attempt to explain the a priori but non-analytical nature of absolute presuppositions by claiming that such knowledge is not conceptual, i.e. not clarificatory but ampliative. Collingwood occasionally described absolute presuppositions as being synthetic a priori[26] but it is clear that the notion of the synthetic a priori, as used by Collingwood, captures a notion of purely explanatory necessity. In *An Essay on Philosophical Method* Collingwood claimed that there are not, as the empiricists and logical positivists claimed, two kinds of propositions, propositions which are hypothetical and universal (propositions about relations of ideas which are necessarily true and cannot be denied without contradiction) and propositions which are categorical and particular (propositions about matters of fact which are contingently true and can be denied without contradiction). According to the traditional empiricist classification of propositions into relations of ideas and matters of fact only propositions which are hypothetical, i.e. propositions which do not predicate existence, can be universal. Examples of such propositions are 'triangles are three sided-figures' or 'bachelors are unmarried men' which could be paraphrased as 'if triangles exist, they have three sides' and 'if bachelors exist, they are unmarried men'. Conversely, propositions which are concerned with existing things, or which relate a concept to spatio-temporal objects, such as 'all the books on the shelves have a hard cover' are categorical (or existential) rather than hypothetical, but not necessarily true or true in virtue of the laws of logic. Against Hume's fork Collingwood argued that there is a third class of propositions. To this third class, according to Collingwood, there belong propositions which are definitive of domains of enquiry propositions which Collingwood refers to as philosophical propositions.[27] Philosophical propositions are definitive of any given domain of enquiry in the sense that they express the kind of explanations which are employed by the practitioners of different disciplines. So, for instance, the domain of enquiry of the historical sciences, for Collingwood, is mind, because explanations in the historical sciences make use of a teleological or purposive notion of causality, whereas the domain of enquiry of the natural sciences is said to be matter because in the natural sciences the cause of an event is not a purpose but an antecedent state of affairs. Collingwood's reasons for arguing that there is a third class of propositions which are neither hypothetical and universal nor categorical and particular is that philo-sophical propositions are not propositions about matters of fact arrived at on the basis of observation and empirical generalisations. The claim that actions are expressions of thought or mind, for instance, Colling-wood would say, is the kind of non-empirical generalisation that makes history possible as an autonomous domain of enquiry with a distinct method and subject matter from that of the natural sciences. Philo-sophical propositions, therefore, for Collingwood, are synthetic a priori not in the weighty ontological sense that they are necessary existential propositions but in the weaker epistemic sense that they are explanatorily necessary.

Another important difference between Kant's and Collingwood's reform of metaphysics concerns their understanding of 'Being'. Kant identified Being with existence and famously stated that 'Being is not a real predicate'.[28] This statement occurs in the context of Kant's refuta-tion of the ontological argument or of any a priori proof for the existence of God which attempts to demonstrate the existence of God by arguing that existence is a mark of its concept, thereby effectively defining God into existence. Kant argued that being is not a real pre-dicate because it is "merely the positing of a thing, or of certain deter-minations, as existing in themselves". In other words, to say of a concept that it has being, is merely to say that the concept is instantiated. Whereas Kant identified Being with a concept's instantiation or extension, Collingwood identified Being with a concept having maximal intension or containing, within itself, an infinite number of 'marks'. Any concept, he says,

> unites within itself two distinct kinds of plurality: First the plurality of its individual instances, and secondly, the plurality of its specific differentiations. Thus the concept colour unites all the individual colours of all the individual coloured things into a

class of which they are members; but it also unites the specific colours red, orange, green and so forth into a genus of which they are species. It may be convenient to refer to the former unification by saying that the concept is general, to the latter by saying that it is generic (EPM, 27-28).

Being, for Collingwood, is the most abstract concept, a concept so abstract that it is unable to have any descriptive power. In *An Essay on Metaphysics*, Collingwood states that metaphysics, traditionally conceived, is the study of pure being or ontology. He adds also that there cannot be such a science as metaphysics if it is understood as a study of pure Being. Collingwood explains why metaphysics, understood as a science of pure Being or ontology, is impossible, by saying that the science of pure being is a science without a subject matter because the concept of pure being is obtained when the abstractive process is pushed to its utmost limit and, when this happens, there remains nothing determinate to investigate. Collingwood claims that

> There is no science except when two conditions are fulfilled. There must be orderly and systematic thinking, and there must be a definite subject-matter to think about. In the 'science of pure being', however admirably the first condition is fulfilled, the second cannot be. In the case of every other science there is a definite subject matter whose peculiarities differentiate it from the subject-matter of every other science. But the science of pure being would have a subject matter entirely devoid of peculiarities; a subject-matter, therefore, containing nothing to differentiate it from anything else, or from nothing at all (EM, 14).

The concept of pure Being, as the end-point of the abstractive process, has no determinate content: the error of traditional metaphysics was to believe that there could be a presuppositionless study of pure Being or epistemically unconditioned knowledge of reality, that the study of what there is, ontology, could be carried out independently of the study of how what there is, is known, i.e. epistemology. Given the impossibility of a study of pure Being, metaphysics for Collingwood, must take the form of an enquiry into the absolute presuppositions which govern any given domain of enquiry. Collingwood's understanding of the concept of Being as the concept which is located at the end point or summit of the abstractive process is also illustrated in the discussion of the nature of philosophical taxonomies in *An Essay on Philosophical Method*. Here Collingwood claims that in the natural sciences classifications are such that the objects which fall under the specific class of a genus cannot overlap with the objects which fall under its coordinate class. To illustrate: natural history subdivides organisms into animals and vegetables. It then subdivides animals into vertebrate and invertebrates. Animals are further subdivided into mammals fish, birds and reptiles. In classifications of this type if x is an animal it cannot be a vegetable and if x is a vertebrate it cannot be an invertebrate. Whereas there can be some degree of cross-over or overlap among subordinate classes and their super-ordinate ones (some organisms are animals, some animals are vertebrates and some vertebrates are mammals), there cannot, as stated, be any cross-over or overlap in the class of objects which form the extension of two coordinate classes (if x is a vertebrate it is not an invertebrate). Philosophical classifications, unlike classifications in the natural sciences, have to do with purely conceptual rather than empirical distinctions. Therefore, whereas in the kind of classifications employed in natural science in moving from specific classes to their super-ordinate class, we increase the number of instances which fall under the genus (there are more animals than vertebrates, and more organisms than animals) in philosophical taxonomies in moving from specific classes to the genus we decrease the internal differentiations or marks of concepts until one reaches a concept, that of Being, which is so abstract as to lack any determinate content and consequently any descriptive power. The concept of Being, following Collingwood's terminology, is not the most general empirical concept (the concept with the greatest extension or number of objects falling under it) but the most generic or abstract concept.

Given these discrepancies between Kant's and Collingwood's philosophical projects, in what relationship does Collingwood's reform of metaphysics stand to Kant's transcendental philosophy? As we have seen, both Kant and Collingwood believed that, in order to be reformed, metaphysics had to be subjected to a critique: they both agreed that the metaphysics of the past was naive or dogmatic and that a reformed metaphysics had to take into account the distinction between the order of knowledge and the order of existence, a distinction overlooked by those scholastic philosophers who took the structure of knowledge to be a sure guide to the nature of things. Writing in the aftermath of the newly drawn distinction between relations of ideas and matters of fact, a distinction which was meant to undermine the possibility of acquiring knowledge of nature a priori, Kant accepted the empiricist notion of Being as existence and remained sceptical about the possibility of knowing the ultimate nature of reality. Whereas Kant, having endorsed an empiricist or materialist conception of Being, was driven to establish a synthetic, non-conceptual connection between concepts and existing things, Collingwood, having identified Being not with existence but with the summit of conceptual abstraction, proceeded to provide, in a quasi-Aristotelian fashion, a *catalogue raisonné* of the various forms of knowledge and of the explanatory principles to which they appeal. Further, Collingwood's understanding of the subdivision of experience in terms of internal differentiations of the concept of Being disrupts Kant's constitutive/regulative distinction and with it the idea that whereas theoretical judgments have existential import, moral judgements do not: for Collingwood, our experience of the world, whether theoretical, as in the natural sciences, or practical, as in the historical sciences, is a manifestation of Being *qua* natural and *qua* historical.[29] Finally, whereas Kant, having identified Being with existence, declared the ultimate nature of existing things to be epistemically opaque, Collingwood, having identified Being not with existence but with the lack of conceptual distinctions or determinations, stated that reality as it is in-itself is not so much epistemically opaque or unknown to us but that it is rather, in principle, unknowable, because there cannot be a science of pure Being and there cannot be a science of pure Being because such a science would lack a determinate subject matter: metaphysics consequently must take the form of an enquiry into the absolute presuppositions of art, natural science, history etc. Like Kant Collingwood acknowledged the need to distinguish between the order of knowledge and the order of existence and the need to subject the metaphysics of the past to a critique for failing to acknowledge the distinction between ontological and epistemological issues. Collingwood, on the other hand, did not fully agree with Kant that some form of epistemological scepticism would be the necessary price to pay for subjecting the metaphysics of the past to a critique. Perhaps more in line with twentieth century attitudes towards the problem of scepticism, Collingwood sought to provide a demonstration not of the falsity but of the futility of epistemological scepticism, i.e. the futility of positing an Archimedean or transcendent standpoint beyond experience. According to Collingwood, outside the conceptual articulation of Being there is not real, i.e. epistemically unconditioned knowledge, but no knowledge: unlike the metaphysicians of the past, in providing a *catalogue raisonné* of the various forms of experience, Collingwood did not assume that the structure of thought mirrors the nature of reality; yet unlike the transcendental idealist he ruled that there could be knowledge outside the science of experience of consciousness.[30.]

NOTES

1 I would like to thank James Connelly and David Boucher for commenting on an earlier draft of this paper.

2 R. G. Collingwood, *The Idea of History*, Oxford University Press, 1946; revised edition, edited by Jan van der Dussen, Oxford, Oxford University Press, 1993.

3 In particular W. H. Dray's 'Historical Understanding as Rethinking', *University of Toronto Quarterly* 27, 1958; 'Historical Causation and Human Free Will', *University of Toronto Quarterly* 29, 1960; 'The Historical Explanation of Actions Reconsidered' in S. Hook (ed), *Philosophy and History*, New York, New York University Press, 1963 and *History and Re-enactment: R. G. Collingwood's Idea of History*, Oxford, Oxford Clarendon Press, 1995, chapters 2 and 3.

4 Collingwood's most important reflections on the method and subject matter of philosophy are contained in *An Essay on Philosophical Method*, Oxford, Oxford University Press, 1933 (abbreviated as EPM) and in *An Essay on Metaphysics*, Oxford, Oxford University Press, 1940; revised edition, edited by Rex Martin, Oxford, Oxford University Press, 1998 (abbreviated as EM).

5 Any comparative study of Kant and Collingwood is riddled with problems not least because of the lack of agreement, within Kantian scholarship, on the precise nature of Kant's reform of metaphysics. As far as Kant's theoretical philosophy is concerned there

appear to be two main lines of interpretation that seem to split on the issue of whether Kant's transcendental idealism is a purely epistemological thesis or whether there still is an ontological commitment in Kant's transcendental philosophy. Often this interpretative split goes hand in hand with certain views concerning Kant's attitude to scepticism.

6 To my knowledge the Kant scholar who, more than any other, acknowledged this influence, is Walsh. See his *Kant's Criticism of Metaphysics*, Edinburgh, Edinburgh University Press, 1975; *Reason and Experience*; Oxford, Clarendon Press, 1947; *Metaphysics*, Hutchingson University Library, 1963 and his 'Categories' in R. P. Wolff (ed) *Kant*, London, Macmillan, 1968.

7 For the purpose of this essay I will presuppose that there are important continuities between *An Essay on Philosophical Method* and *An Essay on Metaphysics*. I cannot, for reasons of space, provide a full account of the internal development of Collingwood's thought and, least of all, a refutation of the view that Collingwood's work can be neatly split into an early and a later phase. My view, on this matter, is that whereas Collingwood's thought developed, his understanding of the task of philosophy remained fundamentally the same and that his account of absolute presuppositions in *An Essay on Metaphysics* is a further exploration of what, in *An Essay on Philosophical Method* Collingwood had referred to as philosophical propositions (propositions which are definitive of domains of enquiry). In this respect I would agree with Rex Martin and Adrian Oldfield on the point that metaphysics is, in the first instance, to be defined as a study of the absolute presuppositions of disciplines rather than epochs. On this point see Rex Martin's 'Collingwood's Claim that Metaphysics is a Historical Discipline' in *The Monist* 72, 1989, published in a slightly different form in *Philosophy, History and Civilization: Interdisciplinary Perspectives on R. G. Collingwood*, edited by David Boucher, James Connelly and Tariq Modood, Cardiff, University of Wales Press, 1995 and Adrian Oldfield's 'Metaphysics and History in Collingwood's Thought' published in the same anthology.

8 Kant, *Critique of Pure Reason*, London, Macmillan, 1985, translated by Norman Kemp Smith, B xvi, p. 22.

9 What occurs in moving from the concept of cause as it is employed in the historical sciences to the concept of cause as it is employed in the theoretical sciences of nature is a progressive removal of a teleological framework of explanation. The main difference between the practical and the theoretical sciences of nature is that whereas in the former the cause of an event is an antecedent state of affairs considered from the point of view of an interest in controlling the natural environment, in the theoretical sciences of nature the causes of natural events are viewed independently of any impact that agents may have on the natural environment. To illustrate the distinction between the concept of cause as it is employed in the practical and theoretical sciences of nature Collingwood uses the following example: "if my car fails to climb up a steep hill, and I wonder why, I shall not consider my problem solved by a passer-by who tells me that the top of the hill is farther away from the earth's center than its bottom, and that consequently more power is needed to take the car uphill than to take her along the level . . . All this is quite true; what the passerby has described is one of the conditions which together form . . . what I call the cause in sense III (*the sense in which it is employed in the theoretical sciences of nature: my note*) . . . But suppose an AA man comes along, opens the bonnet, holds up a loose high-tension lead and says: 'Look here, sir, you're running on three cylinders'. My problem is now solved . . . If I had been a

person who could flatten out hills by stamping on them the passer-by would have been right in calling to the hill as the cause of the stoppage; not because the hill was a hill but because I was able of flatten it out" (EM, 302-3). This example illustrates the difference between the concept of cause in the practical and theoretical sciences of nature. For Collingwood, on the other hand, the main difference between the concept of cause as employed in the historical as opposed to the natural sciences (whether practical or theoretical) is that whereas the practical and theoretical sciences of nature explain (events) by appealing to empirical regularities, the historical sciences explain (actions) by ascribing reasons to agents. The natural sciences are concerned with empirical or external relations between events; the historical sciences are concerned with internal, non-empirical relations between actions and the motives/beliefs they express.

10 For Kant's distinction between an empirical and a transcendental deduction see CPR B118/A86, p. 121.

11 See *An Essay on Metaphysics*, part I, chapter 3.

12 The use of the term history in Collingwood's work differs from the common sense conception of it. In *The Idea of History*, for instance, Collingwood describes history not as that area of knowledge which is concerned with the past, but as the right way of investigating mind (IH, 219). A great part of the Epilegomena, in *The Idea of History*, is an attempt to defend historical method against the experimental method which consists in observation, classification and the use of general laws, a method that Collingwood regarded to be inadequate to the study of history. The term 'history', as Collingwood employs it, is much broader than the vernacular. By historical method Collingwood means not a method specific to practising historians but a method which is common to any discipline in the social sciences which shares a conception of the nature of explanation as distinct from the character of explanation in the natural sciences.

13 See John Locke's 'The Epistle to the Reader' in *An Essay Concerning Human Understanding*, Glasgow, Collins Fount Paperbacks, 1981, p. 56.

14 Kant's anti-Leibnizian point is to be found in CPR A24/B39, p. 68. It is the first argument for the transcendental ideality of space given in 'The Metaphysical Exposition of this Concept'. For an account of Kant's arguments for the transcendental ideality of space see H. Allison, *Kant's Transcendental Idealism*, New Haven, Yale University Press, 1983, pp. 82-86.

15 Kant, CPR B234-A190/B248-A203, pp. 218-227.

16 Ameriks argues that the main feature of the method employed by Kant in the transcendental deduction lies in the fact that "it takes the critique to accept empirical knowledge as a premise to be regressively explained rather than a conclusion to be established" (K. Ameriks, 'The Transcendental Deduction as A Regressive Argument', *Kant Studien* 69, 1978).

17 R. G. Collingwood, *An Autobiography*, chapter 6, Oxford, Oxford University Press, 1939.

18 S. Gardner, *Kant and the Critique of Pure Reason*, London, Routledge 1999, pp. xiii.

19 Barry Stroud 'Transcendental Arguments', *Journal of Philosophy* LXV, 1968, pp. 244 ff.

20 see footnote 16.

21 Kant, CPR, A7/B11, p. 48.

22 Whereas there is much support for the first line of interpretation Kant grants some plausibility to the second interpretation when, in the context of his refutation of the ontological argument, he claims that any reasonable person ought to admit that all existential propositions are synthetic (CPR A598/B626, p. 504).

23 Kant, CPR A152/B191, p. 190.
24 A thorough account of the historical context of Kant's discussion of the analytic/ synthetic distinction is to be found in H. E. Allison, *The Kant-Eberhard Controversy*, Baltimo, the Johns Hopkins University Press, 1973. Through an analysis of Kant's reply to Eberhard Allison shows how the apparent ambiguity in Kant's formulation of the analytic/synthetic distinction is cleared. Eberhard challenged the novelty of Kant's notion of the synthetic a priori from the perspective of dogmatic or pre-critical rationalism by saying that synthetic a priori knowledge is conceptual although not self-identical knowledge. When confronted with an attempt to reinscribe the analytic/ synthetic distinction within the frame of reference of the dogmatic metaphysics which was the objective of the transcendental philosophy to critique, Kant stated that the predicate in a synthetic judgment could not possibly be derived by means of analysis because whereas in analytic judgements the concept of the predicate is brought in a relation to another concept, in synthetic judgments the relationship between the predicate and the subject is a real, not a logical or conceptual relation, i.e., the concept of the predicate is related to an object, not to another concept (Allison, p. 54-55). Another interesting account of the analytic-synthetic distinction is to be found in A. Coffa, *The Semantic Tradition from Kant to Carnap*, Cambridge, Cambridge University Press, 1991, chapter 1.
25 His metaphysics is, as Collingwood says, a metaphysics without ontology which makes no existential claims. It is possible to speak of an expansion of knowledge in Collingwood's case, only in the sense of an increased level of sophistication in the conceptual map of knowledge and in the internal differentiations of the concept of Being as discussed later.
26 To be precise, it is philosophical propositions, rather than absolute presuppositions, that Collingwood refers to as 'synthetic a priori' thereby making an explicit reference to Kant's theoretical philosophy (in 'The Collingwood-Ryle Correspondence', deposited in the Bodleian library). The term 'absolute presuppositions' was coined later and would not have been part of Collingwood's philosophical vocabulary in the immediate aftermath of the publication of *An Essay on Philosophical Method*, when the exchange with Ryle took place. As stated earlier, however, I am, for the purposes of this exposition, assuming that Collingwood conceives of metaphysics as a study of the absolute presuppositions of disciplines, rather than epochs and consequently, that absolute presuppositions, as discussed in *An Essay on Metaphysics* are comparable, at least to a great extent, with philosophical propositions, as discussed in *An Essay on Philosophical Method*.
27 Collingwood's discussion of philosophical propositions is to be found in *An Essay on Philosophical Method*, chapter 6. A clarification of his defence of a third class of philosophical propositions in contrast to the logical positivists' assertion that there are only two kinds of propositions, matters of fact and relations of ideas, is to be found in Collingwood's private correspondence with Ryle in the context of a discussion about the ontological argument.
28 Kant, CPR A599/B627, p. 504.
29 Collingwood's rejection of the constitutive/regulative distinction amounts to the removal of any possible ontological anchor for knowledge or experience and paves the way for the claim that metaphysics studies the nature or structure of *our* experience rather than the structure of *any possible* experience, and consequently is, even if in this rather minimal sense, an historical discipline.

30 This might explain why Collingwood often wavered in his self-representation as either a (Kantian) transcendental idealist or as an (Hegelian) objective idealist. In his (unpublished) 'Commentary on the Preface to the Critique of Pure Reason', for instance, Collingwood praised transcendental idealism and described post-kantian phenomenology as a backward step in the direction of scholastic philosophy, whereas in *An Essay on Philosophical Method* he praised Hegel for his rejection of subjective idealism (subjective idealism being a term coined by Hegel to describe Kant's transcendental idealism). Such dithering in Collingwood's self-representation as either a Kantian transcendental idealist or as an Hegelian objective idealist may be explained by his attempt to overcome Kant's epistemological idealism/scepticism in favour of Hegel's epistemological realism whilst retaining Kant's critique of transcendent realism.

Modes of Visualisation in Neo-Idealist Theories of the Historical Imagination (Cassirer, Collingwood, Huizinga)

DAVID A. WISNER
The American College of Thessaloniki

It is said of G. M. Trevelyan that he was a fiend for direct observation, which led him to travel extensively to gain a greater feel for his subject matter. No reader of his famous essay, *Clio, A Muse*, can likely forget Trevelyan's description of a walking tour past Helvellyn:

> One day, as I was walking along the side of Great Gable, thinking of history and forgetting the mountains which I trod, I chanced to look up and see the top of a long green ridge outlined on the blue horizon. For half a minute I stood thoughtless in enjoyment of this new range, noting upon it forms of beauty and qualities of romance, until suddenly I remembered that I was looking at the top of Helvellyn! Instantly, as by magic, its shape seemed to change under my eyes, and the qualities with which I had endowed the unknown mountain to fall away, because I now knew what like were its hidden base and its averted side, what names and memories cling round it. The change taking place in its aspect seemed physical, but I suppose it was only a trick of my own mind. Even so, if we could forget for a while all that had happened since the Battle of Waterloo, we should see it, not as we see it now, with all its time-honoured associations and its conventionalised place in history, but as our ancestors saw it first, when

we did not know whether the 'Hundred Days' as we now call them, would not stretch out for a Hundred Years.

Such a desire to 'see . . . as our ancestors saw it first' was a common element in Trevelyan's account of the historian's craft, so much so that he felt compelled, as it were, to conclude, 'Every true history must, by its human and vital presentation of events, force us to remember that the past was once real as the present and uncertain as the future.' No faculties of the human mind did he appreciate more in this respect than 'insight, sympathy and imagination of the finest,' which permitted such a vision into the realms of the past.[1]

Modern history is full of similar examples of historians seeking to commune intimately with the past in one way or another. One need think only of Machiavelli donning his toga, or of Gibbon toiling to find the right turn of phrase for a translation out of the Latin. The French artist Louis David believed that were the ancients to visit his studio in Paris round about 1800 they would recognise themselves in his painting. In the nineteenth century an entire generation of historians was weaned on the writings of that veritable luminary, Sir Walter Scott. Nor is the phenomenon limited to bygone eras. Today archaeologists in Italy struggle to rebuild the city of Pompeii using only materials and techniques known to antiquity, while entrepreneurs groom the Viking site of Jorvik as a historian's Disney World. Students in the Western Civilisation surveys taught in American universities are often treated before or during lectures to multi-media shows designed to transport them back – somehow – into the past, even as critics of the practice decry it as anachronistic. And who can deny the impact that film has had on our contemporary historical consciousness? Some of our more resourceful historians have even availed themselves as consultants to the film industries of several Western countries.

More to the point, historians have periodically attempted to include the imaginative dimension as a formal element in their explanations of what exactly it is that the historian does. As Isaiah Berlin has observed, 'Vico in the eighteenth century (*fantasia*) and Herder some hundred years later (*Einfühlung, Verstehen*) gave the first thorough theoretical treatments of the phenomenon of "entering into" minds and situations [of] the past.'² Masters like Thierry and Michelet, Macaulay and Trevelyan, and any number of nineteenth-century Germans all recognised the validity of a personal communion with the past-personal denoting both the conscious projection of one's own values and the admission of extra-rational means of understanding as opposed to what by now has too often been caricatured as the predominant tendency in nineteenth-century historiography toward a purely rational, scientific collection and analysis of historical facts. Round about 1900 and thereafter a number of historians and philosophers, more or less affiliated with the type of relativism implied at the very least in the anti-scientific literature of the nineteenth century, endeavoured to give a systematic philosophical explanation for an approach to history which was based on an imaginative re-experiencing or re-enactment of the past. Indeed, as H. Stuart Hughes has convincingly demonstrated, the neo-idealist historians and philosophers of the so-called 'generation of 1905' – Dilthey, Croce, Weber, etc. – were among the first to grapple constructively with the issue of the creative imagination in their social thought.³ Their legacy is still with us, the problematics of post-structuralism notwithstanding.

An equally important but apparently overlooked stage in the development of a cogent theory of the historical imagination came in the early decades of the twentieth century in the hands of what might be called a second wave of neo- (or post-) idealists. These men, historians and theorists like Ernst Cassirer, R. G. Collingwood, and Johan Huizinga, if not José Ortega y Gasset, Bernard Groethuysen, Herbert Butterfield, Michael Oakeshott, and Isaiah Berlin, sought to build on the work of the preceding generation while explicating some of the problems still inherent in neo-idealism. As such theirs is a chapter to be added to the turn-of-the-century cohort of neo-idealists studied so keenly by Hughes. The grouping of Cassirer, Collingwood, and Huizinga in particular is quite interesting for several reasons in fact. Although all three were practising historians they came to history from different domains – Cassirer and Collingwood from philosophy and Huizinga from philology and linguistics; all contributed in one way or another to broaden significantly the horizon of historical inquiry. All three wrote influential essays on the subject during the critical decades of the 1920s and 1930s, when the nineteenth-century ideal of scientific, positivistic history was still a force to be reckoned with. At the same time all were eventually concerned with the type of excessively nationalistic, mythologising and, to some extent, social scientific histories which were filling the void left behind by the demise of *Historismus*. All admitted that the historian could not but bring to his work the full weight of the values and prejudices of his time. And yet all sought nonetheless to find some rational grounding for their relativism, specifically in a neo-idealist philosophy of knowledge, in which history was seen as a special mode of thought. It is perhaps no coincidence that their efforts should have taken place when they did, in the crucial interwar decades when such endeavours seemed to risk foundering on the shores of an intemperate age, and yet where a tiny but firm voice of moderation and reason still carried over the din: all three men were particularly outspoken and militant critics against the fascist regimes. It was thus that all three also upheld a rigorous ethical standard in the work of the historian, and saw themselves as the depositories, and indeed, the conscience, of Western civilisation.[4]

The imaginative element was a key component in the thought of the second generation neo-idealists. So, too, did their style of thinking contain a distinct visual dimension, which coincides, uneasily perhaps, with what has been called the ocularcentrism of modern Western philosophy; this is precisely what I refer to in the phrase 'modes of visualisation.' By this I mean something more than the common phenomenon of using visual metaphors to describe our intelligence of things, a phenomenon which has been a staple of intellectual culture in the West since the advent of Neo-Platonism at the very least.[5] To be sure, it is commonplace to find this type of metaphor in descriptions of the historian's *métier*. What I have in mind rather concerns at the most fundamental level an attempt to ground the type of imaginative experience described by Trevelyan, for instance, in a systematic theory of knowledge. Put briefly, the question to be asked is the following: What do we do when we try to 'see . . . as our ancestors saw it first,' or, to take another example from Trevelyan, when we distinguish between 'those who see [something] now and those by whom its was once seen?'[6] The authors whose views are examined in these pages all asked this question more or less directly, and arguably gave the most creative answers to it to date.

The following discussion will begin with something of a standard statement on the role of the imagination and, by extension, the place of visualisation in historical research by a younger contemporary of our triad, Herbert Butterfield, whose basic position in this respect, reminiscent as it is after all of that of Trevelyan, reflects more or less their common point of departure and provides us with a convenient place to start our investigation.[7] Then I will consider each of the writers individually for their general theories of the historical imagination and their particular contributions to an epistemology of historical visualisation. Although I am most interested in statements of a theoretical nature, and to no small extent in the *language* used therein (whence my choice to let each author speak for himself, as much as is possible), I will also make passing reference, where pertinent, to the practical application each may have made in their own work as historians. But my purpose is to do more than simply sketch a series of parallels among the three. A progressive analysis of the epistemological writings of Cassirer, Collingwood, and Huizinga should also permit us to draw certain constructive, if not programmatic, conclusions in light of contemporary debate on the nature of history and historical knowledge. Thus I will conclude with some tentative reflections of a rather broader nature with respect to the modes of visualisation evaluated below, notably as these pertain to the ethical dimensions implicit in the neo-idealist philosophy of history.

I

What is it that historians do when they engage in historical research? What is the specific place of the imagination therein? A classic relativist answer is to be found in the pages of Herbert Butterfield's 1931 essay, *The Whig Interpretation of History*.[8] First off, the historian is an observer, engaged in some sort of visualisation: his purpose is one of 'visualising the general course of history or commenting on it' (15). This observation borders on scrutiny: one looks, so to speak, 'at some point in history through the microscope [so] that we can really visualise the complicated movements that lie behind any historical change' (21). But the historian is 'not merely the observer:' he must also perform some 'creative act of the historical imagination' (77, 91). In so doing the historian cannot but approach his subject from the perspectives of his own time. 'Real historical understanding,' however, 'is not achieved by the subordination of the past to the present, but rather by our making the past our present and attempting to see life with the eyes of another century than our own' (16). Only thus can one escape the dangers of the so-called 'whig interpretation of history,' which elsewhere Butterfield calls an 'optical illusion.'

In this instance 'seeing' is generally synonymous with 'understanding,' but there is more. As we have just seen, Butterfield's notion entails an act of the imagination, which implies that the mind is active in its effort to come to terms with the evidence at hand. Butterfield's claims in this respect support his relativist, idealist position against both the whig and the positivist historian. Indeed, some of the author's most luminous passages are to be found in his description of this facet of historical knowledge. The student of history is indeed not merely an observer, he objects (92-93; my emphasis):

> for if he were this only he would be a poor observer. In a special sense he goes out to meet the past and his work is not merely the function of mind, it is a *venture of the personality* . . . The historian is something more than the mere passive external spectator. Something more is necessary if only to enable him to *seize the significant detail* and *discern the sympathies* between events and find the facts that hang together. By *imaginative sympathy* he makes the past intelligible to the present . . . . There is a kind of awareness that only comes through *insight and sympathy*, and is perhaps absent from us when we are too alert for a purely scientific end. It is absent from us if we read our documents only literally, and miss their *innuendo* because we lack the *historic sense*. Something of this awareness is necessary to catch the *overtones in history and in life*, to read between the lines and *touch the human side* of our subject, for which our minds may be too mathematical if mind does not work along with sympathy and

imagination. It will always be something of a *work of art* to
understand the ways of our next-door neighbour, and however
learned we may be in psychology *something like divination will be
necessary* before we can see its bearings upon any particular
human being . . . . It is necessary that we should *go with instinct
and sympathy alive and all our humanity awake.*

To sum up, the historian is a prisoner of his own time, but seeks
nonetheless to place himself in the shoes of his historical protagonists,
fully aware as he is of his limitations. He loves the past for the sake of
the past, partly as a result of 'the emotional drive that is necessary to
make us question conclusions that seem foregone' (94), partly out of
'the desire to bring himself into genuine relationship with the actual,
with all the particularities of chance and change – the desire to see at
first-hand how an important decision comes to be made' (73). And yet
he is also aware that, insofar as history 'is the analysis of all the media-
tions by which the past was turned into our present' (47), there may
well be something essential to be learned about human nature, namely,
'that we ourselves are, in our turn, not quite autonomous or unconditioned, but a part of the great historical process; not pioneers merely,
but also passengers in the movement of things,' that is, 'where . . . we
ourselves, and our ideas and prejudices, stand' (63). History, in short,
represents a 'special mode of thought,' and the historian's description of
change constitutes 'his peculiar contribution to our knowledge of
ourselves and of human affairs' (129).

This condensed account of Butterfield's essay brings us metaphorically to the departure gate, as it were, whence Cassirer, Collingwood,
and Huizinga ventured forth in their quest to distinguish further what
the historian does when he imagines or 'sees' into the past. For Butterfield's account raises a host of philosophical and methodological questions
which he leaves unanswered. What actually transpires when the historian studies his evidence? How does the mind function in its creative act
of imagination? What exactly is so special about the historical mode of
thought? How does the historian know when his knowledge approaches
verisimilitude? Precisely what does the historian contribute to his contemporaries? To be fair to Butterfield, his principal purpose is not to

consider such inquiries. And yet the importance of the position I am attributing to Butterfield, particularly as revealed in the long passage cited above, makes this line of questioning essential, not only if we are to fulfil his exhortation that we continue to ask questions, but also if we are to be able to ascertain the general validity of his thesis.

Ernst Cassirer seems to have engaged in this type of interrogation, principally in *An Essay on Man*, which is our chief theoretical source for Cassirer's views on historical knowledge.[9] Cassirer was what Collingwood himself would have called a younger-generation adherent to the 'neo-Kantian school' of historical criticism which came into prominence in Germany toward the end of the nineteenth century.[10] He upheld an idealist theory of knowledge, and argued in favour of what on the surface at least amounted to a relativist historiographical thesis. His principal contribution as a philosopher was his theory of symbolic forms, which marked the culmination of a life-long historical investigation into the theory of knowledge. In *An Essay on Man* Cassirer claimed that the epistemologist needed to ask, in order to determine the distinctive nature of historical knowledge, not what the 'logic' of historical inquiry might be, but rather what its 'object' was. At stake was nothing less than man's moral core.

Cassirer's answer to the general query, 'What does the historian seek to do?' is relatively straightforward on the surface: to 'see' the men of other days . . . the real life, the drama of history' (220). To be sure Cassirer, like a host of his contemporaries, conceives of sight metaphorically, as a function of the 'mind's eye,' so to speak. And yet he has more in mind when he uses such metaphors of sight. In fact, the chapter on history in *An Essay on Man* can be read, on one level at least, as a primer on how such 'sight' is possible. To begin with, Cassirer adds to his initial statement that the role of the historian is to search for the 'materialization of the spirit of a former age.' Historical facts and laws, if such exist, will never allow us to perceive this aspect of the life of the past: some other *object of cognition* is necessary. That object is 'symbolic' in nature, a component, in Cassirer's scheme of human knowledge, of a hierarchy of symbolic forms by which the human mind comes to know, understand, and interact with its environment. Historical knowledge is thus derived from a 'reading' of all the 'various symbolic idioms.'

Reading, in turn, entails interpretation. Historical knowledge is the product of 'ideal' or 'symbolic reconstruction,' by which the 'living form' of the evidence, those symbolic idioms of past ages through which man expressed and by nature continues to express himself, can be understood in the present. 'History,' writes Cassirer, 'is the attempt to fuse together . . . the scattered limbs of the past and to synthesize them and mold them into new shape' (196). Historical visualisation is in this sense the perception of forms and shapes with various possible meanings. The specific meaning these forms and shapes take for the historian is the product of a 'new intellectual synthesis – a constructive act' (204).

The relativism implied in this position leads Cassirer to claim moreover that the process of synthesis and reconstruction must constantly undergo revision. In a universe of *becoming*, the need for revision is constant (198-99):

> The facts of the philosophical past, the doctrines and systems of the great thinkers, are meaningless without an interpretation. And this process of interpretation never comes to a complete standstill. As soon as we have reached a new center and a new line of vision in our own thoughts we must revise our judgment.

The historian's point of departure is of necessity the present; his own understanding is coloured by his own time. Inasmuch as the past is dead, the 'symbolic universe' must therefore serve as a medium both physical and temporal between past and present. The process of revision is inexorable: 'As soon as we see . . . individual men in a new light we have to alter our ideas of the event' (201).

Metaphors of vision are clearly evident in Cassirer's description of the historian's search. But there is an added dimension to this search which is equally important from our point of view. History, insofar as it is related to art, both in the hierarchy of symbolic forms and as a form of understanding, 'teaches us to visualize, not merely to conceptualize or utilize, things' (188).[11] Considered thus, 'visualisation' is imaginative as much as it is intellectualistic. The historian must 'feel' even as he thinks. On the one hand he must grasp the 'personality and character' of those whom he studies: this is what a 'symbolic interpretation' permits. Yet by the same token he must also strive toward a connection with the 'real life' of history. Thus Cassirer argues that both understanding and feeling are necessary in historical research. 'In history we regard all the works of man, and all his deeds, as precipitates of his life; and we wish to reconstitute them into this original state, we wish to *understand* and *feel* the life from which they are derived' (203).[12]

Yet the historian must bring his *own* feelings to his subject as well. This is in part a consequence of the temporal constraints which determine the nature of historical inquiry. But at the same time Cassirer acknowledges that in his attempt to have a feel for the past the historian's attitude must be something more than dispassionate. 'The historian cannot invent a new language or a new logic [for] a human and cultural life. He cannot think or speak without using general terms. But he infuses into his concepts and words his own inner feelings, and thus gives them a new sound and a new color – the color of personal life' (206). His task thus conceived the historian must engage in an act of intuition, of 'intellectual and imaginative . . . sympathy.' Only in this manner can dead facts and artefacts regain life: the act of 'seeing' restores to historical evidence its 'creative energies;' the act of understanding 'is always an act of the productive imagination' (226).

Stated in even stronger terms, the historian is charged with the sublime mission of 'revivifying the past.' He becomes a 'retrospective prophet' charged with 'a prophecy of the past, a revelation of its hidden life' (197). Such language, like that of Butterfield, is all the more striking given the measured tone of the rest of Cassirer's discussion. Why should this be so? For Cassirer the answer has two basic components. On the one hand, historical imagination falls for the neo-idealist in the same register as did the sublime in Kantian aesthetics, that is, at the very limit of what the mind can know and what language can express: a *creative imagination* is essential to cross this barrier. On the other hand, Cassirer emphasises the impulse toward historical knowledge in the individual, and the ultimately (neo-Kantian) ethical character of the effort to revivify the past. At one level Cassirer falls back on the notion of human nature: man experiences a 'fundamental instinct,' a 'fundamental tendency,' to express himself, to 'break the chain of his individual and ephemeral existence' (203). This is the origin of culture, of the symbolic universe. Apart from this humans have lately discovered in themselves the wherewithal to *remember* past forms, and more importantly to seek out their meaning. The integrity of the initial impulse toward symbolic expression is 'kept alive by the art of the historian.' Thus Cassirer concludes in resolute fashion: 'In order to possess the world of culture we must incessantly reconquer it by historical recollection' (204).

Cassirer here takes his discussion even farther in a direction which seems to stray from his elaboration of the role of imagining and seeing in the historian's work. For he concludes both that we have a moral *responsibility* to do our work well, but also that history as such is a 'form of self-knowledge' and, ultimately, a door onto human freedom (228). Nonetheless we can grasp the critical significance of the special intellectual, imaginative, and, in short, symbolic visualisation in his description of historical knowledge. Within the confines of his chapter on history in *An Essay on Man*, to which I shall return momentarily, he has provided us with a step forward in our quest to define precisely what such visualisation might be. Cassirer's emphasis on the *nature of our evidence* helps us understand the intermediary realm between the past and the present.[13] This is precisely the field of historical vision, that is, of intellection and intuition. Moreover, Cassirer describes in considerably more detail than did Butterfield the relationship the historian has with this evidence. From the starting point of his peculiar brand of neo-Kantian epistemology he also indicates the objective epistemological foundation for the act of the creative imagination so central to this tendency in historical thought. He suggests a more elaborate version of the mechanisms behind our drive to know and therefore see the past. And he endeavours to place historical knowledge, that special mode of thought, in the overall context of human consciousness.

To be sure, there are problems in Cassirer's position as developed in *An Essay on Man*. In the first place, Cassirer himself acknowledges that he has not engaged in a philosophy of history *per se*, but rather in a philosophy of culture, in which history, like art and science, occupies a privileged position. More important, the precise step-by-step function of historical recollection and productive imagination remains to be worked out. At best Cassirer gives us a parallel with art which begs further amplification. Finally, the so-called spirit of former ages continues to be rather vague as formulated here in Cassirer's discussion, particularly with respect to the means by which an understanding thereof can be built up from the symbolic evidence.[14] Man may well attain a special kind of freedom with the proper historical knowledge, but when and how exactly he knows or feels that his interpretation is correct is still something of a mystery.

II

An answer to some of the dilemmas present in Cassirer's chapter of history in *An Essay on Man* may be found in the work of R. G. Collingwood. Indeed, in many ways the perspectives and conclusions of the two men *qua* philosophers of history are remarkably close in spirit. Read together, they provide complementary analyses of many of the phenomena hitherto discussed, particularly with regard to the character of historical evidence, the nature of historical thought, and the autonomy of historical knowledge, Collingwood even going so far as to claim that history was a 'necessary form of experience.'[15] Both worked from an idealist, if not broadly neo-Kantian, epistemological standpoint. Both argued in favour of what on the surface seemed to amount to a relativist historiographical position, although both sought to give objective grounding to this same position. Both were profoundly interested in the what and how of history, and both were acutely aware of the recent vintage of critical historical method, to which both endeavoured to resolve pressing problems. From our point of view in particular the 'logic of question and answer' which Jan van der Dussen, the recent editor of Collingwood's best known work in the field, *The Idea of History*, considers to be so important in all of Collingwood's work on the philosophy of history,[16] dovetails very neatly with Cassirer's discussion of the nature of historical evidence. Thus if on one level Cassirer tells us what we see, Collingwood tells us how we see it.

Collingwood's work on the philosophy of history, while more ample than Cassirer's, also contains a number of difficulties which are worth mentioning at this point. As van der Dussen has commented, Collingwood's thought went through several stages, and has been subjected subsequently to a bewildering variety of interpretations.[17] On some points, such as the standing of historical evidence, so critical in Collingwood's exposition, there is considerable divergence, if not occasional contradiction, in the texts. Given the editorial history of *The Idea of History*, which van der Dussen attempts to sort out, it would seem that on certain such points Collingwood never quite gave his final word.[18] On a purely doctrinal level, finally, there is some question as to how far Collingwood went beyond the position upheld by Butterfield or Cassirer, for example, with regard to the autonomy of history as a mode of knowledge, to embrace the claim of Croce that 'all reality is history and all knowledge is historical knowledge,' or, as Collingwood himself puts it in one of his early lectures, 'all philosophy is the philosophy of history' (197, 425).

These apparent discrepancies do not present major obstacles to an initial intelligence of Collingwood's contribution to the present line of inquiry, however. For the following discussion I will be interested in one principal essay in *The Idea of History* entitled 'The Historical Imagination' (231-49). The essay was included by T. M. Knox in the original edition of *The Idea of History*, although it had initially been delivered and published in 1935 as Collingwood's inaugural lecture as Waynflete Professor of Metaphysical Philosophy at Oxford University.[19] This chapter of *The Idea of History* has not attracted the commentary that other, more famous sections of the book have, especially those that deal with re-enactment. That Collingwood should have given the lecture on such an occasion is nonetheless proof of the importance he assigned to the ideas contained therein, even if in later years he seemed to have progressed beyond certain notions expressed in the original lecture.[20]

Specifically, this chapter provides us with a detailed elaboration on the role of the imagination and the nature of the creative act in historical knowledge, both of which are distinctly vision-oriented in character. Like Cassirer, and perhaps even more so like Butterfield, Collingwood often uses visual metaphors in his philosophy of history. Thus for example he states that on a very elementary level historical thought 'is like perception,' which is to say that it has a distinctly personal, or individual, to use Collingwood's term, character. Or, as he put it in one of his early lectures, the historian focuses his microscope on the evidence needed to fill his monograph, realising as he does that there will always be some 'ultra-microscopic . . . pieces of evidence' which remain undetected, along with 'those which the magnification itself removes from his field of vision' (457). The goal of the historian, finally, as stated in the essay on the historical imagination, is to draw a 'coherent and continuous picture . . . of the past' (245). But such cases almost always have a more immediate functional and methodological value as well. For throughout Collingwood implies that there is an objective content to historical vision. This stems first from the means by which we examine the evidence, and second from the *mental processes of inference* from this same evidence.

History, wrote Collingwood in 1926 in a passage similar in spirit to Butterfield's later essay, 'is the explanation of how the actual world in which we live has come to be what it is' (468). As he pursued his inquiry Collingwood modified this initial definition substantially. Thus by 1936 he could write, in a justly famous passage, that 'all history is the history of thought' (215). Leaving aside for the moment the development Collingwood's own ideas underwent in the intervening decade, a more formal question awaits us: How is this thought known? According to Collingwood it is re-enacted in the historian's mind. As he looks at the evidence the historian 'has to discover what the person who [left behind certain relics] meant by them. This means discovering the thought (in the widest sense of the word . . .) which he expressed by them. To discover what this thought was, the historian must think it again for himself' (282-83).[21] Whereupon Collingwood elaborates in common-sense fashion on the mechanism of such re-enactment (283; my emphasis):

> Suppose, for example, he is reading the Theodosian Code, and has before him a certain edict of an emperor. Merely reading the words and being able to translate them does not amount to knowing their historical significance. In order to do that he must *envisage* the situation with which the emperor was trying to deal, and he must envisage it as that emperor envisaged it. Then he

must *see for himself,* just as if the emperor's situation were his own, how such a situation might be dealt with; he must *see the possible alternatives,* and the reasons for choosing one rather than another; and thus he must *go through the process* which the emperor went through in deciding this particular course. Thus he is *re-enacting* in his own mind the experience of the emperor; and only in so far as he does this has he any historical knowledge, as distinct from a merely philological knowledge, of the meaning of the edict.

Or again, suppose he is reading a passage of an ancient philosopher. Once more, he must know the language in a philological sense and be able to construe; but by doing that he has not yet understood the passage as an historian of philosophy must understand it. In order to do that *he must see what the philosophical problem was,* of which his author is here stating his solution. He must think that problem out for himself, see what possible solutions of it might be offered, and see why this particular philosopher chose that solution instead of another. This means *re-thinking* for himself the thought of his author, and nothing short of that will make him the historian of that author's philosophy.

To be sure, on the surface at least this vision is meant metaphorically as much as methodologically. Moreover, stated as such it is open to serious criticism. Quite apart from the fact that Collingwood is hereafter obliged to fight through a thicket of epistemological difficulties relative to the *logical possibility* of re-enacting the thought of a historical actor, the general theoretical explication offered in this passage seems overly intellectualistic, inasmuch as the men of the past may not always have deliberated in the rational manner implied by Collingwood (we shall return to this problem below).[22] Nonetheless, taken as the historian's desideratum Collingwood's statement provides the point of departure for an understanding of the historical imagination, which makes the faculty of historical sight possible. Stated otherwise, were it not possible to *envisage* it would be equally impossible to *re-enact.*

According to the intermediary position taken by Collingwood in the chapter of the historical imagination, this latter should be taken as an *a priori* structure of thought, and thereby a constructive criterion for historical knowledge.[23] The immediate problem which Collingwood attempts to resolve in this chapter is that of inferential thinking in history, which he had grappled with inconclusively in an earlier lecture. As is nearly always the case with Collingwood, the problem arises from the nature of historical evidence. Having rejected uncritical history, in which the historian accepts the evidence at face value, Collingwood now goes on to examine the critical stance the historian needs to take vis-à-vis the evidence. Certain statements of fact lead us to the tentative conclusion that history is a 'web of imaginative construction stretched between certain fixed points provided by the statements of authorities' (242), that is to say, as Collingwood has already specified elsewhere in this essay, is thus actually a construction built upon the evidence remaining after the historian has assumed his critical stance.

Collingwood will later go on to add that in essence none of the presumed fixed points upon which he has spun his web are veritably fixed, an idea to which I will return momentarily. For the moment it is the role of the imagination in the spinning of the web which interests me. This web is the product of a mental activity which Collingwood calls the '*a priori* imagination.' Common sense tells us that from two separate facts related by the evidence (Julius Caesar was one day in Rome and a later day in Gaul) we interpolate that he actually travelled from one place to the next. Yet Collingwood argues that such interpolations are correct on more than a common-sense basis alone. On the one hand, our conclusion is legitimate if necessitated by the evidence. On the other hand, it is a product, or, to use Collingwood's terminology, a construction, of the imagination, which in fact is a *structure* of thought, without which all telling of history would be impossible.

It is on this plane that Collingwood takes a great step beyond the claims of earlier historians like Macaulay (and more recently Butterfield) for whom the imagination was an essential tool of the historian – assuming, of course, that descriptive narrative is the proper means of relating historical knowledge. For Collingwood this historical imagination is neither fiction nor fantasy, but is necessary in a specific sort of way: 'we cannot but imagine what cannot but be there.' It is a construct of the mind, analogous to the type of imagination employed by the artist who creates a work of art, with the exception that where the artist's imagination is 'pure or free' the historian must direct himself to 'imagine the past' (242). This is the web which is perceived, seen, envisaged, by the historian prior to the effort of re-enactment.

From these initial conclusions Collingwood explores further implications which are indirectly relevant to our investigation. First, he goes on to claim that none of the fixed points over which we stretched our web are in fact fixed: 'they must be achieved by critical thinking' (243). This is a point which Collingwood repeated in yet another context in a lecture given in 1936, but which he seems to have advanced beyond in sections of *The Idea of History* composed at an even later date. For the moment Collingwood is content to maintain simply that the historian must constantly review the evidence, which entails a continuous process of rewriting history. As his own standpoint changes so does the view he is able to produce in the historical imagination; no single view is a final one. Although this statement, reinforced elsewhere in the book, tends toward relativism, we must constantly bear in mind that the *mental activity* which makes it possible for us to see into the past is objective and *a priori*. Moreover, Collingwood further concludes in this essay that some additional criterion must be sought to guide the historian in his endeavour to understand and use those morsels of evidence over which he constructs his imaginary web. As we read and study our evidence, we accept or reject bits and pieces of it according to whether we as historians are able to incorporate it 'into a coherent and continuous picture' of our own. Thus as we imagine what happened we find ourselves in the possession of a tool which can also be used to criticise our sources. 'The *a priori* imagination which does the work of historical construction supplies the means of historical criticism as well' (245).

Collingwood pursues his discussion of this specific criterion by comparing once more the work of the artist, in this case the novelist, with that of the historian. Whereas both are meant to be 'self-explanatory, self-justifying . . . product[s] of an autonomous or self-authorising activity,' that of the historian must also produce a picture which is 'meant to be true.' He further claims that the process of obtaining historical knowledge is self-perpetuating. 'The enlargement of historical knowledge comes about mainly through finding how to use as evidence this or that kind of perceived fact which historians have hitherto thought useless to them' (247). History therefore can be said to be a peculiar and essential inheritance of mankind, like art, science, philosophy, or morality, something continually sought after but never attained in its totality or finality. Collingwood does not despair at this thought, however, for it leads him to his ultimate conclusion, spelled out moreover in language very close in spirit to that of Cassirer and Butterfield, namely that the constant study of history reveals one final dimension of history, the history, and thus the idea, of history itself (248-49; my emphasis):

> the discovery that the historian himself, together with the here-and-now of which forms the total body of evidence available to him, is part of the process he is studying, has his own place in that process, and can see it only from the point of view which at this present moment he occupies within it.
>
> But neither the raw material of historical knowledge, the detail of the here-and-now as given him in perception, nor the various endowments that serve him as aids to interpreting this evidence, can give the historian his criterion of historical truth. *That criterion is the idea of history itself: the idea of an imaginary picture of the past.* That idea is, in Cartesian language, innate; in Kantian language, *a priori.* It is not a chance product of psychological causes; it is *an idea which every man possess as part of the furniture of his mind, and discovers himself to possess in so far as he becomes conscious of what it is to have a mind.* Like other ideas of the same sort, it is one to which no fact of experience exactly corresponds. The historian, however long and faithfully he works, can never say that his work, even in the crudest outline or in this or that smallest detail, is done once and for all. He can never say that his picture of the past is at any point adequate to his idea of what it ought to be. But, however fragmentary and faulty the results of his work may be, the idea which governed its course is clear, rational, and universal. *It is the idea of the historical imagination as a self-dependent, self-determining, and self-justifying form of thought.*

To sum up, historical visualisation takes on a number of interrelated guises in Collingwood's account. Seeing is first of all putting oneself in the proper context. To see well, however, one must have the appropriate formal training. As a critic, then, one must read into the evidence, which implies a wealth of experience leading one beyond the stage of formal training. Finally, and most essentially, historical visualisation is the mental projection of an 'imaginary' series, I am almost tempted to say in the form of a cinematic sequence, of events in the mind's eye. If, furthermore, this step-by-step process is followed through, the next phase in Collingwood's philosophy of history, re-enactment, appears both more reasonable and more attainable *as a methodological premise*.[24] At the same time Collingwood offers striking parallels with and advances upon the positions developed by Butterfield and Cassirer. Visualisation is now more firmly grounded in the activity of the mind and more clearly related to the evidence upon which the historian bases his tale, while the epistemological and moral standing of the discipline itself is more solidly established. History is a necessary form of thought and experience, a necessary tool for self-knowledge.

Nonetheless there are certain points where Collingwood's theory is particularly susceptible to criticism. I shall leave out the obvious critique which opponents of historical narrative would be likely to address to Collingwood. Taking as given the position advocated in the essay on the historical imagination, which, as I have incidentally tried to show, can be made to appear to be consistent with later developments in Collingwood's thought, there does remain the painful possibility that this position does not represent Collingwood's final say on the matter. Even more important from my point of view is the means by which certain evidence is acknowledged as useful or accurate, for here and there Collingwood seems to admit certain procedures which are at odds, on the surface at least, with the criteria he posits elsewhere.

The overall impression given by Collingwood throughout *The Idea of History* is one that discounts 'mere' experience as a criterion for judging historical evidence. Likewise, he rejects any number of naïve theories which fail the rigorous test of his notion of the *ideality* of his-torical knowledge, most of all the 'mysterious flair' which allows a historian to 'transport' himself back into the past. In this sense Collingwood's philosophy does risk appearing overly intellectualistic. Now Colling-wood does try, unconsciously perhaps, to occupy some middle ground which might offer a logical way of escaping from the narrowness of his position in this regard. Like Cassirer, he often balances between such poles as universal/particular, subjective/objective, real/fictional, nature/spirit, critical/constructive, and so on. Moreover, he does at a crucial juncture admit of the principle of 'imaginative sympathy,' which in the hands of Butterfield and Cassirer, as we have seen, acquires an extra-rational character. But in theory Collingwood is not entirely able to square his theory of historical knowledge with the means of acquiring it. His historian needs practice, and judges by instinct (387):

> The fisherman who found his way home in a fog by smelling the lead, after sounding with it, was hardly more independent of book-learning than the archeologist who rubs his thumb along the edge of a potsherd and says 'they never feel like that much after the reign of Domitian'.[25]

This 'feel' the historian has for his evidence enables him, paradoxically perhaps, to approach a 'logic,' if not a 'science,' of history, which for Collingwood is based, implicitly at the very least, on the application of archaeological methodology. Yet if, as Collingwood writes of Croce, the historian must only 'assert what the evidence before him obliges him to assert' (204), how finally does one come to acknowledge this obligation?

III

To recap briefly in a constructive vein, I have been trying in this essay first to outline the positions assumed by certain twentieth-century historians and philosophers of history regarding what I have called modes of visualisation in historical knowledge, arguing along the way that for these writers an imaginative sort of visualisation constituted an important element in their account of historical thought. That histor-ians in general see metaphorically does not seem to be in doubt, although even at this level there may yet be room for further elaboration. At the same time I have also implied, at the very least, that it may be possible to formulate a more comprehensive theoretical account of historical visualisation, by attempting to resolve certain problems inherent in the systems examined thus far. These problems, as we saw in the section on Butterfield, include the nature of historical evidence, the functioning of the creative imagination, the means by which we test the truth-content of our account of the past, and finally the moral dimensions of historical knowledge. I have furthermore justified this exercise by claiming that it may well help us garner support for the type of idealist, seemingly-relativist (but anti-sceptical) historiographical positions assumed by people like Herbert Butterfield, Ernst Cassirer, and R. G. Collingwood.

As I see it the historian who provides the final piece to the puzzle I have been piecing together is the Dutchman Johan Huizinga. Huizinga is a particularly apt figure to study in this regard. As Francis Haskell has noted, he formulated an implicit set of ground rules for the use of imagery as historical evidence, one which has yet to be surpassed despite its obvious inner contradictions. As an amateur epistemologist Huizinga acted as a bridge between the great German school of Rickert and Dilthey on the one hand and a second generation of neo-idealists on the other; yet although Huizinga was profoundly influenced by the previous generation's debate over knowledge in the *Kulturwissenschäften*, he was even more deeply stirred by his own personal vision of historical truth. Nonetheless, Huizinga presents a number of striking similarities with Cassirer and Collingwood. Although Huizinga first lectured publicly on the phenomenon of the historical imagination in 1905, and his career, like that of Croce, spanned more or less the first half of the century, his most influential work came arguably in the 1930s. Philosophically speaking he was an idealist and a relativist, although he, too, fought rigorously against historical scepticism and sought rather to provide some objective grounding for historical knowledge. His lectures and essays give ample testimony to the fact that he was deeply aware of and concerned over the state of modern historical consciousness. Huizinga was a highly active historian, and his epistemology, if less rigorously logical than those of his peers, was even more descriptive of his actual work in the field. More important still, Huizinga made a singular effort to practise what he preached and preach what he practised. In his eyes the historian had a moral mission to uphold the high status of historical knowledge and to prevent it and the culture which produced it from falling into decadence and decay. A close reading of his theoretical work, scattered though it may be, reveals the extent to which Huizinga anticipated both the linguistic and the pictorial turns in contemporary historiography (just as he seems to have anticipated the turn toward the social sciences, especially anthropology), all the while remaining faithful to an older model of the historical imagination. It may be that his work on historical knowledge, like his use of imagery in writing history, still constitutes the most advanced statement made on the subject on contemporary theory.[26]

Visual metaphors are indeed abundant in Huizinga's theoretical and practical work, as is a more explicit discussion of historical visualisation. The historian 'draws a picture,' 'calls up images,' and so on (Task, 46, 53). Yet like Cassirer, Huizinga also claims more specifically that the historian must formulate in his mind an image of the *forms and shapes* of the life of the past. Here, however, Huizinga tells us as well how these forms and shapes might actually appear. Not only is the mental reconstruction of the past a difficult exercise in and of itself, he argues, but in certain cases 'this vision of an epoch resulting from the contemplation of works of art is always incomplete . . . [because] we lack the actual sight' of the objects in question (Task, 212 ff., 233, 237). Whence no doubt was born Huizinga's famous notion of 'morphologies,' that is to say, the 'forms . . . and patterns of thought and life' (Task, 28, 51 ff.). 'A dramatic interpretation based on a morphology of human society,' writes Huizinga, 'would probably in the final analysis provide the most balanced definition for expressing the nature of history, as long as it places special emphasis upon its unsystematic, descriptive character and upon the necessity of *seeing its object in action*' (Idea, 293).[27] Yet Huizinga goes even farther still in his attempt to explain exactly what this experience consists of. For whereas Cassirer and Collingwood reflected at length on the nature of historical evidence and the interpretation thereof (in short, on what in the first instance we see and how in the second we see and/or project it) Huizinga sketched out a theory of how the historian ultimately evaluates this evidence, one which also accounts for both the special vocation of the historian and the various frames of mind he is apt to generate as he engages in his study, one might almost say the existential relationship he has with his material. Finally, Huizinga informs us how these visions might be best verbalised, and in so doing gives us a criterion for judging the merits of a given piece of historical writing.

In his famous essay entitled 'The Task of the Cultural Historian' Huizinga writes (Task, 58):

> History is the interpretation of the significance that the past has for us. Implicit in this character of history is that of arrangement. In order to understand a fragment of the past as reflected in his own culture, the historian must always and everywhere attempt to see the forms and functions of that fragment . . . Every event . . . conceived by the faculty of historical cognition presumes an arranging of the material of the past, a combining of a number of data out of the chaos of reality into a mental image.[28]

This brief passage gives a general definition of history and, more important, summarises Huizinga's point of departure in the area of historical knowledge, which here and elsewhere he calls 'historical cognition.' Historical cognition consists above all in forming mental images; a piece of work which succeeds in turn in conjuring up such images should be the goal of all historical research and writing. The images must moreover be graphic and concrete, yet seen in context. As in other intellectual endeavours – philosophy, literature, jurisprudence, science (here Huizinga echoes Cassirer and, to a lesser extent, Collingwood) – the image is a *form* imposed by the mind. The particularity of historical understanding is that it is seen 'in and through the past' (Definition, 5).

History has the further peculiarity that the precise means by which the mind produces its image is the *imagination*. 'History,' writes Huizinga, is 'a form of knowledge with power to fill the imagination.' By imagination Huizinga means 'not fancy, but that image-making force which recreates an original thing so that others may seem to see the features and hear the voices of the billions of people who once lived.' Historical visualisation is thus a vital force, rather than a static 'photographic' representation which lacks the power to excite the imagination. It is a sense with an aesthetic and dramatic character, a character that is best captured and communicated through narrative (*relatio*) (Forms, 217-18). Here Huizinga reveals himself incidentally to be a precocious critic of the rising tide of social scientific analysis in history, which he relates also to a general lack of historical stimulation in contemporary society.[29]

Huizinga's real contribution, however, lies in how he grounds the truth-content of his images. In a number of particularly illuminating passages he argues that the historian must feel a special conviction, and convey a sentiment of earnestness or genuineness with regard to his material (Idea, 43 ff.; Definition, 6). Here Huizinga moves somewhat beyond Cassirer and Collingwood, deftly linking their idealist and seemingly relativist tendencies with elements of both classical philosophy and German romanticism. It is in particular on this latter plane that Huizinga has a decisive contribution to make to our discussion. History becomes what Michelet called a 'resurrection.' The historian must exercise a certain talent for calling to life the dead matter of the past. He knows that his endeavour has some validity first and foremost if he himself has striven toward the truth, if he has experienced an 'impulse,' an 'absolute craving to penetrate to the genuine knowledge of that which truly happened, even when we are aware of the inadequacy of the means to the end' (Idea, 23-24). This striving is not far from what Cassirer might have called the *desire to understand*, which for him constituted one of the two poles of the 'unity of the will.'[30] Here Huizinga wades further into seemingly murkier waters. For however genuine the desire to know the truth may be, the historian must always create an image of the 'shape of things gone by' (Definition, 6). Huizinga insists that this image is both fleeting and approximate. Are we then to rely on what Collingwood disparagingly called a certain 'flair' on the part of the historian to sniff out the truth (keeping in mind that as an archaeologist this is precisely what Collingwood advocated, almost despite himself)? Is not Huizinga merely recasting the psychologism of some late nineteenth-century German theorists?

Are we to accept the contemporary accusation that Huizinga was merely a dilettante, despite his obvious interest in certain areas of the social sciences, notably anthropology?[31]

The answer to these queries, I think, brings Huizinga especially close to Cassirer's style of thinking, as I have already suggested. The interplay between past and present, which is part and parcel of historical knowledge, breeds what Huizinga calls a mental tension, not unlike that which exists for all knowledge when the mind creates an image of an imperfectly apprehended, and knowable, external reality. 'The impetus and value of this mental tension and of its product, history,' suggests Huizinga, 'lie in the complete earnestness which distinguishes it' (Definition, 6). Thought operates not in a vacuum but in a state of dynamic flux, in which certain moments of lucidity make possible a clearer glimpse of man's environment. Moreover, and here he rejoins Collingwood too, Huizinga also finds a *moral* dimension to this thirst for and consequent conviction of the truth: it is a vital need. When history degenerates into a mere play of numbers civilisation has revealed itself to be lacking in some essential quality. Like E. H. Carr a generation later Huizinga claimed that the relative health of a civilisation manifested itself in the vitality of its historical vision.[32] 'History,' the Dutchman concludes, 'is the intellectual form in which a civilisation renders account to itself of its past' (Definition, 9).

It would seem to me that Huizinga starts thus with the simple wish of avoiding the dangers of both positivism and relativism, by building on the epistemological and moral implications of his idealist philosophy. But as we have just seen his perspective quickly broadens. Huizinga's ideal was a society with sufficient stimulation and taste, with a flair and a thirst for the dramatic, and he thought in the 1920s that such characteristics were on the rise, albeit precariously. Thus he was inclined to link that feeling of earnestness he so applauded with an equally praiseworthy 'heroic sincerity' in even the most minute area of historical work. Not surprisingly, then, he also reflected on the qualities inherent in good historical research and writing. In this instance, too, he can be said to add to the observations proffered by Cassirer and Collingwood. First, he says, one must be imaginative and have a suitable temperament. Although Huizinga does not develop this idea we may suppose that he means in part that the historian must to a degree be able to empathise with the objects of his study; this is precisely what Cassirer prescribed when he wrote that the historian must of necessity be a judge, but above all he must strive to be a *juge d'instruction*.[33] Moreover, the historian must ask appropriate questions and choose his subject well. Too much historical work, claimed Huizinga in 1926, was of mediocre quality due to the simple fact that the questions put to the evidence were ill-conceived, that the scope of the matter was not fully appreciated, that, to put the matter in visualistic terms, the image called to mind was not properly focused; here, incidentally, we approach Collingwood's description of historical interrogation. As opposed to those who would claim that no historical knowledge is possible, Huizinga would answer in common sense terms that the historian was the ultra-sceptic *par excellence*: none more than the historian used such hyper-critical means to determine the truth content of a given historical fact, and such was in truth the best defence *against* scepticism.

More important, no doubt, was the emphasis Huizinga placed on the means by which we recount our historical research. As much as he favoured an epic imagination, he did not necessarily advocate popular literary forms for the telling of history, in part because a society that found solace in this type of writing had probably reached a decadent stage in its moral relationship with its past. Like Collingwood, Huizinga distinguished between literary creation and historical narrative, the one allowing flights of fantasy, the other clearly moored to historical evidence. But for Huizinga, we recall, part of the epistemological dilemma faced by the historian was still how to arrive at a suitably convincing picture of the past based on this evidence. Huizinga's answer to this question can be found in his discussion of one of the basic tools in the historian's repertory, the concept of periodisation. The historian is bound to use terms like 'Renaissance,' but should do so only in such a way as to retain a certain 'flavor,' 'pith,' or 'savo,' in his language. History writing is thus the art of applying the imagination to some fragments of the past and deriving a lively story therefrom which nonetheless appeals by means of that force of conviction that the images it brings to the reader's mind are vivid and compelling, that is meaningful and thus valid.

Live, Huizinga seems to be telling us, and write like a visionary
regardless of how big or small the slice of the historical pie you are
serving up. One almost *hears* in this context the famous words of Henri
Pirenne, whom Huizinga cited as an exemplar, to his younger colleague
Marc Bloch relative to the historian's need to live in the present.[34] For
indeed, Huizinga did not merely consider the historian's task to be
exclusively visualistic, and thereby intellectualistic, but rather thought
that all the historian's senses had to be called into play. In this respect,
we might say that in his description of 're-experience' Huizinga adds
something of an existential, almost sensual dimension to the intellec-
tualism inherent in Collingwood's account of re-enactment. Huizinga
again rejoins Cassirer in the lists against those who merely recount or
merely analyse, or seek to judge based on something more than imperfect human knowledge, or worse yet use this fallibility as an excuse for
weak-kneed scepticism. There are biological and moral criteria for writing
good history, and the ability to 'see' into the past is a key factor in the
process.

IV

Huizinga might appear to some as the great dandy in modern historiography. To be sure, his work is less systematic and in some senses
more speculative than that of a Cassirer or a Collingwood, of a Croce
or an Ortega y Gasset. But this same *préciosité*, combined with the fact
that Huizinga acted as a living link with the debates of the previous
century, also endows his work with a certain potential for moving beyond
the standard critiques of idealism and neo-idealism. Thus even as he
advocated a type of imaginative vision of the past (*Ahnung* was the term
closest to what he meant, based directly on late German romantic
theory)[35] he also urged us to see in multiple ways, in a manner which
prefigured contemporary advocacy of 'stereoscopy.' He proposed likewise to engage all the senses in historical cognition, and not just sight.
At the same time, Huizinga realised that even if the historian's knowledge is based on an *intuition* of the past, he still needs to use *language*
as the medium for his mental constructs; but he also implied that there

is no sense telling any historical tale if it has no graphic anchor in the mind. Like his fellow neo-idealists, Huizinga affirmed that historical knowledge is of necessity imperfect and fleeting, and thus that the historical imagination bordered on the sublime, yet he also suggested that the historian take a realist, as opposed to a purely nominalist, stance vis-à-vis the world around him, for this is precisely what distinguishes history from fiction. The common-sense experience of life (which after all was the basic stuff of history) required no less.

But in fact Huizinga was not really alone in any of this. Nor was his ultimate emphasis on the ethical dimensions of good historical work unique. Indeed, for those fans of woolly moralising there may yet be a humanistic moral to be told here, one which bears repeating given the fundamentally critical juncture at which it was initially formulated. The type of self-knowledge provided by good historical thinking might no longer be at the premium our authors seemed once to think it was. Nonetheless, should we be inclined to believe that ours is a culture with an acute historical consciousness, then if we argue in any way that this culture is worth fighting to preserve, so too must the historical component therein. Moreover, if we accept Huizinga's claim that such historical consciousness is also the sign of an advanced civilisation, Eurocentric as the notion might sound, then we might also reflect more deeply on what it means to engage in historical research. All three of our authors, in one way or another, realised on the one hand that the 'consumption' of historical knowledge was something which needed to bring all aspects of society and its productive cycles together, from the lowliest antiquarian buried in some local archive to the worldly publisher with commercial outposts across the globe. The historian has a responsibility to ensure that the grist given to the mill is both pure and nourishing. The recent debates over the popular reception of historical work on the Holocaust, not to mention the press often given to Holocaust denial, are warning enough that such responsibility need be met.[36] By the same token, the historical imagination as described above can allow us both to use fruitfully and to advance beyond what cinematic and video technology might have contributed to our modes of perceiving the world, and especially to take cognizance of and transcend the pathos of 'historical consciousness' fed to us in the form of contemporary movie-making (this includes the serious and the not so serious, among the latter Monty Python springs to mind). But Huizinga also gives us another variation on the theme. By restoring the epic dimension to history through the effort of visualisation, he tells us, we are helping *save* civilisation; moreover, as Cassirer, Collingwood, and Huizinga would all have been prepared to argue, we are thereby maintaining the integrity of the realm of human freedom. The stakes in this battle are immense, and take on added value when we consider how tempting it is to see today's post-modernists in the same light in which Collingwood portrayed the Oxford 'realists' in his own day.[37] The following words by Collingwood might moreover hold a sobering thought in this respect: 'we ought by now to realise that no kindly law of nature will save us from the fruits of our ignorance.'[38] More prosaically, if the historian, often compared to a detective or a judge or whatnot, *qua* historian has a type of knowledge which is recognised as a special mode of thought unto itself, should we not consider that this same historian, called upon to set a standard in the preservation of human culture and civilisation, also engages in a special mode of inquiry, in an *autonomous discipline*? Be like a judge or a lawyer, be like a detective, like an archaeologist, or even a prophet, we are often told, and no doubt we tell our students. To which, the historian who sees into the past may well respond, be like a historian.[39]

NOTES

1 G. M. Trevelyan, *Clio, A Muse* (1913), cited in *The Varieties of History from Voltaire to the Present*, 2nd ed., ed. F. Stern (New York, 1972), 234-35. Cf. also D. Cannadine, *G. M. Trevelyan: A Life in History* (London, 1992), ch. 5, especially 190-92.

2 I. Berlin, 'The Divorce between the Sciences and the Humanities,' in *Against the Current: Essays in the History of Ideas,* ed. H. Hardy (Oxford, 1981), 106.

3 H. S. Hughes, *Consciousness and Society: The Reorientation of European Social Thought 1890-1930*, revised ed. (New York, 1977), ch. 6. For the German school in particular cf. also T. E. Willey, *Back to Kant: The Revival of Kantianism in German Social and Historical Thought, 1860-1914* (Detroit, 1978); K. C. Köhnke, *The Rise of Neo-Kantianism: German Academic Philosophy between Idealism and Positivism*, tr. R. J. Hollingdale (Cambridge, 1991); G. G. Iggers, *The German Conception of History: The National Tradition of Historical Thought from Herder to the Present* (Middletown, 1968); and L. P. Thiele, 'Heidegger, History, and Hermeneutics,' *Journal of Modern History*, 69 (1997), 534-56.

4 All three were also interconnected through literary channels, specifically the *Festschrift* for Ernst Cassirer published in Oxford in 1936 (cited *infra*), to which Huizinga contributed, articles from which Cassirer and Collingwood cited in published works, and on which Collingwood wrote an important review (*English Historical Review*, 52 [1937], 141-46).

5 See generally M. Jay, *Downcast Eyes: The Denigration of Vision in Twentieth-Century French Thought* (Berkeley, 1993); and also M. Moran, 'Metaphysical Imagination,' in *Dictionary of the History of Ideas: Studies of Selected Pivotal Ideas*, ed. P. P. Weiner *et al.* (New York, 1973), III:208a-223b.

6 *Clio, A Muse*, in *The Varieties of History*, 238.

7 Cf. however Cannadine, *Trevelyan*, 208-12, for a nuanced picture of the relationship between Trevelyan and Butterfield.

8 H. Butterfield, *The Whig Interpretation of History* (London, 1931). References to this and other sources will generally be made in short form directly in the text.

9 E. Cassirer, *An Essay on Man* (New Haven, 1944), 189-228.

10 R. G. Collingwood, *The Idea of History*, revised edn., ed. J. van der Dussen (Oxford, 1993), 166.

11 In the chapter on art in this same book Cassirer concludes first that art teaches us to see and intuit sensuous forms, in the sense of Leonardo da Vinci's *sapere vedere* or of what Cassirer calls 'sympathetic vision.' But he adds that art is also a mode or process of perceiving, the product of a 'constructive eye' which permits us to discover the 'realm of pure forms.' *Essay on Man*, 159, 162-63, 167, 188.

12 This fusion of understanding and feeling was a characteristic trait in Cassirer's mature philosophy, which elsewhere took the form of a synthesis of reason and will. I refer here to my paper, 'Ernst Cassirer, Historian of the Will,' *Journal of the History of Ideas*, 58, 1 (1997), 145-61. See also *Ernst Cassirer de Marbourg à New York. L'itinéraire philosophique*, ed. J. Seidengart (Paris, 1990), 17-114, where attention is drawn to the problematic character of Cassirer's early historical endeavors, namely a penchant to treat history schematically, as opposed to empirically and/or teleologically.

13 The realm of historical symbols is moreover strikingly akin to the rationally intelligible realm of nature, as conceived, for example, by the Cambridge Platonists ('Plastick Nature'). See Cassirer, *The Platonic Renaissance in England*, trans. J. P. Pettegrove (Lon-

don, 1953), 141-42. For a post-modernist take on this same type of middle ground, see M. A. Holly, *Past Looking: Historical Imagination and the Rhetoric of the Image* (Ithaca, 1996), 17-24, 139-43.

14 To Cassirer's credit, this is what he attempts to do in his principal works on the history of philosophy from the Renaissance to the Enlightenment, especially *Individual and Cosmos in the Renaissance* (originally published in German in 1927), *The Platonic Renaissance in England* (1929), and *The Philosophy of the Enlightenment* (1932).

15 *Idea of History*, 159; and cf. 175-76, 184, 186, where Collingwood keenly describes the state of German scholarship on the philosophy of history at the time he (and Cassirer) began his mature work on the question.

16 *Idea of History*, 'Introduction,' in particular xxviii, xxxi.

17 *Idea of History*, xxxii-xlii, xxiii-xxviii, respectively.

18 In this respect see also D. Boucher, 'The Significance of R. G. Collingwood's *Principles of History*,' *Journal of the History of Ideas*, 58, 2 (1997), 309-30; and J. van der Dussen, 'Collingwood's Lost Manuscript of *The Principles of History*,' *History and Theory*, 36, 1 (1997), 32- 62. Both Boucher and van der Dussen have had access to Collingwood's manuscripts at Oxford University Press, long thought disappeared.

19 *The Historical Imagination; an inaugural lecture delivered before the University of Oxford on 28 October 1935* (Oxford, 1935).

20 Mention must be made in this respect of Collingwood's *An Autobiography*, reprint (Oxford, 1978); as well as another collected set of Collingwoods writings, in this case a number of articles entitled *Essays in the Philosophy of History*, ed. W. Debbins (Austin, 1965), which is briefly discussed in van der Dussen's introduction to *The Idea of History*.

21 It is precisely on this plane that Cassirer's work on symbolic forms complements Collingwood's argument regarding the function of historical evidence; and cf. in this vein the comments in the 1928 lecture (491 ff.), where Collingwood likens historical method in general to archaeology.

22 For a related critique see Karl Popper, 'On the Theory of the Objective Mind,' in *Objective Knowledge: An Evolutionary Approach*, revised ed. (Oxford, 1979), 188, where Popper objects also that certain acts might be 'beyond the historian's capacity for action and therefore for re-enactment' (Popper was generally critical of the idealist – or 'second world' – approach to historical knowledge in Collingwood's account). Cf. also the reservations voiced by Hughes with regard to similar difficulties in Croce's theory of history, *Consciousness and Society*, 212-13, 226-27. As Boucher and van der Dussen have both recently shown, at the time of his death Collingwood was trying to work out a revised theory of re-enactment, in concert with his *Principles of Art*, which would also take into account human emotions.

23 On this account cf. also W. H. Dray, 'R. G. Collingwood on the A Priori of History,' *Clio*, 12 (1982), 169-81.

24 See in this vein the comments in van der Dussen's 'Introduction,' *op. cit.*, xxv-xxviii.

25 Cf. also *Idea of History*, 139. It is worth noting here that the lectures contained in the revised edition of Collingwood's work contain interesting and valuable, if occasionally contradictory, comments on the teaching and learning of history. I refer in passing to my review of the new edition of *The Idea of History* in the *Journal of Liberal Arts*, 2, 2 (1996), 99-107.

26 The sources consulted for the following discussion include J. Huizinga, 'The Idea of History,' in *The Varieties of History*, 290-303; 'The Task of Cultural History,' in *Men*

and Ideas: History, the Middle Ages, the Renaissance, trans. J. S. Holmes and H. van Marle (Princeton, 1959); 'History Changing Forms,' *Journal of the History of Ideas*, 4, 2 (1943), 217-23; and 'A Definition of the Concept of History,' in *Philosophy and History: Essays Presented to Ernst Cassirer*, ed. R. Klibansky and R. Paton (Cambridge, 1936), 1-10 (cited in abbreviated form in text). See also F. Haskell, *History and its Images: Art and the Interpretation of the Past* (New Haven, 1993), ch. 15, especially 468-95; and cf. David Gary Shaw's review of the new English translation of Huizinga's *Autumn of the Middle Ages*, 'Huizinga's Timeliness,' *History & Theory*, 37, 2 (1998), 245-58.

27 This notion of morphologies is inherently visualistic, almost in a neo-Platonic vein; cf. also in this instance Huizinga's repeated reflections on the traditional realist/nominalist dichotomy, e.g., in 'The Task of Cultural History,' 20, and 'The Idea of History,' 290-91. In his later article 'History Changing Forms,' 217, Huizinga further specified that he had three distinct types of form in mind, the first a sort of mental inquiry, the second a historical pattern, and the third the aesthetic judgment of the past.

28 For a discussion of this particular essay see R. L. Colie, 'Johan Huizinga and the Task of Cultural History,' *American Historical Review*, 69, 4 (1964), 607-30.

29 Indeed, Huizinga represents well what Geoffrey Barraclough might have distinguished as a neo-idealist opponent to the rise of the social sciences; see G. Barraclough, *Tendences actuelles de l'histoire* (Paris, 1980), ch. 3, especially 94.

30 See E. Cassirer, *The Myth of the State*, 2nd ed. (New Haven, 1974), 58.

31 See especially Jacques Le Goff's editorial remarks in J. Huizinga, *L'automne du Moyen Age*, tr. J. Bastin (Paris, 1975), x; and cf. Collingwood, *Idea of History*, 165 ff., 389.

32 E. H. Carr, *What is History*, 2nd ed., ed. R. W. Davies (London, 1987), 132.

33 *Essay on Man*, 209; and cf. Collingwood's famous detective image of the historian, *Idea of History*, 266 ff.

34 Recounted in M. Bloch, *The Historian's Craft*, tr. P. Putnam (New York, 1953), 46-47.

35 'The Task of Cultural History,' 53-54; and cf. E. Breisach, *Historiography: Ancient, Medieval, and Modern* (Chicago, 1983), 233.

36 I am thinking in particular of the polemics caused as a result of the publication of D. J. Goldhagen, *Hitler's Willing Executioners: Ordinary Germans and the Holocaust* (New York, 1996).

37 *Autobiography*, 15-21, 44-52, 166-67.

38 *Idea of History*, 334.

39 It is my pleasure to acknowledge the debt I owe to Donald R. Kelley, under whose guidance I first began to explore the issues discussed herein; to my colleagues at the American College of Thessaloniki, Deborah Brown-Kazazis and Anna Challenger, for decisive input; and to the readers of *Collingwood Studies* for instructive comments on an earlier draft of the paper.

T. H. Green's Theory of the Common Good

Maria Dimova-Cookson

Introduction

I argue that Green's common good theory contains two legitimate but distinguishable senses of the common good. The first is the common good as the principle of personal moral growth, while the second is the common good as the society of equal individuals. The first and, as I shall argue, the more important way of defining the common good describes the formal conditions of a moral act. The second way in defining the common good is substantive: it names it as the society of equal individuals. While the first (the formal) definition leaves the common good substantively undefined, the second fixes it into a particular object.

This observation contributes both towards a better understanding and a reconstruction of Green's common good theory. So, on the one hand, it responds to the standard challenges of the kind 'Is there such a thing as a common good?', 'What is this common good?', 'Does the common good theory give a credible representation of human nature?' On the other hand, it develops new criticisms and offers reconstructions of his philosophy. By revealing the shortcomings of Green's common good theory this article unlocks its full potential. Green does not spell out that the pursuit of the common good represents a process of moral growth as opposed to a mere factuality of human moral nature. If the best spirit of his own common good theory is being followed, we shall see that the common good does not reflect the innate moral nature of human agency, as Green believes to be the case, but rather the innate *possibility* of moral behaviour. Green's common good theory reveals the formal conditions of moral conduct.

The double usage of Green's common good has been registered in the critical literature.[1] What has not been done and is offered by this article is an analysis of the reasons why Green has ended with two definitions of the common good; an explanation why this dichotomy is a necessary one; and an assessment of the dialectics between moral good and ordinary good. The article uses aspects of Green's common good theory as a foundation for further analysis of the nature of moral good. It introduces the concept of 'ordinary' good and thus offers an explanation of the genealogy of moral good. Depending on whether Green uses 'the common good' in its formal or in its substantive sense he is referring to two different generic types of good: moral and ordinary. In other words, the extent to which the common good is a moral good, and the extent to which it is an ordinary good varies as to which sense the common good is being referred. Green equates the common good exclusively to the moral good and thus (i) 'loses' the concept of the ordinary good; (ii) fails to assess the dialectics between ordinary and moral good; (iii) does not see that the meaning of the common good changes depending on the perspective from which it is being defined.

As mentioned, I have gained the philosophical grounds of my criticism of Green by employing elements of his own moral and common good theories. My claim that the pursuit of the common good is a result of a process as opposed to being an intrinsic feature of the human character, as well as my analysis of the genealogy of moral behaviour, are based on the 'salvation argument' which is the main component of Green's common good theory.

The article takes the following strategy. Section one explains why Green has developed two, instead of one, concepts of the common good. A brief review of Green's moral theory that precedes the introduction of the common good, reveals that he has already developed two distinguishable definitions of the moral ideal. I argue that Green has followed the same strategy in the analysis of the common good by offering, first, a formal account, and second, a substantive one. Section two discusses the first sense of the common good. I argue that the primary purpose of Green's common good theory is to reveal the process through which an individual acquires the motivation to act as a moral agent. That is why the common good in the first sense reveals a process of personal growth. I argue that Green himself has not articulated in a straightforward manner the meaning of the common good as that of a process of personal development because he wants to present human morality as firm and unconditional, rather than of dynamic in nature (subsection 2.1). In section two I also investigate the implications of my interpretation of the common good. Subsection 2.2 discusses the unique position of the self in the pursuit of the common good, and subsection 2.3 discusses Green's loss of the concept of the ordinary good. Section three addresses the second sense of the common good and argues that in its substantive use the common good is not a moral good but an ordinary good.

1. OUTLINING THE TWO PERSPECTIVES IN DEFINING THE COMMON GOOD

Green's common good theory is developed in Chapters III and IV of Book III of *Prolegomena to Ethics*, entitled 'The Moral Ideal and Moral Progress'. The first two chapters of this book explain the nature of the moral good and the moral ideal and offer the foundation of Green's moral theory. Chapters III and IV (of Book III) focus on the common good and thus offer a continuation of Green's theory of the moral ideal. So, in the first two chapters of Book III, i.e. just before starting his discussion of the common good, Green has already laid the foundations of his moral theory by making very substantive philosophical claims. I will briefly present and analyse his theory of the moral ideal because it throws light on his strategy of defining the common good.

Green has defined the moral good by distinguishing it from the good. While any object, which satisfies desire, is good, only those objects, which bring true satisfaction, are morally good. So the individuals pursue self-satisfaction in different objects. Only some of these objects are *truly* good, i.e. morally good. In order to explain the nature of the morally good object Green describes the personal attitude from which this object has to be pursued. A person acts morally if she acts out of a self-disinterested disposition, i.e. if she acts with 'good will'. Green notices the circular format of his definition of the moral good:

> If, on being asked for an account of the unconditional good, we answer either that it is the good will or that to which the good will is directed, we are naturally asked further, what then is the good will? And if in answer to this question we can only say that it is the will for the unconditional good, we are no less naturally charged with 'moving in a circle'.[2]

Green points out that in explaining the nature of morality, one ends up moving into a circle. While a philosopher is defining moral practice he is, by necessity, defining two mutually determined, yet *distinguishable* elements. The first is the personal attitude out of which a moral action is undertaken or the inner moral disposition. Green calls it the 'good will'. The second is the concrete object of moral pursuit, the very action or thing that is considered to be moral. Green calls it the un-conditional good. Such an object which he believes to be intrinsically moral is the perfect character. Green's concern is that a moral theorist is, by necessity, 'trapped' between these two elements: he has to define the second through the first and vice versus.

I call this circle a 'phenomenological circle' and argue that Green has made a philosophical achievement by registering it. The 'phenome-nological circle' reflects the fact that whichever way of defining a moral good a philosopher chooses, he should be aware that this is one of two possible ways, none of which is complete on its own, or independent from the other. Green has defined the moral ideal in two ways. The first definition is given from the perspective of describing one's inner attitude, i.e. by explaining the inner moral disposition. The actual objects in which this disposition can be practically enacted can vary and that is why they are left unspecified. That is why I call this first definition of the moral ideal a 'formal' definition, and argue that it is philosophically primary to the second, the 'substantive' one.

Green also defined the moral ideal from a second perspective – from the perspective of specifying the actual object in which the moral good is to be found. As a moral philosopher, Green felt that he had to be able to give direct answer to the question 'What is the moral good?' He knew that his theory could be seen as inferior to the utilitarian one which clearly and unambiguously named 'the greatest sum of pleasures' as the true good. That is why Green also gave a name to the moral good by claiming that the only true good is the perfect character. Thus, Green believed that he escaped 'the circle.' It seemed that 'the perfect character' defined the moral ideal from the two perspectives simultaneously. It could represent both the disposition for moral action (people with perfect character always act with good will) and the object of the moral action (the perfect character seen as the achievement of a moral effort). My criticism of Green is that he should not have tried to 'overcome' the phenomenological circle. Defining morality from two perspectives has been a philosophical achievement. Green's attempt to avoid a circular definition of the moral good has left him unaware that his theory has offered two, rather than only one, definitions of the moral ideal.

As has been the case with the moral ideal, Green defines the common good from two perspectives. And again, he has felt uncomfortable with each of them separately, that is why he has tried to unify them in a single, straightforward theory. Andrew Vincent also points out that Green has given us two definitions, both with respect to the true good and to the common good: 'On the one hand, the true or common good can be seen as a permanent interest which is non-competitive, namely a formal will to be good. On the other hand the true good can be explicitly identified with the realisation of individual capacities'.[3] Vincent believes that this duality is the 'central problem in Green's idea of the true good which also permeates his discussion of the common good'.[4] Geoffrey Thomas speaks about "a logically harmless but expositionally awkward ambiguity in Green's use of 'common good'".[5] The first use of the common good adds another aspect of the definition of the true good, the aspect of 'compossibility'. The second use refers to 'a network of social roles'. Thomas believes that the ambiguity of these different uses 'creates no confusion in Green's argument'.[6] I argue that this ambiguity is itself a result of confusion. It is a consequence of Green's tendency to shift between a formal and a substantive definition; or, in other words, it is a result of his failing to keep in focus the phenomenological circle while analysing moral phenomena. I will review the two definitions of the common good in turn.

2. THE COMMON GOOD AS PERSONAL MORAL GROWTH

The first sense of the common good should be understood along the lines of the formal, the non-substantive, definition of the moral ideal. It outlines the conditions of a moral conduct without specifying the actual moral deed itself. The formal conditions of a moral act are to be found in the personal disposition of the agent. In this sense, the common good is a state of mind, an attitude, a personal insight into the contents of the true good. So, explained in this way, the common good is not being located in any particular object; it should not be understood as something that is good for all. This explanation invalidates the claim that people will never agree on what the common good is, as the common good is not to be found in a specific object. *I pursue the common good when I act upon a presentation of the good of others as being my good.* The theme of the common good is a continuation of the discussion of what constitutes moral conduct, of what is, in more concrete terms, my inner state while I am pursuing my ideal for perfection. Green advances us towards the idea that our state of perfection consists in an attitude of perceiving our good as united to that of others.

Green's theory of the common good describes, in essence, a person's transition from pursuing her ordinary good towards pursuing her moral good. By ordinary good I mean what Green means by 'good'. I refer to good which is good to oneself only, as opposed to moral good which is intended by its agent as a good common between him and the others. The reason why it is not immediately obvious that Green's common good reflects *a process* of moral growth is that he has been reluctant to acknowledge the dynamics of moral conduct. Green views moral nature as fixed, as firmly embedded in the human personality. He wants to present the aspiration towards the common good as a trait of human character. He claims that all people have a genuine interest in the well-being of others – what I would call a 'noble social interest'.[7] The noble social interest implies that the individual takes an interest in her fellow human beings for their own sake, i.e. regardless of whether this brings her any personal benefits. There is, however, an ambiguity about whether this interest is a quality which individuals develop, cultivate and achieve, or a quality which they inevitably possess on the grounds of their human nature. The shortcomings in maintaining the latter and the advantages of advancing the former will subsequently become clear.

Green's desire to assert the 'factuality' of the noble social interest (the interest in other people as ends in themselves) leads him to under-value the aspects of the interest in the common good which belong to one's personal experience. These aspects he rather presents as belonging to some prehistoric development which had already been completed with the emergence of the rational man. However, Green's theory contains a description of *a process* in which a person has started to perceive other people's good to be as valuable as her own. Green explains this process by advancing the interesting argument that *in his desire to overcome his transient nature, every human being tends to invest his moral energy into social projects.* I will present this particular argument in more detail. For the purpose of convenience, I call it 'the salvation argument'. I demonstrate that this argument expresses Green's ambivalent attitude towards the fact that the noble social interest gradually emerges, i.e. that it is an outcome of a process.

2.1. THE SALVATION ARGUMENT: CRITICISMS AND DEFENCE

I claim that Green both reveals and disguises a process which is bound to take place within the development of the human individual. On the one hand, he wants to present the individual's devotion to the good of the others as an inborn aspect of human nature. This, however, contradicts his theory of the moral ideal as the effort for self-perfection, as 'a life of becoming, of constant transition from possibility to realisation, and from this again to a new possibility . . . '[8] On the other hand, Green's intuition about the developmental nature of human personality re-emerges throughout his entire philosophy. It is also present in the salvation argument.

Green's salvation argument consists as follows. We, as human beings, may sometimes pursue pleasure, but we never think of our ultimate good in terms of pleasure. Utilitarians are wrong to believe that the individual imagines his happiness as a 'sum of pleasures'.[9] Pleasures cannot add up. A repetition of the same pleasure does not necessarily increase the feeling of being pleased. Pleasures are transient and after their expiry they leave a feeling of dissatisfaction. So when one thinks of an ultimate good, one does not imagine a maximum number of pleasures, but something radically different. One looks for an object which is permanently good, for an 'abiding satisfaction'.[10] Thus a person seeks his ultimate good in 'ideal objects, with which on the one hand he identifies himself, and which on the other hand he cannot think of as bounded by his earthly life, objects in which he thinks of himself as still living when dead'.[11] An example of such an object is the wellbeing of one's family. A man has an 'interest in permanent good' and together with it, an interest in his own permanency. He sees his permanent good in providing for the well-being of his 'kindred', and his permanency in the fact that his kindred are going to outlive him: 'Projecting himself into the future as a permanent subject of possible well-being or ill-being – and he must so project himself in seeking for a permanent good – he associates his kindred with himself.'[12] The emergence of the family Green believes dates as far back as the human interest in the permanent good.[13] The institution of the family presupposes a person's ability to think of others as of herself.

Further, Green argues that the same link which exists between the individual and her kindred, exists between her and society in general. This special type of link expresses Green's understanding of the individual's social nature. Society gives the individual an opportunity for immortality:

> At a stage of intellectual development when any theories of immortality would be unmeaning to them, men have already, in the thought of a society of which the life is their own life but which survives them, a medium in which they carry themselves forward beyond the limits of animal existence.[14]

The common good is the person's chance for transcending the 'perishing nature of pleasures' and the finite nature of her individual self.[15]

Green claims that there could be no contradiction between one's true good and one's dedication to the good of others, as these two, by definition, are identical. There may exist a tension between what constitutes my pleasure and someone else's pleasure. But because *my true good* is the object in which my permanent satisfaction is sought, it is something different from pleasure. It is good for me, on account of being good for others, on account of my desire to associate myself with them. The possible contradiction between me and the rest can occur within the quest for pleasure, but never in the quest for the true good: 'the distinction of good for self and good for others has never entered into that idea of a true good on which moral judgements are founded.'[16] Green's thought is not 'the good of all has to be good for me as well'. It is 'my true good is possible only as a contribution to, only in alliance with, the good of the others'. Green's 'common good' is the individual's 'true good'. Apart from a society a person has no permanent wellbeing.

The conclusion of the salvation argument is that every human being can achieve salvation only through his integration with society. It asserts something as a matter of fact, rather than as a possibility. Several serious objections can be raised against it, and I will consider two. The first one is that, if one's true good as a disinterested service to others is simply a matter of course, then one deserves no moral approbation for performing it. Alan Milne points out that presenting the true good as non-contradictory to one's inclinations 'obscures the real sacrifice of personal self-interest which meeting moral demands may involve'.[17] He adds that this account of human nature leaves no place for the possibility of 'immorality as distinct from moral error'.

The second objection focuses more sharply on the dogmatic form of this argument. Presenting moral conduct as if it were a mere fact betrays Green's intentions to actually bring forward the complexity of moral life. In its form, his argument is vulnerable to all claims testifying states of events which do not coincide with the assertion that in her urge to overcome her finiteness, an individual seeks an integration of herself with society; that '[h]is own well-being [a person] thus necessarily presents to himself as a social well-being'.[18] There are several plausible assertions which can be made to present a challenge to Green's claim. The following three statements are examples: 'there are people who understand the transient nature of human life and are prepared to accept it', 'there are people who grow to be more and more self-indulgent and who dedicate their lives to the pursuit of pleasure as a matter of principle'; 'there are people who need to break through their liaisons with the social environment in order to find their true self-identity'. Each of these claims poses a threat to Green's argument by denying its universality. It is difficult, I would say, impossible, to assert complex phenomena as universal facts as Green does. To argue that the phenomenon of human beings seeking their salvation through a process of social integration is a fact of human nature is a poor way of presenting a valuable insight. The truth of this observation should not depend on its applicability in every single human life.

Green's argument, however, contains a universal message. It explains why and how human beings are capable of acting as moral agents. The salvation argument is a practical application of the abstract philosophical assertion developed earlier in *Prolegomena* that in all his actions an agent follows an idea.[19] There Green argues that human beings do not act upon instincts but always follow an idea of self-satisfaction; that they always 'distinguish' themselves from their desires; that even when they succumb to easy pleasures they are always aware of the costs of their choices. The salvation argument gives flesh and thus reveals the strength of the theory of the will. To remind, according to the salvation argument, when individuals want to increase their wellbeing they pursue some form of lasting self-satisfaction, which is not to be seen in any 'sum of pleasures'. What Green demonstrates through this argument is that a human being's idea of self-satisfaction constantly develops. Initially one's idea of wellbeing can coincide with simple pleasures, but this idea will, by necessity, develop towards a radically different object. Because simple pleasures are transient and their expiry leaves a sense of dissatisfaction they will gradually 'disqualify' as being someone's idea of what is good for himself. The quest for permanent self-satisfaction can find rest only in some kind of good which transcends ordinary pleasure. Only by seeing the good in a new way, i.e. only by changing her concept of her wellbeing, can a person find lasting happiness. Moral behaviour is possible because human beings are capable of pursuing an idea of a good which is not only good for themselves, but a good that is common between them and the others. So the salvation argument reveals the principle of moral action. It explains the genealogy of moral motivation and thus the possibility of moral conduct.

Both the salvation argument and the principle of moral action reflect a process. Green reveals the logical steps of the process in which one adopts the common good as his own good: people are aware that pleasures are transient; they need permanent satisfaction; they look for objects where lasting wellbeing can be found; they find these objects in the unification of their wellbeing with that of others. All these logical stages are actually stages of human experience, each of them building on the preceding one. So, in a sense, Green's argument is not dogmatic at all, it does not *presuppose* the noble social interest, it demonstrates it by disclosing its genesis.[20]

The backbone of the salvation argument consists in describing the process by which an individual comes to 'think of' others as of himself. This process is difficult to explain because, in a sense, it is 'counterfactual'. Obvious facts are that individuals distinguish themselves from others and act in their own interests. The cases of disinterested service to others are rather exceptional. Yet to prove the possibility of the common good as disinterested service to others, Green does not have to reject obvious facts. Once he describes the process through which one's concept of self grows to incorporate others within itself, it becomes clear how a self-interest can simultaneously be an interest in the good of others. The strength of Green's argument is that he describes the human character as dynamic, rather than as fixed. The weakness is that he wants to assert moral attitudes as facts. Thus, although he makes important discoveries about human nature, he ends up with a distorted picture. Green asserts the 'factuality' of people being loving, caring and noble, at the expense of denying the 'factuality' of them being self-centred and antagonistic to others. He does not need to deny the latter in order to assert the former. On the contrary, humans become noble and good to others in their attempt to overcome their selfish impulses. A full account of the generic nature of morals requires admission of the fact that individuals pursue pleasures and prioritise their own wellbeing over that of the others.

Admitting the dichotomy between personal pleasures and the concern for the wellbeing of others does not pose such a threat to Green's common good theory as many critics believe.[21] His mistake is confined to the fact of not registering that this difference exists at least at some level. Avital Simhony argues, in defence of Green, that all those who believe that there is a tension between egoism and benevolence pre-suppose a 'dualist moral framework' which precludes the possibility of a 'non-contingent connection between the two personal and moral good'.[22] I believe that Green's common good theory should not be defended by thoroughly denying the conflict between the personal and the common good, but by emphasising the fact that this theory represents a process of moral growth. The pursuit of the common good is not a fact, it is a moral achievement. It reflects a process whereby the moral agent has overcome his habitual pursuit of simple self-satisfaction. In other words, the synthesis between my good and the common good is not given, but achieved. Green is very good in explaining the process in which a person's concept of her own good grows to embrace in itself the good of others, but he fails to see the implications of this theory. The synthesis in the end does not preclude the dichotomy at the beginning; the former is based on overcoming the latter.

2.2. THE UNIQUE POSITION OF THE SELF

An important implication of the observation that the primary purpose of the common good theory is to reflect a process of moral growth is the recognition of *the unique position of the self* in the process of finding the common good. Because Green does not make sufficiently clear that the common good, in essence, represents a principle of moral action, he also does not see the necessity of distinguishing between what is *my* ultimate good and what is the good I can do for *others*. As a matter of principle, these two cannot be the same.

Green maintains that a person should not distinguish between his own true good and that of others. Once we are aware 'what it is that we desire in desiring our own true or permanent well-being, it would seem we have already answered the question, what it is that we desire in desiring the well-being of others'.[23] Once we have established that permanent wellbeing cannot be found either in pleasure or in any sum of pleasures, then we should know that it is not pleasure that we have to provide for others in our desire to do them good. It has already been ascertained that the individual attains his true wellbeing by conceiving of his good as common between him and others. It is the same kind of wellbeing, Green believes, he should aim to achieve for others.

There is one sense in which what Green says is correct. An individual should not judge the good of others by a criterion different from that by which she judges her own. She should not think of the wellbeing of her fellow human beings in any terms inferior to her own. However, Green is wrong in advancing the view that she should act towards other people's permanent good in the same manner as she acts towards her own. This is impossible by the definition of what the true good is. If I find a permanent satisfaction in caring for others, I can act upon my belief. Yet if, for instance, my brother would find his true good in caring for others, I could not achieve this for him. As the true good is acting upon your moral ideal, it is non-transferable. As 'the only true good is the good will',[24] the true good, exists only as performed.

We are again facing the phenomenological circle. Keeping a clear vision of the dichotomy between the good will and the actual good done is very important. Whatever contents of the good is asserted, it can only be legitimised from the perspective of the manner in which it is pursued. A generous deed is also a moral deed only if it is performed out of a moral disposition. Nothing is truly good on its own: its moral character is always invested into it by an individual who searches for a permanent satisfaction by identifying himself with the others. The contents of the actual true good cannot be separated from one's motives for seeking it, and then declared as a standard object of moral pursuit. If Green's idea of true good is properly understood, it should become clear that my true good can never be your true good. What is truly good for me may be truly good for you as well, but the very object in which I seek my true good cannot be the same as yours. You cannot exercise my high faculties, neither can you do good to others instead of me. The true good cannot be given or taken.

This controversy has often been disputed among the critics of Green's work. What does he mean by 'good', the objects aimed at or the way in which an object brings gratification? Prichard argues that it is the latter.[25] He makes a point very similar to the one I am offering. He believes that on Green's initial definition of good as something that satisfies desire, the consistent use of the term should signify a 'feeling of satisfaction and gratification' and not 'the *realisation* of the thing desired'.[26] He observes that a feeling of satisfaction and gratification can be excited only by a state of our own activity, and concludes that 'there cannot be such a thing as a good common to two different persons, unless the two so-called different persons are really one and the same, and so not different persons'. If Green is consistent in his presentation of the 'good' he should not use it in the sense of an object, but in the sense of a subjective feeling.

Peter Nicholson marks the dichotomy in Green's usage of the term 'good' as a 'substantive' and 'adjectival' use.[27] He argues against Prichard that it is not true that Green means the good in an adjectival rather than a substantive sense. Nicholson believes that Green's more impor-tant definition of the good is as an object, not as a source of satisfac-tion.[28] He reveals the internal connection between the two approaches in defining the good. Nicholson argues that the adjectival use is only a means to a further and richer definition of a substantive concept. As Green's concept of good develops into a concept of moral good, Green has legitimately moved from one substantive use to another. It is for the purposes of this transition that Green analysed the good as a source of satisfaction: "Green has moved from a substantive to an adjectival use of 'good', and this enables him to reach a new substantive use."[29] Nicholson believes that as the good should be understood as an object, not as a source of satisfaction, Prichard's argument fails. My disagree-ment with Prichard is slightly different. I believe the good should be seen as both these things, and therefore, Prichard is partly wrong, partly right. He is wrong to argue that the common good can never be com-mon. The object in which the agent, who seeks the common good, finds satisfaction, is good for her in common with others. The way in which I believe Prichard right is as follows.

Prichard's argument, however imprecise in its fulness, still makes a valuable point. The good understood as a source of satisfaction cannot be common. The common good, seen as the true good, can only be mine, never ours. It is common as between me and others, but not common as belonging to each of us in an equal way. As I have said, against Prichard, I can argue that the use of 'common' is still legitimate if carefully specified. I can aim at a good which is common, like being a good teacher, because in attaining it, many people benefit. My good is also good for my pupils. Yet, this good stays in a different relation to me and to the students. It is my, but not their, true good. This 'common good' is not their true good, because in attaining it they have not yet become involved in activity contributing to the wellbeing of others. We can see that by definition the true good as common good implies that the object, in which satisfaction is sought, satisfies not only the subject of the action but a wider circle of people.

Green's theory of the common good is a further explanation of his views on the moral ideal. In the same manner as the moral ideal, the common good is not necessarily fixed into any particular object. The common good can express itself in pursuit of objects, which on the surface, may seem very different. '[K]eeping a family comfortably alive, without reference to the well-being of any wider society' is an expression of the common good in the same way as 'composition of a book on an abstruse subject', or organising the 'sanitation of a town'.[30] The particular objects in which the common good is sought 'vary in different ages and with different persons, according to circumstances and idiosyncrasy'.[31] What unifies all quests for the common good is a principle. It always reveals an interest in an object which is good both for the individual and her fellow human beings. In other words, this principle is: the common good is always to be found in an object which can be desired only if the individual identifies himself with a wider range of human beings. In clarification of this principle, Green argues that this object in which the common good is to be found is not a part of one's experience: it is an anticipation, it is an image projected into the future. As was the case with the moral ideal, it acquires its particular meaning throughout the process of its pursuit:

> The idea of the good, according to this view, is an idea, if the expression may be allowed, *which gradually creates its own filling.* It

is not an idea like that of any pleasure, which a man retains from an experience that he has had and would like to have again. It is an idea to which nothing that has happened to us or that we can find in existence corresponds, but which sets us upon causing certain things to happen, upon bringing certain things into existence.[32]

We can see that an important part of the definition of the common good is its 'open-endedness', its conditionality on the manner of its quest. It comes into existence only as 'crowning with success' someone's effort towards it. Green's claim is that the common good is not part of our experience, it is always a projection into the future ('it rest[s] not on instinct but on self-consciousness – on a man's projection of himself in thought into a future, as a subject of a possibly permanent satis-faction').[33] One conclusion of this claim is that whenever the common good is a 'fact', whenever it has already happened, and is thus part of experience, it should always be seen as an achievement. The unity of my wellbeing with that of the others, and respectively, my identity with a wider social environment is never a 'mere fact', it is an attainment. And it is an attainment from the perspective of a self-conscious subject.

With respect to the common good, the common good seen as one's true good or as a moral ideal, its agent is always in a unique position. The synthesis between one's welfare and that of others, between oneself and society, the synthesis which is the core of the common good, is always achieved, never pregiven. Through the identity with society the agent achieves something which he did not have before, and he becomes something which he was not. It is true that the common good attained in the end is meant to be, and is, good in common to the agent with others. Organising the sanitation of a town makes the life of everyone, of the agent and of her fellow-dwellers, more comfortable. However, this is good to the agent in one more sense, additional to that of increasing comfort. It is good for her as it is also her self-fulfilment. The common good is good for all but it stays in a different relationship to its performer and its beneficiaries.

Green is wrong to argue that a person can work for other people's true good in the same way as he works for his own. He says that the individual can contribute to the true good of others by 'the realisation for them of the same objects' in which he finds his own happiness.[34] I have shown, by referring to Green's theory of the common good as a moral ideal, that it is impossible to realise the true good on behalf of someone else.

2.3. THE LOSS OF THE CONCEPT OF THE ORDINARY GOOD

Observing this particular inconsistency in Green's theory, the impossibility of the common good as a moral ideal to be common to all in an equal manner, can bring forward other controversies. In the assertion of the true good Green 'loses' his concept of the ordinary good. This loss is caused not by a lack of insight into human nature (Green himself had introduced a perfectly acceptable concept of good) but by his unjustified eagerness to reject entirely the hedonist utilitarian theory of pleasure. With the progress of his theory of the moral ideal Green rejects a notion which initially served as a foundation: the notion of the ordinary good. In the process of elucidating the nature of the true good, Green effectively disqualifies the ordinary good from being good at all. This devaluation of the ordinary good is in parallel with his neglect of the importance of the self-centred framework of general human practice. If these two are neglected, the theory of the common good/true good/moral good loses its foundation. Additionally, their practical fulfilment becomes impossible. To reiterate, by ordinary good I mean what Green means by 'good'. I refer to good which is good to oneself only, as opposed to the moral good which is intended by its agent as a good common between him and the others.

There is a benign paradox implicit in Green's theory of the noble social interest. Revealing and resolving this paradox offers a key to resolving the difference between ordinary and moral behaviour. Green says that it is characteristic of the noble social interest 'that, to the man who is the subject of it, those who are its objects are ends, in the same sense in which he is an end to himself'.[35] This popular appeal to which Green subscribes, the appeal to treat 'thy neighbour as thyself' would have, I argue, no meaning if there were not something special to the way one treats oneself. The paradox is the following. How can I treat others as I treat myself, if what generally characterises my treatment of myself is the unarticulated belief that I am the centre of the universe?

What is so special about the individual's treatment of himself? I hope not to raise much controversy by claiming that what defines one's self-perception is the unconditional value of an individual to herself. Everything she does, bears directly or indirectly on her own self. This represents an essential part of Green's theory of the will where he claimed that human practice is based on a 'self-seeking' principle.[36] The individual is always the final end of her actions. A person does not have to justify to himself repeatedly the fact that everything he does is aimed at increasing his wellbeing: his wellbeing is of unconditional value to himself. He treats himself as if he were the most important person: to himself, he *is* the most important person. This is the meaning of the concept of an end. 'The end' is what marks the upper limit on an ascending line of things of importance. 'The end' is the absolutely valuable in relation to which other things acquire their significance. That is why speaking about a plurality of ends always entails some contradiction. If the end is the ultimate purpose, or the absolutely valuable, how can this be multiple?

Now we have spelt out the implications of a person's self-perception as an end to himself, we can see that the appeal for treating others as ourselves is a controversial one. This paradox can be resolved, but I believe it should first be admitted. It is possible to treat others as ends, but this will entail a change within one's self-perception. When I treat someone else as an end, that means that my self-awareness as an absolute end has been challenged. The self-centred framework of my action has been 'questioned', and as a result, 'weakened'. It is a powerful message of Green's moral philosophy that human beings as rational can 'distance' themselves from themselves and overcome their habitual attitudes. The individual has 'this power of contemplating himself as possibly coming to be that which he is not', he has the power to 'bracket' his self-perception as absolutely valuable.[37]

What Green fails to see is that even when overcome, the self-centred framework is not invalidated. As we saw, it is this framework that underpins one's concept of an end. It is because we are ends to ourselves that we understand that other people are also ends to themselves. The possibility of bracketing my absolute value and pursuing goods solely on account of them being goods for others, does not preclude the possibility of me also pursuing goods which are goods only to myself. I will develop this further. The elimination of the self-centred framework would simultaneously imply a destruction of the possibility of doing good to others. In other words, by disqualifying the ordinary good, one also makes the common good impossible. Only if ordinary good exists, am I in a position to fulfil my common good. To the recipients of my production of good, the good I produce is ordinary. It is meant to satisfy them not as part of a wider community, but as ends to themselves. To me, my production of good to others is the true or the common good, because it is meant to satisfy me not as a sole subject, but as a subject who has identified herself with others.

We can reach the conclusion that a good which is common to a number of people and stays in equal relation to all of them cannot be a common good in the sense of true good, but can only be an ordinary good.

3. THE COMMON GOOD IN THE SECOND SENSE – AS THE SOCIETY OF EQUAL PERSONS

Now we are in a position to see that the two senses in which Green uses the term 'common good' differ in an important way. When Green refers to the common good as an object which stays in equal relationship to all individuals, this object, on analysis, represents not the moral good (i.e. the common good in the first sense) but the ordinary good.

We have seen that Green uses the common good in the meaning of the process of moral growth. Additionally he also speaks of the common good in terms of some 'common end' which all individuals should unitedly pursue.[38] In more abstract terms this common end is described as 'a spiritual activity in which all may partake, and in which all must partake, if it is to amount to a full realisation of the faculties of the human soul'.[39] In more concrete terms the common end is a type of society where all men are equal, it is a 'development of society into a state in which all human beings shall be treated as, actually or in promise, persons – as agents of whom each is an end equally to himself and to others'.[40] The second sense of Green's common good is based on *a particular vision* of justice and happiness. Here the common good is not a spiritual or altruistic activity in which an individual can find self-fulfilment. It is clearly seen as a form of social life:

> It [the ultimate good] must be a perfecting of *man* – not of any human faculty in abstraction, or of any imaginary individuals in that detachment from social relations in which they would not be men at all. We are therefore justified in holding that it could not be attained in a life of mere scientific and artistic activity, any more than in one of 'practical' exertion from which those activities were absent; *in holding further that the life in which it is attained must be a social life, in which all men freely and consciously co-operate* . . .[41]

The 'common good' comes to express Green's vision of how the perfecting of the individual soul should be achieved in practical social terms. However abstract the ideal of the ultimate good is, however much we can find out its concrete content only in the process of its unfolding, Green asserts that the common end is a particular type of society with particular institutions. We should understand the true end of our human moral effort 'not as determined merely by an abstract idea of law, but as implying (what it must in fact imply) a whole world of beneficent social activities'.[42]

What I call the second sense of the common good Avital Simhony takes to be its main meaning. She argues persuasively that Green's common good 'is about a certain kind of society, social union which both underpins relation of mutual interest and gives it effect'.[43] I believe that this is a legitimate interpretation of the common good and, as Simhony proves, it offers both solutions to difficult practical dilemmas and answers to unfair criticisms against Green. I will not pursue this aspect of the common good further in this article.

I argue that the first and the second senses of the common good differ in an essential way. The common good as the effort of seeking one's own good in conjunction with the good of others is different from the common good as the society of equal persons which is the only means through which the human soul can perfect itself. In the first sense, the common good is a principle of moral action. The objects in which it can find expression can be sought and achieved only by an agent exerting moral effort. The common good as a moral good is exclusively related to a particular person. Each individual should seek her own 'common good'. She should find out for herself the object in which her true good resides. As can be seen in the first sense of the common good, the use of the term 'common' is very specific. The common good is common as a result but personal as an aspiration, as an effort, as an act of self-fulfilment.

The common good as the society of equal persons is common in a different way. Although Green attempts to present his idea of the just society as a development of that vein of thought which has already introduced the common good as the moral ideal, his message departs from its starting point. In other words, although he presents the equal society as a moral objective in the pursuit of which the individuals can seek fulfilment, this does not express the full value of social equality. The just society is not a moral good. Its 'goodness' cannot be seen primarily as that of a moral achievement. When Green describes the value of social equality he may emphasise the moral effort involved in its attainment; however, he places much stronger emphasis on the benefits this equality will bring to the general improvement of humankind. The social equality is good to all in common and to all alike. It is not good because it could be someone's self-fulfilment: its value does not consist in its being a moral ideal. To individuals the good society is an ordinary good, not a moral good. It aims to satisfy a person as a private self, not as an extended common self – the self which one acquires only within a moral act. The ordinary good is a good which is meant to be good for oneself – not to the exclusion of the others, but not necessarily to their inclusion. According to Green's definition, in the perfect society everyone is treated as an end: each person is valued simply on account of his human nature. This implies that everyone is deserving social welfare and justice regardless of whether he acts as a moral agent or not.

Green's just society is 'commonly' good to all. All are recipients of its goodness. To those who contribute to its creation in a moral way, by means of overcoming their personal inclinations, the just society is both an ordinary and a moral good. However, the exclusive value of the social equality is its unrivalled capacity to provide ordinary good, in Green's estimation, it can provide more good than any other social formation or human artefact at all.[44]

Pinning down the inadequacies of Green's common good theory contributes to unlocking its full potential. We can see that Green's arguments can simultaneously carry a powerful message and its own negation. Green fails to emphasise the personal character of the moral ideal and the common good, and he loses the concept of the ordinary good. However, he provides the practical and moral theories which I have employed to analyse his common good theory and detect its errors.

CONCLUSION

I argue that Green fails to underline that his common good theory reflects a process of moral growth because he is concerned to present the noble social interest as a fixed trait of the human character. Whether he has defined the common good from the inner personal perspective, or from the outer, objective one, he has always tried to present it as something firm and unconditional: that is why he has not seen his definitions of the common good as essentially different from each other.

Green's common good theory can be fully understood in the light of his preceding theories of the will and of the moral ideal. There Green gives formal accounts of general human behaviour and of moral behaviour, in particular. A formal definition of an object defines the conditions of its pursuit, and these conditions are to be found in the inner disposition of the agent who has adopted the object as an object of his own pursuit. An object becomes what it is only as being involved into someone's experience. Green defines the good as that which satisfies desire; he defines the moral good as that which is sought with a self-disinterested attitude. In the same vein of thought, the formal conditions of the common good are to be found in the possibility of the human agent to pursue the good of others as part of her own good.

In his overall philosophy Green has always given priority to the formal over the substantive definitions of the good, the moral good, or the common good. That is why, I have argued, the formal definition of the common good holds a priority over the substantive one. This gives an answer to a widespread challenge against Green claiming that people will never agree on what the common good is. If the common good is understood in its non-substantive version, i.e. as a principle of moral action, then it holds universal character and thus bears no dispute. This article offers a solution to the debates about what exactly Green's understanding of the good is, as well as, how common the common good is. By explaining the genealogy of the moral good, I reach the conclusion that a particular object is morally good only with respect to the person who has produced it. The same object is ordinarily good to those who simply benefit from it. If the common good is understood only in its substantive sense, i.e. as a particular object that is good to many people in common, then it represents an ordinary, not a moral good. Green would not have been satisfied with a concept of the common good that does not reflect the moral character of the individual. That is why, I believe, that the substantive version of the common good on its own does not render the fullness of his common good theory.

NOTES

1 See Colin Tyler, *T. H. Green (1836-1882) and the Philosophical Foundations of Politics*, (Lewiston,The Edwin Mellen Press, 1997), 96-137; Geoffrey Thomas, *The Moral Philosophy of T. H. Green* (Oxford, Clarendon Press, 1987), 254; Andrew Vincent, *The Philosophy of T. H. Green*, (Aldershot, Gower Publishing Company Ltd, 1986), 13.

2 T. H. Green, *Prolegomena to Ethics*, (Oxford, Clarendon Press, 1890). Hereafter *Prolegomena*; in quoting, the first figure will refer to the number of the page, the second, to the number of the section. *Prolegomena*, 204, 194.

3 Vincent (ed.), *The Philosophy of T. H. Green*, 13.

4 Vincent (ed.), *The Philosophy of T. H. Green*, 13.

5 Thomas, *The Moral Philosophy of T. H. Green*, 254.

6 Thomas, *The Moral Philosophy of T. H. Green*, 255.

7 Green uses the terms 'social interest' or 'distinctive social interest' (*Prolegomena*, 211, 200).

8 *Prolegomena*, 210, 199.

9 See *Prolegomena*, sections 221-228.

10 *Prolegomena*, 246, 230.

11 *Prolegomena*, 245-6, 229.

12 *Prolegomena*, 247, 231.

13 See *Prolegomena*, sections 229-232.

14 *Prolegomena*, 247, 231.

15 *Prolegomena*, 242, 228.

16 *Prolegomena*, 248, 232.

17 Alan Milne, 'The Common Good and rights in T. H. Green's Ethical and Political Theory', in *The Philosophy of T. H. Green*, ed. by Andrew Vincent, (Aldershot, Gower Publishing Company Ltd, 1986), 62-75, 69.

18 *Prolegomena*, 249, 232.

19 See Book II ('The Will') of *Prolegomena*.

20 In this context, I would like to mention that David Brink addresses Green's salvation argument as a major theoretical resource to his own concept of 'metaphysical egoism' (David Brink, 'Self-Love and Altruism', *Social Philosophy & Policy*, 14:1, 1997, 122-57). He believes this concept resolves the shortcomings of the 'strategical egoism' theory which 'can justify other-regarding duties only towards partners in systems of mutual advantage' (123). The conception of metaphysical egoism 'should lead us to see people's interests as metaphysically, and not just strategically interdependent'. Brink acknowledges the legacy of two traditions: of Plato's discussion of love in the *Symposium* and the *Phaedrus* and Aristotle's discussion of friendship and political community in the *Nicomachean Ethics* and the *Politics*, and of Green's discussion of self-realisation and extension of common good in the *Prolegomena to Ethics*. These two traditions offer the insights which help Brink to develop his theory of '*interpersonal psychological continuity*', and to explain his idea that 'the separateness or diversity of persons is not so fundamental' (141-2).

21 Milne, 'The Common Good and rights in T. H. Green's Ethical and Political Theory', 69; Melvin Richter, *The Politics of Conscience; T. H. Green and his Age*, (London, Weidenfeld and Nicolson, 1964), 254-61; Henry Sidgwick, *Lectures on the Ethics of T. H. Green, Mr. Herbert Spencer and J Martineau*, (London, MacMillan, 1902), 69-72.

22 Avital Simhony, 'Colin Tyler, Thomas Hill Green (1836-1882) and the Philosophical Foundations of Politics. An Internal Critique.' *Bradley Studies*, 5:1, 1999, 87-106, 100.

23 *Prolegomena*, 251, 235.

24 *Prolegomena*, 257, 240.

25 H. A. Prichard, *Moral Obligation. Essays and Lectures*, (Oxford, Clarendon Press, 1957).

26 Prichard, *Moral Obligation*, 71.

27 Peter Nicholson, *The Political Philosophy of the British Idealists*, (Cambridge, Cambridge University Press, 1990), 66.

28 Nicholson, *British Idealists*, see Study II, Section II.

29 Nicholson, *British Idealists*, 66.

30 *Prolegomena*, 256, 239; 252, 235.

31 *Prolegomena*, 256, 239.

32 *Prolegomena*, 259, 241, emphasis added.

33 *Prolegomena*, 258, 240.

34 *Prolegomena*, 253, 236.

35 *Prolegomena*, 211, 200.

36 See *Prolegomena*, 104, 100.

37 *Prolegomena*, 258, 240.

38 *Prolegomena*, 309, 286.

39 *Prolegomena*, 309, 286.

40 *Prolegomena*, 292, 271.

41 *Prolegomena*, 311, 288. The italicising of the last sentence is mine.

42 *Prolegomena*, 311, 288.

43 Avital Simhony, 'T. H. Green: The Common Good Society', *History of Political Thought*, 14:2, 1993, 225-47.

44 See *Prolegomena*, Book III, Chapter V: 'The Greek and the Modern Conceptions of Virtue'.

Bradley and Sidgwick on Philosophical Ethics

ANDREW VINCENT
University of Wales, Cardiff

In the 1870s there was a peculiar episode in British philosophy which still has odd resonances. Two philosophers were working simultaneously on treatises on ethics. The first to be published was Henry Sidgwick's *Methods of Ethics* in 1874. The second was Francis Bradley's *Ethical Studies*, published in 1876. According to Bradley, one of the more famous essays within *ES* ('Pleasure for Pleasure's sake') was already completed by 1874. Bradley, however, added a note to the end of the essay. Though brief, it concluded that Sidgwick 'had left the question [of utilitarianism] exactly where he had found it'. Sidgwick reviewed Bradley's *ES* in *Mind* in 1876, noting the addition to Essay III. Bradley immediately responded in the same year of *Mind*. Sidgwick quickly fired a reply. Bradley then followed this with a pamphlet in 1877. In redrafting his 2nd edition of *ME*, Sidgwick changed some passages in relation to Bradley's objections, although it is not explicit. Sidgwick did not, however, actually respond to Bradley's pamphlet. Schneewind comments here that 'perhaps he [Sidgwick] felt he would not maintain a proper tranquillity of temper himself if he tried a direct reply' (*SE*, 400).

Neither Sidgwick nor Bradley appear to refer to each other in an autobiographical sense. This silence obscures the relation between the two thinkers. Although never reaching anywhere near the heights of invective of, say, the Ruskin and Whistler debacle, Bradley's and Sidgwick's disputation still has all the qualities of finely honed viciousness. Rather than follow the minutiae of the debate, I will discuss it through the following themes: the nature of philosophy, ethics, common sense, the social organism, reason and pleasure.

PHILOSOPHY

One root to the problem between the two thinkers seems to be on the nature of philosophy itself . The matter, however, is not as simple as an analytical utilitarian and idealist in contest. There are some definite similarities between them. Both prided themselves on their analytical rigour. In many ways, Bradley was the most sceptical and analytical of all the British Idealists. As such he remained an enigma to many of his Idealist contemporaries. Equally, Sidgwick was so concerned to maintain a self-critical analytical stance that he tended, at times, to undermine his own work. The careful, inconclusive, hedging ending to *ME* highlights this style. As Maitland remarked, 'I sometimes think that the one and only prejudice that Sidgwick had was a prejudice against his own results' (see *M*, 306).

It is a hackneyed criticism of Hegelianism, and some manifestations of analytic philosophy, that they both tend towards a philosophically conservative imprimatur on what is – the Owl of Minerva usually hoots dismally at this point. Bradley thus remarks: 'All philosophy has to do is "to understand what is", and moral philosophy has to understand morals which exist, not to make them or give directions for making them' (*ES*, 193). Philosophy looks at the world cut and dried. Philosophy, also, to Sidgwick, introduces clarity into established conventions. It can only make explicit the rational foundation of what is. This is essentially a form of underlabourer conception of philosophy. Sidgwick was often quite depressed by this limitation.

Another implication of this analytical expository style is a logical unease in both thinkers with normative moral philosophy and the role of theory qua practice. In fact, one might have expected utilitarianism, *prima facie*, to have subscribed to the normative dimension. However, Sidgwick is ambivalent here and clearly smarts when Bradley suggests he is fostering hedonistic utilitarianism. Yet, oddly, one can almost see a contest between the two as to who could be the most distanced from the path of moral edification. The stakes are high, since both sense in the other an underlying normative proposal.

There is, in addition, something puzzling in Sidgwick's conception of philosophy. His assumption of the importance of established common sense was also a quasi-Hegelian judgement. Ironically, Sidgwick's 'Owl on Minerva' sensed the moral *Sitten* of England as utilitarian. His *ME* was painting its grey on grey. This was Benthamism, as has been remarked, 'grown sleek and tame'. Sidgwick was using Bentham to justify Burke. The upshot of this position was theoretically and practically conservative. Sidgwick, in the late 1880s, had moved on a very practical level from Millean radicalism to quite explicit Burkean conservatism. In the 1886 election, he returned early from a holiday in Europe specifically to vote conservative in a notably safe conservative parliamentary seat. Bradley, also, less publicly, was giving his philosophical benediction to Victorian culture, although it was not quite utilitarian. His caricatured reputation for conservatism also has roots in an 'underlabourer' Hegelianism. Both men also clearly shared a mutual detestation of Gladstone.

Overall, one might describe both philosophers as engaging in a form of underlabourer, hermeneutic, expository and critical approach. One crucial difference here is that Bradley's approach is dialectical. His conception of philosophy at this stage is quite definitely Hegelian in texture. There is, thus, an underlying sequential development to the exposition. Sidgwick's conception of philosophy hovered more uncertainly between a deep analytical scepticism, a confident Millean positivism and an odd and touching faith in Kantian practical reason. Sidgwick, however, had already made up his mind on post-Kantian idealism well before reading Bradley. Writing to a friend in 1866 from Germany, he commented that the whole Idealist enterprise was a 'monstrous mistake' (*M*, 151). Thus, although aware of the Hegelian approach, he intentionally ignores the dialectical aspect to *ES*.

ETHICS

It is no surprise that there are different conceptions of Sidgwick's ethics. In one reading, Sidgwick's ethics is an *ex post facto* philosophical reflection upon 'methods'. In the second interpretation, ethics is a normative universalist utilitarianism which can provide clear ethical guidance. In a third view, utilitarianism is embedded in common sense, which, if criticised, clarified and refined provides ethical guidance.[1] The third view is the most persuasive interpretation, but it is not clear that it can be completely reconciled with the first account, which also undoubtedly figures in *ME*. We might call these three perspectives the hermeneutic, normativist and integral readings.

In the hermeneutic view, ethical science is an abstract discipline focusing on the ends of practical reason. It is free from metaphysics, psychology, religion and practical edification. Sidgwick thus claims fiercely not to have been promoting *any* one particular position in ethics. The ethical thinker empathetically enters into and expounds the varying methods used in daily practice and criticises them from an 'impartialist perspective'. Ethical methods are divided into three types: egoistic hedonism (every man ought to seek his own pleasure/happiness in any volition), universalistic hedonism or utilitarianism (every man ought seek the general happiness/ pleasure) and intuitionism (which largely premises itself on self-evidence). All three methods to Sidgwick, are 'more or less vaguely combined in the practical reasoning of ordinary men' (*ME*, 496). No complete synthesis is attempted in *ME*.

Ideal utilitarianism, to guide the enlightened agent through moral issues, was something he found problematic. He was clear that those who attributed to him an ideal utilitarianism were mistaken. For example, he noted in the preface to the 2nd edition of *ME*, that many critics have assumed that he is an 'assailant of two of the methods . . . and a defender of the third'. He continued, pretty certainly against Bradley, that one writer 'has gone to the length of a pamphlet under the [wrong] impression . . . that the "main argument of my treatise is a demonstration of Universalistic hedonism"' (*ME*, x). There is a strong sense of sceptical modernity in Sidgwick, particularly in terms of twentieth century moral philosophy. Basically, he serves up a limited smorgasbord of conflicting ethical positions (flavoured with microscopic critical analysis) and then appears powerless to recommend any. He assumes, in fact, in the final chapter of *ME* that no method or approach can be proved or shown without some metaphysical or theological notion and that none are philosophically available. His obsessive interest in psychical research is related to this latter detail.

There is another dimension to this repudiation of edification, focused on Sidgwick's occasional remarks on history. He developed a conception of ethics which was also historically sensitive (an uncharacteristic move in the utilitarian tradition), suggesting that one could not attain any 'ethics' outside a particular community and moral tradition, although the roots are still loosely utilitarian. Philosophical ethics is thus rooted is an existing moral order (see *ME* , 497). There is a close intellectual parallel here with Bradley (see *ES*, 196-7).

A strong normativist perspective can also be identified.[2] However, an unqualified normativist conception would be a misreading of Sidgwick. Yet, at the same time, Sidgwick's ethics are still a form of demure Benthamism. They lack the brash confidence of Bentham, yet his 'empirical-reflective-method' was essentially a much more tempered form of Bentham's felicific calculus. The theorist consults the common sense of the normal 'Benthamite Mensch'. This leads to the 'integral perspective. In the integral perspective, common sense embodies utilitarianism. It reveals moral beliefs, providing 'axiomata media' for potential prescription. These moral beliefs, if refined, do provide utilitarian norms.

Bradley's critique of Sidgwick inevitably gets strung out between these perspectives. It is not surprising that Bradley complains that he 'can find no unity of principle which holds its [*ME*] parts together' (*SH*, 124). Oddly, in concurrence with the hermeneutic Sidgwick, Bradley holds that ethics, like philosophy, is not concerned with practical edification. Ethics is about *understanding*, with clarity, the day to day communal practices of morality. There is one other niggling element, though, even within this hermeneutic parity between Sidgwick and Bradley. For Bradley, theory starts from and is verified in experience, yet, as Bradley remarks 'it is *not* mere experience. It is reflection and interpretation; and when mere experience pronounces on the abstract conclusions of science, then it ceases to be experience and, becoming theory, must itself stand and fall by the theoretical test' (*SH*, 114-5). The epistemology embodied in these points is suspicious of unalloyed empiricism and the confusion of modes of understanding. Sidgwick's position on this issue is far less clear.

Bradley takes Sidgwick to be a normative utilitarian. Sidgwick consequently complains about misinterpretation, and he has a point, but Bradley is not wholly to blame. At root, for Bradley, a normative 'ethical science does not exist yet'. He raises a number of objections to this conception of ethics, but most congregate around his contention that Sidgwick's conception of ethics is 'jural'. For Bradley, whereas law regulates a diversity of situations with a rule, morality does not. In morality, we take a particular case and ask is it right or wrong (see *SH*, 104-7). It is tempting to suggest, against Bradley, that morality also has a jural dimension. Yet, his argument gains more bite as he continues. Bradley finds, in the 'normative utilitarian Sidgwick', a strong suggestion of a moral 'almanac', namely, an abstract reflective code, which tells us what we ought to do on a practical level.

First, for Bradley, such a code would have to cover all possible moral contingencies to be viable. Yet, to have such complete knowledge is impossible. Second, the background assumption in Sidgwick is that it is the individual who makes moral judgments. One way out of this isolated subjectivity is to appeal to an ideal utility. For Sidgwick, many of the puzzles he deals with would go in an enlightened utilitarianism. Bradley, again, finds this puzzling, namely, does Sidgwick want to maintain a distinction between the 'enlightened' and 'vulgar' (*SH*, 111-3)? In fact, Sidgwick does discard 'Ideal utilitarianism'. Once the 'Ideal' perspective is rejected subjectivity remains. In addition, to even suggest something is objectively right is to imply no other course is open, which, for Bradley, is plainly ridiculous. Third, there is a dilemma on the question of moral theory and practice. For Bradley, when ethical science ceases to understand and proposes to alter the facts with such rules, then something has gone badly wrong. Sidgwick simply gives us casuistry or Jesuitry.

Of course, this whole critique may be nugatory if the hermeneutic Sidgwick is a more accurate assessment. Yet, Sidgwick's ethics hovers between the hermeneutic and integral perspectives, with some occasional forays into a fulsome normativist view. If Bradley appears to misread Sidgwick, it is with some justification.

THE STRUGGLE OVER THE ORDINARY

Both thinkers focus on the 'ordinary' or 'common sense' as a touchstone for morality.[3] However, many moral philosophers have felt uncomfortable with the idea of the probative force of common sense. For Sidgwick, however, all the common sense virtues we use in everyday practice are utilitarian. Ordinary practice provides the 'middle axioms' for utilitarianism. When carefully criticised these axioms give ethical guidance. Sidgwick claims, surprisingly, that the decisive influence in formulating this perspective was Aristotle (*ME* 6th edition preface, xix-xx). Utility is embodied in the 'ethos' of English culture (no doubt conservatively determining the station and duties of citizens).

Sidgwick's review of *ES* does make some telling points, although his purposeful avoidance of certain key assumptions in Bradley's approach inevitably weakens his case. First, he ignores the dialectical sequence. This allows him to express surprise at Bradley's own self-critique in later essays. Secondly, he continues, on the same assumption, that Bradley's 'Ideal morality' conflicts with the ordinary morality of a community. Hence, what has happened to Bradley's much vaunted common sense? He thus turns the tables on Bradley's comments on Ideal utilitarianism, suggesting Bradley himself wants to refine ordinary morals. Sidgwick argues that Bradley also acknowledges the authority of 'cosmopolitan morality' which transcends country or state. The 'Station and Duties' theme thus loses all its distinctiveness and is 'reduced to little more than a vague and barren ethical commonplace, dressed in a new metaphysical formula' (*CN*, 549). Thirdly, given the perception that morals can be refined, Sidgwick suggests that even Bradley's ordinary unreflective man would be surprised by the ethical standards he is supposed to agree with. In fact, such surprise is almost inevitable (from point two). Sidgwick then twists the knife, suggesting, in effect, that Bradley is surreptitiously fostering his own normative conception (*R*, 126).

Bradley's response to this is uncharacteristically weak. He does not complain about the misreading of the 'dialectical sequence'. Bradley's sensitivity to Hegel's influence (which gets more pronounced in later years) may well have been in the background. He simply asks where Sidgwick gets the quotation on 'unsophisticated common sense' (*SES*, 124). Sidgwick admits in his next response that he invented the phrase (and thus is prepared to give up the inverted commas), but still thinks it appropriate for Bradley's argument (*R*, 126).

In summary, Bradley has little complaint about the content of common sense, but he worries as to exactly what Sidgwick is doing with it. He suspects him of wanting to modify it with abstract jural rules. For Bradley, moral philosophers are not authoritative guides to what 'ought' to be done in morals. Given Bradley's conception of the nature of philosophical ethics, his view is hardly surprising. Sidgwick, on the other hand, conscious of the close parallels between his own and Bradley's approach, is determined to damn Bradley for proclaiming the importance of the unrefined 'ordinary' morals. He thinks that Bradley also signals his own unease with unreflective common sense and is determined to push the contradiction. Sidgwick does put his finger here on a problem with Hegelian ethics which is better examined under the rubric of the social organism.

THE SOCIAL ORGANISM

There is a sequence of complex related arguments focusing on the relation of practice and theory, individual and community and, later, public and private reason. In this section it is the community/individual angle which will be focused on. The gist of the debate between Sidgwick and Bradley relates to distinct ontologies. Bradley's ontology is communitarian and Hegelian, Sidgwick's lies in Millian and Benthamite empirical individualism.

First, Sidgwick notes that self-realisation is a central theme of *ES*, yet, Bradley appears to admit that he does not know what 'self' means, an admission which, Sidgwick says, 'disarms satire' (*CN*, 545-6). Sidgwick's criticisms rely, once again here, on an avoidance of dialectics. Bradley responded by claiming that he had not attempted to solve the problem of the origin or full character of the self, but, suggests that his view is not thereby 'incoherent' (*SES*, 123). The problem seems to be that Sidgwick's Millian self is a fairly static sentient being, whereas Bradley's self is a 'process'. This would account for Sidgwick's impatience with Bradley's mutations. The root to Bradley's 'process self' lies in the conception of self-realisation. For Bradley, action is thought translating itself into existence. Any action 'I' perform must be something that I posit as an end. In fact, 'I' can posit is my self in another state. Thus, any action is self-realisation, since it is an end posited by me. Nothing can be foreign to me since 'what we desire must be in our minds' (*ES*, 82). Therefore, to will is to self-realise. As Bradley put it, 'The will must be in the act, and the act in the will' (*ES*, 34). Bradley's self changes with each end it places before itself.

Second, Sidgwick takes issue with Bradley's idea of the 'self as a whole' (an inclusive end which embraces other ends). As reasoning creatures, humans try to systematise, but Sidgwick comments, do we gain 'anything by calling the object of our search "the true whole which is to realise the true self"' (*CN*, 546-7)? Bradley views this differently. The self is envisaged as an 'incompleteness' with an underlying sense of systematic completeness. The premise behind this is that human beings cannot logically abide contradiction. The human self develops by positing greater and more systematically inclusive ends. The sequence of *ES is* the gradual development of more systematic and inclusive 'wholes'.

Third, Sidgwick pushes the above point, asking what Bradley's idea of a systematic whole means? Taking the argument directly to the 'Station and Duties' essay again, Sidgwick claims that Bradley 'accepts a merely relative universality as a sufficient criterion of goodness' (*CN*, 547). Bradley quite legitimately responds to this, noting, 'that this is what I do *not* say' (*SES*, 123). For Bradley, it is both relative and absolute. Sidgwick once again ignores the dialectic sequence and contends that the social organism is neither a relative nor an absolute whole, that is, 'it is not the universe and we have no reason to identify its will – granting this to be real and cognisable – with the universal or Divine Will to which our wills should conform' (*R*, 126). This point misses the logic of the 'concrete universal'. However, Sidgwick sees the 'concrete universal' as nothing but the 'old doctrine . . . that the individual man is essentially a social being'. Bradley, thus, does not really advance beyond crude sociological relativism. (*CN*, 547-8).

Bradley, in reply, notes that if his view is like another, is that an objection to it? There is a sense here that Sidgwick simply casts aspersions. Sidgwick however refines the point in replying, complaining this time that Bradley does not distinguish the cruder view of society, simply being a natural organism, from society as organism possessing a rational will. Thus, he concludes, 'the result of the non-distinction is that much of this polemical argument – as far as I can trace it through the fold of rhetoric – is directed against an individualism which will find no defenders: the individualism, namely, to which the "Social Compact," belongs, and to which Utilitarianism long since gave the *coup de grâce*' (*R*, 126). In effect, Sidgwick claims he has a more sophisticated conception of moral and social theory, unfortunately what it is is never made clear.

When one reconstructs Sidgwick moral theory (and by inference his political theory), it is clear that he alternates between two methods, egoism and universalistic utilitarianism. The third method, intuition, appears largely as cheering chorus for utilitarianism. Sidgwick's egoist is one who produces the maximum amount of his own pleasure. Universalistic utilitarianism suggests that the egoistic individual can rationally inculcate self-sacrifice. It was obviously deeply irritating to Sidgwick that Bradley insisted that any consistent hedonism must remain egoistic and egoism is irreconcilable with morality. This undermined his whole strategy. Instead, he tries, for Bradley, to use egoism up to a certain point, then suppresses it surreptitiously to get to the next step, universalistic hedonism. For Bradley, Sidgwick's egoistic hedonist could never *logically* assert something as objectively desirable without refuting herself. Sidgwick is thus hoisted by his own philosophical petard. Egoism is both ontologically crucial *and*, at the same time, fatal. Despite Sidgwick's denial, the single sentient individual hovers at the unexamined ontological root of *ME* (*SES*, 124).

For Bradley, there are ways around egoism. One path is for Sidgwick to give up all claims to 'my' or 'yours', thus egoism goes out of the frame altogether. For Bradley, this would be a position close to Schopenhauer's. He thinks that Sidgwick would not be comforted by such an idea. Another alternative for Sidgwick would be to appeal to intuitions. Sidgwick does this. In this case, every 'single sentient' being must have an intuition 'of my pleasure as pleasure in general'. Yet, intuition is, at the best of times, a tricky philosophical device. Bradley thinks the idea of such 'mass' coincidence of egoistic intuitions ridiculous. Utilitarianism may be intuitively true for Sidgwick, but, Bradley remarks that this is not his intuition (*ES*, 128).

For Bradley, within the moment of the 'social organism', the self-realising individual is not asked to personally 'invent' a universal moral content, conversely, the content comes to the individual in a pre-existing form of life. It arises in social habits, conventions and traditions, which are assimilated, at first by rote and play and then by reflection. A moral vocabulary, *per se*, only makes sense in the context of existing forms of life, containing well-defined rules, which agents progressively place before themselves. The agent knows what is right or wrong in moral conduct by a 'subsumption, which does not know that it is a subsumption' (*ES*, 196). The community is a larger and more systematic whole, containing sedimented rules and social functions, which humans posit to themselves. All morality is, though, an imperfect realisation of human wholeness. This implies some degree of relativity of morality to historical communities, a point recognised by the hermeneutic Sidgwick.

Many of Sidgwick's criticisms make palpable hits. A characteristic difficulty with the Hegelian argument is the manner in which morality comes to the individual. Morals appear from the 'relative' communities and from 'outside' the autonomous will of the individual. Yet, Bradley's thesis does not deny the autonomy of the individual. It does not imply, as Sidgwick suggests, that others can therefore determine my actions (a critical point on positive liberty arguments which has been repeated thereafter by critics up to Isaiah Berlin). It is true that for Bradley morality has no place or situation outside of a community. It is *also* clear that no social function, state or community is perfect. An ethos may be corrupt and all communities are limited by other communities. The human self is subject to many unpredictablities. 'Ideal Morality', and later essays in *ES*, address some of these problems and move the argument beyond the station and duties thesis. Morality always implies imperfection. It tries to gain an end which makes it (morality) impossible. Morality is, thus, an effort after non-morality. Morality is always trying to cease to exist. Unless the agent divined herself to be a whole she could not feel the sense of her own imperfection and try to pass beyond it. This is one reason why religion figures at the end of *ES*. Religion, in effect, gives us what morality cannot.

THE DUALISM OF REASON

There is an elusive problem in Sidgwick which we have already encountered in the contrast between egoism and universalistic utilitarianism. The problem reappears in two notions of rationality. Sidgwick calls the latter issue the 'dualism of reason'. The central question is what does reason require of us in an ordinary [moral] life? There appear to be two answers in Sidgwick's *ME*, one optimistic and integral, the other pessimistic and pluralistic. Bishop Butler and Kant jostle for attention here. The focus for this debate is, first, on reason understood as generic tool of logic. In effect, Sidgwick takes up the 'universalisability rule', formulating it thus: 'That whatever is right for me must be right for all persons in similar circumstances' (*ME*, xvii). For a utilitarian, this introduction of Kantian practical reason is novel. In other words, in moral terms, reason directs that we should treat others equally unless relevant reasons can be shown why one should be treated differently. The second use of reason is calculative. It directs us from maxims to actions. This is more instrumental and prudential in character.

Sidgwick's integral reading sees no problem with reason. There is a confident rationalism in his writings. The argument develops as follows: reason provides self-evidence through direct intuitive insights. It directs us initially to seek our own good. But, it also implies, self-evidently, that one should prefer, prudentially, a greater future good to a present lesser one. It is reasonable to seek self-interest, but reason also directs us to treat like cases alike, namely, to consider the good of others as equal to our own and to consider others' happiness with our own. How does the reasonable egoist arrive at these conclusions? In effect, it is an intuition derived from reason itself. Sidgwick was particularly impressed by Kant's rule of practical reason (*ME*, xx). Sidgwick also suggests other contributory factors which weaken the rationality of egoism. Excessive concentration on one's own interest is not seen as quite sane. Further, to focus so much on one's self produces rapid satiety and ennui (*ME*, 501-2).

Yet, for Sidgwick, even linking Kant and Butler cannot fully explain matters. He suggests that it was rereading Aristotle's *Ethics* that set his argument on track. His *ME* was uncovering, hermeneutically, the structures of moral experience within common sense. Intuitively, we feel that it is reasonable to move beyond self-interest. As a rational being I ought therefore to aim at the general good, since every one's good is the same as any others. Benevolence means that each one of us is bound to regard the good of each individual as much as his own. One seeks the good of all, including one's own good. Self-love and benevolence are not therefore automatically in contention.

Focusing immediately on the two senses of reason, Bradley sees 'a strict and a loose use of reason' (*SH*, 74-5). Bradley concentrates on what 'reasonable' intuition leads to in Sidgwick, in terms of the 'Rule of Equity' and 'Rule of Benevolence'. The first refers to the universalizability rule, namely, like cases should be treated alike. For Bradley, this is just tautologous. The reasonable is the *universal*. It has no *particular* content. The 'Rule of Benevolence' (the good of any one individual cannot be any more desirable than the equal good of other individuals) invokes another tautology, namely, that 'X cannot regard his own happiness as more desirable than the equal happiness of X'. For Bradley, this is either another 'tautology' or 'nonsense'. Sidgwick's analysis of reason gets his argument nowhere. In these 'rules', Sidgwick has reiterated 'the postulates which he [the egoist] denies'. The rational egoist could not logically universalise his particular position (*SH*, 99-101).

What does 'reason' direct the individual to do? For Bradley, Sidgwick's argument gives different answers. It is reasonable both to seek one's own maximum pleasure and that of the whole creation. The central arguments of *ME* rest, therefore, on a contradiction. It appears to be a matter of life and death to Sidgwick's whole enterprise to show that the only true selfishness is morality. The solution, for Sidgwick, is that 'certain quantities of pleasure and pain should be attached to individuals, that they should be adequately rewarded for obeying the rule of duty and punished for violating it' (*SH*, 117). Yet, Bradley continues, how is this attachment of pleasure and pain to be achieved? Average individuals appear in Sidgwick to be often stupid, impulsive and egoistic. It needs, Bradley suggests, a utilitarian *deus ex machina*, but, unfortunately 'the days of Paley are long gone' when a god guaranteed the felicific calculus.

Bradley's critique oddly underscores Sidgwick's own pessimism. This is the 'other Sidgwick', flailing about in psychical research. In this 'despair mode', the conflict of rationalities literally *explains* the whole character and layout of *ME*. Sidgwick raises the question himself. How can the egoist be reconciled with the general happiness? Reason appears to be linked to both methods. In effect, the rationality of self-regard and the rationality of self-sacrifice were both 'undeniable'. Sidgwick commented, 'I could not give up this conviction, though neither of my masters, neither Kant nor Mill, seemed willing to admit it' (*ME*, xviii). In other passages of *ME* an even more despondent Sidgwick acknowledges a resilient and 'fundamental contradiction in our apparent intuition of what is Reasonable' (*ME*, 508). Further, no religious grounds or sanctions can be invoked. All the gods are *in absentia*. There is also no possibility of demonstrating any linkage empirically. The problem of reason, for Sidgwick, is that if we admit that we cannot demonstrate the connection between duty and self-interest and that the notion we have of what is reasonable is not ultimately demonstrable, then we must realise that although we do not abandon morality, we *cannot* completely rationalise it (see *ME*, 508). In effect, this is a *fin de siecle* conception of ethics, which even looks towards some postmodern angst.

PLEASURE

The confrontation over pleasure is part of a larger package. It would take too much time to unravel all the arguments on the issue, thus only the highlights will be examined. The debate can be subdivided between, firstly, the metaphysics of pleasure, second, terminological issues, and third, the ability of pleasure to guide practice (a point glossed earlier). Each of these arguments are nascent within the previous sections of this essay.

Firstly, the metaphysical argument refers back to the earlier discussion. For Bradley, pleasure-based arguments all tend to rely on the 'single sentient individual' to make morality possible. For Bradley, the whole of *ME* is premised upon this metaphysical dogma. It is no wonder that Sidgwick keeps saying that he wants nothing to do with metaphysics.

Utilitarianism and hedonism, basically, have not understood the nature of the self. There is no way that any of us could really imagine (except in our wildest flights of fantasy) being utterly alone and still thinking morally, especially in abstract utilitarian terms.

Furthermore, this abstract 'sentient individual' is too conveniently rolled back into the universal (see *ES*, 127). In Sidgwick, pleasure for each becomes, by magic sleight of hand, pleasure for all. Where precisely the limitations on the egoist come from remains a mystery. Consequently, Sidgwick's argument always has the tendency to collapse back into egoism, unless some other factor is injected, like intuition or 'higher and lower' pleasures. Sidgwick rejected the latter. The 'greatest happiness' therefore has a fictional status. As a particular individual, my pleasures remain mine. On the individualist premise, I can only desire things which relate to *my* feelings. As Bradley comments, the 'pleasure of others is neither a feeling in me, nor an idea of a feeling in me' (*ES*, 129). Bradley thus claims that the notion of disinterested action in Sidgwick is meaningless. Individual pleasure is either the end or it is not. Interestingly, Bradley suggests that the more honest statement of the tendency of this metaphysical egoism can be found in Max Stirner's writings (*ES*, 128).

The second issue concerns the vagueness of pleasure terminology. Pleasure is seen as too abstract and contentless to be of much use. Pleasure and pain are transient feelings. Concepts are abstractions of these feelings, feelings which are infinitely coming into being and perishing. A number of points arise from this. Primarily, Bradley complains that Sidgwick initially separates pleasurable feelings from the conscious self which feels them. Yet, at the same time, in making a case for pleasure, he tries to make it synonymous with the conscious self (*SH*, 81). Consciousness, in Sidgwick, is thus 'the same as feeling and yet includes [unaccountably] thought and action' (*SH*, 82). This bears again upon the debates about the nature of reason. Similarly, Bradley accuses Sidgwick of sliding together (definitionally) 'I desire' with 'what I ought to desire', 'I like' with 'what I ought to like', and 'preference' with what 'I ought to prefer'. He notes that the overall thesis to be proved in *ME* is 'that mere pleasure is the end', yet adds, 'Mr Sidgwick writes conscious life for pleasure and adds desirable (which *means* end) to the definition'

(*SH*, 93). The basic point which Bradley drives home repeatedly is that Sidgwick continually imports his conclusions into his premises – classic *petitio principii*. Sidgwick never gives an account as to how (genealogically) pleasure, feeling and desire incorporate reason and thought (other than by stipulative initial definition). In addition, for Bradley a 'series' of transient feelings is impossible to configure. The idea of a 'sum' of such feelings is conceptually strange. How could I have a *sum* of infinitely passing moments, which are still proceeding? The greatest sum of pleasure or happiness is thus a wild fiction. Pleasure may supervene on morality, but is not coincidental with it.

Third, Bradley suggests that a series of transient pleasures, in diverse sentient individuals, cannot function as a guide to conduct. An infinite quantity of pleasures is incoherent if postulated as an end. A realisable end should be, at least, realisable (*SH*, 85). Consequently, the idea of any clear normative guidance premised on a calculus of pleasures strikes Bradley as meaningless. This is the point Bradley developed under the critical rubric of a 'moral almanac'. Bradley's suggestion that calculative utilitarianism is just downright odd seems quite sensible, regardless of whether or not he is Hegelian.

CONCLUSION

In terms of the relative merits of the above debate, one can find in Bradley's critique many of the late twentieth-century criticisms of utilitarianism, although the maximand 'pleasure' has now been replaced by 'preferences', 'interests' or 'welfare', partly because of the kind of criticism that Bradley (and others) offered. Utilitarianism is now no longer 'hedonic'. Sidgwick, however, also offered a more morally eclectic and analytical argument, which not only looks to later utilitarian thought, but also to many of the developments in twentieth century analytic moral philosophy. Bradley's argument also relates closely to late twentieth century arguments for communitarianism, although his thought is more subtle and nuanced. However, it is also important to see that both thinkers reveal, in the course of the debate, the strengths and weaknesses of nineteenth century utilitarian and communitarian perspectives.

Since both Bradley and Sidgwick were such powerful polemical thinkers, capable of detailed clear-headed analysis, the confrontation between them reveals a philosophical fragility (of sorts). Both cut through each other's arguments so quickly that it is almost alarming to find oneself at the frail-looking metaphysical roots. In this sense their confrontation is immensely revealing.

REFERENCES

ME *Methods of Ethics*, Henry Sidgwick (London, Macmillan 1907)

M   *Henry Sidgwick: A Memoir* by A. S. and E. M. S. Sidgwick (London, Macmillan, 1906)

CN 'Critical Notice of *Ethical Studies*' by Henry Sidgwick, *Mind*, Volume 1 (1876)

R   'Response' [Note on Bradley's note] by Henry Sidgwick, Notes and Discussions, *Mind*, Volume 2 (1877)

SE *Sidgwick's Ethics and Victorian Moral Philosophy* by J. B. Schneewind (Oxford, Clarendon Press, 1977)

ES *Ethical Studies* by Francis Bradley (Oxford, Clarendon Press, 1962).

SES 'Mr. Sidgwick on "Ethical Studies"', by Francis Bradley, Notes and Discussions, *Mind* 2 (1877)

SH *Mr. Sidgwick's Hedonism* in Francis Bradley, *Collected Essays*, Volume 1 (Oxford, Clarendon Press, 1935).

NOTES

1   The terminology surrounding this debate is not helped by the fact Bradley occasionally suggests separating out utilitarianism and hedonism. He has no objection to utilitarianism, qua happiness, being subsumed under the Aristotelian or Greek notion of happiness. He does, however, object to its reduction to pleasure. He suggests that the hedonistic view is the more pervasive reading and thus, at other times, dismisses both hedonism and utilitarianism.

2   Even Sidgwick's sympathetic interpolator Schneewind remarks that 'there are places where Sidgwick seems to be saying quite plainly that utilitarianism is the best available ethical theory. From his other writings we know that he thinks of himself as committed to utilitarianism, and that he assumes it in analysing specific moral and political issues' (*SE*, 192).

3   Oddly, Bradley admits that he and Sidgwick appear to *agree* on what ordinary morality contains, however, he adds 'the difference [between them] is one of principle, not detail. I object not to the things he teaches us to do, but to the spirit and the way in which he teaches us to do them' (*SH*, 116). Whether Bradley is being coy here is open to question.

Social Policy and Bosanquet's Moral Philosophy[1]

WILLIAM SWEET
St Francis Xavier University

Bernard Bosanquet was one of the most prolific and wide ranging of the British idealists. He was the author of some 20 books and over 200 articles and reviews, and his writings included major work on logic, epistemology, aesthetics, political philosophy, metaphysics, and religion. But one further area of interest (indeed, one to which he devoted much of his life) was social policy. In this paper, I want to address a question that arises out of a study of Bosanquet's concern with social policy and social issues in general, and that is, what are the ethical principles that underlie his views?

I will argue that the answer is more complex than one might think, that Bosanquet's writings on social policy and social reform reflect a practical ethics, and that this is distinct from a formal or theoretical ethics or moral philosophy. And I will also suggest that this explains, in large part, the diverse recommendations that one finds in Bosanquet's remarks on ethical and social concerns.

I

To begin with, the question of what ethical theory or principles underlie Bosanquet's views on social policy is not at all a simple matter. This is because it is at the very least not clear what his ethical theory is. In fact, some have proposed that there is no consistent ethics underlying Bosanquet's views, or that he was neither willing nor able to articulate a moral theory or a set of foundational ethical principles of his own.

Let me be more specific here. Several scholars have suggested that it is difficult to discern whether there are any consistent principles or any coherent theory that underlie Bosanquet's remarks on social policy, the function of the state, the purpose of law and punishment, and the rights of (or the respect due) the individual human person. Some, like Ellen Jacobs, have described Bosanquet's ethics as, at best, eclectic, that they are 'Hegelian' but also reflect a Kantian view of the individual.[2] And Andrew Vincent has noted that there are incompatible teleological and deontological elements in Hegelian and British idealism as a whole;[3] and one may think, therefore, that this is something characteristic of Bosanquet's thought as well. Others, like John Dewey, have argued that the 'incoherence' in Bosanquet's ethical theory is more radical, that he misunderstands the relation of moral theory and moral practice, and that his approach to moral philosophy is fundamentally flawed. (Dewey argued that Bosanquet had 'a radically false notion of moral theory';[4] that there is no rigid line between 'ideas about morals' – i.e., 'those implied truths or general facts which lie behind the existence of man as a moral being',[5] such as the principle that self-sacrifice is virtuous[6] – and 'moral ideas'[7] – i.e., 'leading ideas in life', such as 'the idea of a particularly good thing to be done'.[8] And, further, W. D. Lamont claimed that Bosanquet ultimately abandoned moral discourse, by (Lamont alleges) proposing a notion of morality that transcends a concept of duty.[9]

Now there is no denying that Bosanquet's views on ethics are complex and that there are teleological and deontological elements in his discussion of social questions.

To begin with, as noted above, there certainly does seem to be a mixture of the teleological and the deontological in some of Bosanquet's remarks on social philosophy. Consider Bosanquet's view of punishment.[10] Punishment is retributive in justification or explanation (for it is based on will and, hence, has a deontological character) but deterrent when it comes to determining how far one should punish (and, hence, is consequentialist and teleological). This 'mixture' is seen as well in Bosanquet's comment that 'Will and effect are two inseparable sides of every action [. . .] A

Will which does no good at all surely cannot be a good will.'[11] Again, this emphasis on will would suggest a deontological element in morality, whereas the concern with effect would imply a teleological dimension.

Yet Bosanquet would not hesitate to describe his views as simply teleological, though in the following sense. In *The Philosophical Theory of the State*, he writes that, by 'teleological,' he means a view or approach that 'recognises a difference of level or of degree in the completeness and reality of life, and endeavours to point out when and how, and how far by social aid, the human soul attains the most and best that it has in it to become.'[12] And there is certainly a *telos* that is present in Bosanquet's discussion of politics (as there is, more generally, in his metaphysics[13]). Here, he talks about the 'end' of society, the state, and ethical institutions. Bosanquet also speaks of the purpose or objective of social life as the 'rational' or best life, 'the existence and perfection of human personality,'[14] and says that human nature works towards 'a certain kind of completeness.'[15] And, of course, in some of his 'metaphysical' texts and reviews, Bosanquet refers to this *telos* as 'the Absolute,' which is the principle of value.[16]

Still, there are clearly deontological elements in Bosanquet's work. For example, in his late essay, 'Life and Philosophy,' he refers to 'the permanent value of Kantian ethics.'[17] And, specifically, one sees throughout Bosanquet's work on social policy and social reform a concern for the value of the individual, and particularly for the development of individual character, in spite of the fact that such a concern might be sometimes inexpedient. Indeed, the focus of the London Ethical Society, to which Bosanquet devoted much of his energy from 1886 until 1897, was the improvement of moral character, and not simply the realization of a particular set of social and economic conditions. There are other indications of deontology present in Bosanquet's writings on social philosophy and social policy as well. He acknowledges that 'an individual must ultimately follow his conscience to the end'[18] and, in his discussion of punishment, he refers to the 'rights' of which the offender must not be 'defrauded'[19] (e.g., a right to the recognition of one's bad will) even if it would serve no obvious good. Such a concern in preserving the value of the individual is also suggested by Bosanquet's opposition to policies of eugenics or of the 'extermination' of those of the 'unhelpable poor.'[20] And while Bosanquet recognises the imperative character of some *telos* or end (the perfection of human personality), he says there always are limits on what one is allowed to do in pursuit of this end.[21] Finally, for Bosanquet, simply showing that an act serves a common good is not conclusive in establishing that one ought to do it, because he recognises that there can be real conflicts in duties, conflicts that cannot, as a utilitarian might have it, be resolved by reference to some ultimate principle.

There are also remarks in Bosanquet's writings on social and political philosophy that suggest 'moral perfectionism' or a nascent virtue theory. And one might think that this could explain the presence of both the Kantian or deontological and the teleological elements in his work. The 'moral end' is said by Bosanquet to be 'the perfecting of the soul'[22] or 'the excellence of human souls,'[23] and pursuing such an end is not a matter of following universal moral rules; one is simply 'to respond adequately to the situation.'[24] And, while he does not say so explicitly, it seems that this amounts to doing what the Aristotelian 'practically wise person' would do.[25]

This end of 'perfecting one's soul' may appear to have an almost individualist character when we see it described as 'the finite spirit' becoming 'what it had in it to be'[26] or as attaining 'the most and best that it has in it to become,'[27] and when we note comments such as 'self-affirmation is the root of morality.'[28] Still, though some might think that such a focus on 'self' reflects a kind of 'egoism,' it is evident that Bosanquet rejects a fundamental individualism. For the aim of self realization[29] is said to be, at the same time, the best life of the whole.[30] By perfecting ourselves we are promoting a 'form of life'[31] and not just an individual life, and it is for this reason that this moral end is called, as noted earlier, 'the perfection of *human* personality.' In fact, the problem with socialism, in Bosanquet's view, is not that it emphasises the social, but its underlying individualism.[32] Moreover, one notes that Bosanquet also defends the value and importance of self *sacrifice*; such an action, which he frequently alludes to in the words of Goethe, '*stirb und werde*' – 'die to live,' is a moral principle.[33] Consequently, while rejecting individualism and while clearly concerned with the well-being of others, Bosanquet is not arguing for altruism either.

One finds, then, remarks in Bosanquet's writing on social policy and social philosophy that reflect all manner of ethical theories, and so it is no surprise that some have concluded that Bosanquet in fact does not hold a consistent or coherent ethic.

There is, however, an alternate hypothesis of why there are such apparently different tendencies in Bosanquet's remarks on social policy, and on ethics and social philosophy in general. Rather than claim that Bosanquet has no consistent moral theory, some have argued that he was uninterested in ethical theory or that he had no distinctive ethical theory at all.

In the first place, one notes, Bosanquet was rather critical of 'mere morality'[34] and moral philosophy, which he considered individualistic and incomplete, especially in comparison with religion.[35] And so one might see in this an indication of a lack of interest in articulating an ethical theory. Besides, when one examines Bosanquet's work, one notices frequent references to F. H. Bradley's *Ethical Studies*, and it has been suggested that Bosanquet had no need of a *distinctive* ethical or moral theory of his own. This, some have argued, explains why, while he appears to have considered writing a book on moral philosophy several times, he ultimately chose not to. In his 13 August 1876 letter to Frank Peters, written while he was a young tutor and fellow at University College, Bosanquet remarks: 'the book I was to write must wait; perhaps forever. At first on reading Bradley's book [*Ethical Studies*] I felt as if blown to the winds.'[36] And, some 40 years later, we see Bosanquet's letter of 25 April 1915 to J. H. Muirhead, in which he again considers that he may have a duty to 'write a book on Moral Philosophy.' But, he continues 'even this, [. . .] I doubt I shall undertake. It would not be really new, and as Bradley is going to republish Ethical Studies, I doubt if anything more would be useful.'[37] These and other remarks have led some to see Bosanquet as, at best, merely extending Bradley's ethical theory to social philosophy.

In light of the preceding comments, then, it is understandable why some would hold that there is no consistent ethic or no developed ethical theory present in Bosanquet's writings on social policy and social philosophy and, perhaps, not even in his philosophy as a whole. And so there would be no question of there being a set of *underlying* moral principles. But are either of the two preceding hypothesis in fact correct?

II

The range of justifications for social action given by Bosanquet in his comments on social policy and social philosophy may suggest, then, that he had at least a rather casual attitude about ethics and ethical theory. But it would be odd if this were in fact so, given that he was deeply concerned about ethical issues, wrote on ethical problems throughout his life, and was (as is clear from his logic and metaphysics) a highly systematic philosopher. His 1893 volume, *The Civilization of Christendom*,[38] and his inaugural lecture at St. Andrew's in 1903, 'On the practical value of moral philosophy,'[39] are early attempts to articulate an account of the nature and role of ethics in daily life. One notes, as well, his 1918 volume, *Some Suggestions in Ethics*, which he prefaces by saying that its purpose is to serve 'ordinary thoughtful persons who are interested in reflecting on morality,'[40] and his many essays on social policy, and even *The Principle of Individuality and Value* and *The Value and Destiny of the Individual*, discuss ethical concerns.

Again, it is certainly true that Bosanquet was influenced by Bradley, and the remarks from the letters cited above, along with his acknowledgement, in 'Life and Philosophy,' that 'For many of us the publication of Mr. F. H. Bradley's *Ethical Studies* in 1876 [. . .] was an epoch-making event,'[41] would argue for there being significant agreement between them. But to see Bosanquet's social philosophy as just an extension of Bradley's ethical theory to the practical sphere is implausible, for it is far from clear that Bradley's considered ethical views would be consistent with many of Bosanquet's comments on social policy. Indeed, on some issues, such as punishment (as I have argued elsewhere[42]), Bosanquet and Bradley seem to be rather far apart from one another.

The key to understanding Bosanquet's varied remarks on social policy and on social issues in general is, I think, that while he recognises the importance of moral theory, he is also concerned, indeed, is more concerned, with moral practice. I would, therefore, propose the following: that Bosanquet *did* have a coherent moral theory, but that (as his work on social philosophy and social policy suggests) he also had what one might call a practical ethics, and that this is quite distinct from (though not inconsistent with) what his moral theory would be.

One description of ethical life that is often given by Bosanquet is that it is 'the *art* of living together'[43] (emphasis mine). It is something quite distinct from a 'science.' And Bosanquet frequently says that what interests him most is 'the concrete unity of life as it is lived'[44] – 'what makes life worth living.'[45] This is the 'concrete content' of, again, something distinct from that life, namely, 'Ethical Science.'[46] These remarks indicate, then, that there are *two* kinds of ethical concerns that a philosopher might explore: how, concretely, people are to act morally in daily life and 'live together' and, second, what the principles of ethical science or moral philosophy are.

Now, Bosanquet held that one did not need to be able to articulate universal moral principles in order to have an objective guide to moral action. He says, for example, that if one understands or sees how the moral world is, one will note at least two kinds of things. First, in looking at concrete moral life and moral behaviour, we can find basic 'moral ideas' at work (he calls these 'dominant ideas'[47]) which, while necessary to moral activity, can generally be said to be characteristic of particular cultures. And, second, Bosanquet would say that we can also see that individuals have a series of socially recognised roles or functions with corresponding duties, and that these provide guidelines on how one should act. These guidelines are objective, though they are far from universal.

And so Bosanquet talks of a morality of 'my station and its duties.' This notion was first explicitly appealed to by him in 'The Kingdom of God on Earth' (1889)[48] (and, indirectly in *The Civilization of Christendom* [1893]), and it is frequently referred or alluded to throughout his writings.[49] Indeed, in *Some Suggestions in Ethics* (1st edition, 1918), Bosanquet writes that 'my station' (i.e., one's various functions in social life) is the main root of individual morals.[50] Such a view, found in both T. H. Green and Bradley before him,[51] has obvious deontological and teleological elements.

This morality of 'my station' focuses on 'moral ideas' (morality) and not 'ideas about morality' (moral science); or, to put it slightly differently, it focuses on the art of living and not on the science of ethics.

Unlike some theories, a morality of 'my station' is acutely attentive to the existence of practical limits: 'No man in any position can do and leave undone precisely what he would like, so to speak, to do and not to do, if he were free to give full effect to his customary moral ideas.'[52] Specifically, it acknowledges that sometimes there can be a 'conflict of moral obligations and the inevitable sacrifice of some among them.'[53] Such conflicts of duties may have the form:

> I can do no other. It is not I who would be sacrificed; it is my mates, my class, the good cause, the unity and welfare of mankind so far as we grasp it and are working for it. In these great operations of great organisations some individuals must be injured. Our duty to the cause conflicts with our personal duty to them, and is superior to it.[54]

There are, then, 'solutions' or proper responses to moral problems, but they may be far from ideal. And, in general, living an ethical life is the exercise of an 'art' that may involve appeals to rules of thumb, or conventions or practices, practices that are rooted in a conception of a common good, but which are not derived in a scientific way from universal axioms.

This account of ethical life, then, is as much a description, as a prescription. It is akin, Bosanquet holds, to what Hegel calls *Sittlichkeit*. Although it has an objective character, it is not based on a set of ethical principles having a universal form. But one cannot expect anything more in attempting to determine what underlies ethical life. One's stations and functions change throughout one's life and, therefore, the theory of 'my station' does not, and indeed cannot, provide any absolute, unchanging principles.

This distinction between Bosanquet's practical ethics (what follows from 'my station') and moral philosophy will enable one, I would suggest, to make sense of the diversity of the remarks he makes on social issues and social philosophy, noted above. If it is true that 'No man in any position can do and leave undone precisely what he would like [. . .] to do and not to do,' then sometimes what one may be called to do may look as if it is justified on consequentialist grounds. At other times, one's station may require one to carry out a specific duty, and at other times, the moral hero may even be able to discern, and carry out, what goes beyond her or his duty. In such cases, Bosanquet is speaking of *morals*, not *moral science*, and his advice reflects what is indicated by one's 'station,' the description of ethical life and of what allows such a life to be led. It does not by itself rest on the *principles* of any particular moral theory. And this is consistent with the view that, in his writings on social policy and social work in particular, Bosanquet's primary interest was in ethical education and in having people act morally, not in stating or defending moral principles.

Many of the remarks that Bosanquet makes on ethics and the moral life (this ethics that features 'my station and its duties') plausibly reflect, then, what one might call a *practical* ethics and not a theoretical or formal ethic, or an 'ethics according to general principles'[55] like Kantianism or utilitarianism. But this is not to say that Bosanquet held that there can be no moral theory or no moral science at all. Still, one might ask, why didn't Bosanquet develop such a moral theory at any length? And where does Bosanquet present his moral theory in his work?

On this first matter, one reason why Bosanquet is not primarily concerned with moral science or moral theory when he addresses concrete ethical issues is that he is rather sceptical of the actual influence that ideas about morality have on ethical behaviour. As noted above, for Bosanquet, one of the basic principles, if not the end, of human life is self perfection, and this implies the development of moral character. So the key ethical question for Bosanquet is how to promote this. What is it, in other words, that can move individuals to seek their own improvement? Bosanquet's response is that it isn't moral theory. In 'Will and Reason' (an essay preliminary to a series of articles in his volume on social policy, *Aspects of the Social Problem*), for example, he cites Aristotle's remark in the *Nicomachean Ethics* (VI.2 439 a 36) that 'intelligence as such moves nothing.'[56] Again, in one of his early essays, 'On the Communication of Moral Ideas,' Bosanquet writes that 'we must not suppose that the supports of any moral theory are the supports of morality.'[57] To be well informed about ethical principle and ethical theory, Bosanquet would say, matters little in acting ethically or, to be more precise, in being a good person.[58] And his wife Helen, in her biography of him, notes this as well, that he held that (as he says in an early pamphlet for the London Ethical Society) moral theory or moral science are not central to moral education.[59] Bosanquet, then, is principally concerned with how to move people to act morally, and moral theory has at best a minor role in that.

Besides, as noted earlier, moral science isn't really necessary to moral action. On Bosanquet's view, guidelines for moral conduct are already present in some form and to some extent in the various institutions and dominant ideas that exist in the world, and thus he emphasises looking at concrete moral life, which already contains an indication of what it is that individuals should do. (Since it is always in the 'concrete' that some principle is a genuine 'universal,' this is simply a reflection of Bosanquet's general position on the existence of 'concrete universals.') Individuals can, then, determine what they ought to do without the articulation of universal laws or principles.

There are other problems that Bosanquet would note arise when one focuses on moral theory over practical ethics. For example, Bosanquet would point out that moral theory, by itself, can never give a complete account of the ethical life, of whether an action is, indeed, the right action.

In the first place, Bosanquet writes,

> to know whether a subordinate rule or a particular action is, or points to, the best course under all the circumstances of the given case, we should have to include as part of our experience the entire context which makes up the individuality of the moral agent in that action. And in morality there is the peculiar difficulty that the most important part of this context lies within the agent's own mind, and cannot possibly be known to any one else, and is indeed imperfectly known to himself. It is, therefore, a degree more impossible for Moral Philosophy to prescribe or pass judgment on particular actions or courses of action than it is for Logic to contrive or pass judgment on the special theories of the particular sciences.[60]

Moreover, Bosanquet argues that ethical science focuses on principles and on deduction or inference from principle, whereas determining what the right or appropriate thing to do in certain situations is not something that can be 'deduced.' This is not to say that there are no principles in ethics, but rather that what principles there are, are going to be too 'general' and, therefore, too limited in providing guidance on how individuals should act. Bosanquet writes:

> There are general principles in it [the content of the moral life], but it [that life] could not – so I have been led to think – be deduced from general principles; and therefore the argument from general principles of morality, though it demands to be treated with respect, continually fails, to my mind, to reach the root and the essence of the matter. It fails, in my view, because it does not sufficiently consider in what way the individuals whose conduct is being discussed are likely, or are not likely, to make the most of their lives, and do the best with the complex of relations which form their ethical being.[61]

And he concludes that 'we cannot construct the reasonable world of morality from a theoretical view of men in general and of nature.'[62]

The appropriate way to help one understand ethical life or to lead people to act morally, then, is not going to be found in moral science. Indeed, rather than speaking of proving or demonstrating ethical principles or even particular ethical beliefs, Bosanquet uses the language of 'awakening' moral ideas in 'consciousness.'[63] In 'The Communication of Moral Ideas,' Bosanquet advises that 'you must make [the moral life] grow from within.'[64] And such an approach is just the same as that which he uses to describe how to produce 'self government', that it is something that must be 'grown.'[65] Moral theory is not necessary here, and it seems that Bosanquet would hold that the development of moral character could take place even where there are quite different views of moral science. It is revealing that Bosanquet had no particular difficulty in working with Henry Sidgwick (someone with whom he had significant theoretical disagreements) when the latter was President of the London Ethical Society;[66] this suggests that the development of moral character (the objective of a practical ethic) could be carried out effectively (at least, in the short term) and independently of theory. (How specifically this 'awakening' of moral ideas in consciousness is to take place and proceed is another question, and one that also lies outside of moral theory;[67] for it involves determining how individuals can be led to carry out what 'practical ethics' demand, that is, to fulfill their respective stations and the corresponding duties.)

Bosanquet, then, distinguishes between a practical ethics and a moral theory, and it is plausible to hold that it is the former that underlies many of his remarks on social policy and social issues in general. But such a practical ethics is in no way inconsistent with moral theory. While the latter is distinct from the former (for there are practical limits in moral action, and 'in every course of action something must be forfeited if anything is to be achieved'[68]) the object of moral theory and ethical life is, Bosanquet would hold, ultimately the same.

III

But if moral theory doesn't provide a full account of ethical life and has little, if any, role in leading people to be moral, is there any point to theory and the analysis of ethical life at all? Bosanquet's answer is that there is a point, and that is to *understand* moral life, what lies behind it, and what is involved in it. This, for Bosanquet, is something that idealism is particularly equipped to carry out. For idealism, he writes in his 1898 essay 'Idealism in Social Work,' 'is the spirit of the faith in real reality, and its way of escape from facts as they *seem* is to go deeper and deeper into the heart of facts as they *are*.'[69] An idealist moral philosophy seeks to look beneath the surface of phenomena and to thereby discern and provide a statement of what animates existing moral activity and, perhaps, to note certain guiding principles.

Again, moral theory serves to examine and to ascertain the connexions among 'the great moral ideas of the world,' such as 'Life is the practice of dying,' 'Man has natural rights,' 'the end is the greatest happiness of the greatest number,' and so on, and their relation to 'the realities of human nature.'[70] Its purpose is not so much to show that a particular theory is true, as to help to make individuals more aware of the various principles of conduct, and to show that 'a false or fanatical theory *is* a hindrance to conduct. [. . . for . . .] We do see every day that bad theories produce bad observations, and bad observations produce dangerous actions.'[71] As important as this is, however, such an investigation does not make people moral. Bosanquet writes that 'our work is based upon our principles, but does not consist in giving our principles as pills.'[72]

What, then, is Bosanquet's moral theory? Providing a statement of Bosanquet's approach to and conclusions in moral science, and elaborating his views on the various subsidiary issues involved, would be a lengthy task. It would require pursuing such questions as the nature of human freedom, the nature of the individual will, the general will and the relation between them, the source of ethical obligation, the character of dominant ideas, and the 'principle of value,' and more. It would also require explaining how a practical ethics that is rooted in an account of one's station and duties can change and yet remain ethically authoritative. In fact, a theoretical analysis of what ethical life involves would require an investigation into issues that extend beyond 'ideas about morality.' Such an investigation would, clearly, be beyond the task of the present paper. Nevertheless, by way of illustration, let me just briefly indicate one element that one might find in such an analysis.

As we have seen already, on Bosanquet's view, observation of the moral world can show the presence of reason and of certain ideas that are dominant in the consciousness of the participants. Now Bosanquet would argue that, if one looks at what the moral life is, indeed, what any 'life' is, one will see, for example, 'that it is an organized movement in the direction of self-consistency of purpose.'[73] Specifically, if we look at moral activity (as with all behaviour), we see that what underlies it, and what constitutes moral reason itself, is 'a body of intellectual ideas which are in fact predominant as purposes, [. . .] having become predominant by the power they have shown of crushing out or adjusting to themselves the active associations of all other ideas.'[74] This notion of dominant or predominant ideas is founded on what Bosanquet calls in his psychology 'appercipient masses,' and is central to his analysis of human consciousness and of the individual (and 'general') will.

Idealist moral science, then, attempts to describe how and why this 'body of ideas' is organised as it is. And this requires, as we have just seen, an account of human mind or consciousness, that 'Every individual mind, so far as it thinks and acts in definite schemes or contexts, is a structure of appercipent systems or organised dispositions.'[75] The idealist will also enquire into the *character* of such systems, and will find that each such system is a 'set of ideas, bound together by a common rule or scheme, which dictates the point of view from which perception will take place, so far as the system in question is active.'[76] Thus apperception and these dominant ideas provide the means by which perception, visual and even moral, takes place. And, Bosanquet would argue, the idealist will also find that those participating in the same social institution or social group, who share the same moral life, will be seen to possess similar appercipent systems. The fact that their minds are similarly organised, then, accounts for the existence of the ethical community in which one will have stations and corresponding duties.

As this brief illustration shows, the task of moral science is to reveal what goes on 'behind' moral life and to see what principles are or might best serve to describe the direction of ideas in consciousness. These psychological or metaphysical (and related) questions are clearly quite different from those which a practical ethics would raise, for the principal concern in this latter case is how to bring about ethical behaviour and action.

Moral theory or moral science, then, is a valuable activity. It seems fairly clear, however, why it was that Bosanquet did not 'write a book on Moral Philosophy.' First, the elaboration of a fully-developed ethical theory simply may never have seemed necessary. For example, it is likely that Bosanquet thought that the criticism of other moral theories had been thoroughly done by Bradley, and thus there would be no need to repeat this. Moreover, moral theory could provide no complete set of principles from which one could determine unequivocally what to do, and whatever universal principles one might arrive at would not be sufficient for the moral education and social reform that interested him.

But there were also more incidental factors involved in Bosanquet's decision as well. His initial reluctance to write on ethics was motivated, it should be noted, not by Bradley's arguments in *Ethical Studies* (in fact, T. H. Green encouraged Bosanquet to write on the topic afterwards[77]) but by the press of other work, and in his 1876 letter to Peters he goes on to sketch out the distinctive kind of approach to morality and moral science he would take. (This early sketch indicates already that, for Bosanquet, an account of moral science requires the kind of psychological and metaphysical foundation indicated above.) And Bosanquet suggests as much again when he adds by way of explanation to Muirhead, in the letter of 1915 referred to earlier, that he thought he should shun controversy and 'husband my time', especially in 1915, when his health had been long failing (he had been in convalescent homes, on and off, since October 1910)[78] and when he thought that he had little time left to write. Such considerations, therefore, would account for Bosanquet's reluctance to write on the topic of moral philosophy. While a volume on moral philosophy would, of course, have been useful (and would have been more useful for us now), one can see why Bosanquet might not have felt particularly pressed to provide it. Finally, one might add that Bosanquet does leave his public with several indicators of what his moral theory involves. He carries out the project of providing the principal aspects of a moral theory, in a limited way, when he discusses the principle of value in his Gifford Lectures (though this discussion was, of course, part of a larger, metaphysical, project).

In short, then, what one finds 'behind' Bosanquet's remarks that touch on ethics, social philosophy, and social policy, is not a fully developed ethical theory, but a set of 'suggestions' rooted in the contingently-based considerations of a practical ethics of 'my station and its duties.' If one looks at his work in this way, I would argue, at least some of the alleged tensions or inconsistences in Bosanquet's ethical views, described at the beginning of this paper, can be plausibly resolved. Still, even in recognizing the limitations of moral science, Bosanquet certainly would not think we can or should ignore it. While it is not *central* to *his* concerns, as a philosopher he recognises the importance of saying what we can know or understand about the moral life.

IV

There is, then, an ethics that underlies Bosanquet's remarks on social policy and, more broadly, social philosophy. It is an ethics of 'my station and its duties.' It is a practical ethics, i.e., one that focuses on how to act morally in concrete situations and that emphasises (since one of Bosanquet's principal concerns was the improvement of character) the moral education of the individual. Such an ethic takes account of why Bosanquet thought (correctly, some would argue) some ethical problems can be practically intractable, and why the appropriate response here is not an appeal to theory but to 'being equal to the situation' or to determining what 'the reasonable man' would do. Still, this is not a moral philosophy with general and absolute moral principles. A person's 'stations' in life may change, and that which determines his or her stations (the general will, the precise character of moral consciousness, and the state) will change too.

I have also suggested that, for Bosanquet, moral science does not have much of a role in the development of individual character. It is not, as noted above, that Bosanquet thought that there was no theory or science underlying his views on social policy, or that such a theory was unattainable, but that it was insufficient in explaining or justifying how one should act. Nevertheless, the idealist philosopher does have the responsibility of helping people to understand the moral life, its presuppositions, and its motivating values, and so moral philosophy cannot be ignored either.

If we keep the distinction between 'practical ethics' and 'moral philosophy' in mind, then, we can see how the wide range of remarks that Bosanquet makes on ethical and social concerns may be consistent. What he offers on issues such as punishment, poor law reform, and the conditions for charity and relief, is often a practical response, a response distinct from, but not inconsistent with, his moral theory. And Bosanquet does, in fact, provide some direction as to what moral theory must discuss and what its characteristics are. But unpacking this moral philosophy or moral theory at length was a project that, in the end, he did not live to undertake.

NOTES

1   An earlier version of this paper was presented at a symposium on 'The Moral, Social and Political Philosophy of the British Idealists,' held at the Annual Meeting of the Political Studies Association, University of Nottingham, in March 1999. I am grateful to David Boucher, Peter Nicholson, Stamatoula Panagakou, Colin Tyler, Andrew Vincent, and other participants for their comments and questions.

2   Ellen Jacobs, *Bernard Bosanquet: Social and Political Thought*. PhD thesis, City University of New York, 1986, 100-101.

3   Andrew Vincent, 'The Individual in Hegelian Thought', *Idealistic Studies*, 12 (1982): 156-168, especially 165-6.

4   John Dewey, 'Moral Theory and Practice,' *International Journal of Ethics*, I (1890-91): 186-203, at 191. Dewey here is reacting to Bosanquet's 'The Communication of Moral Ideas as a Function of an Ethical Society,' *International Journal of Ethics*, I (1890-91): 79-97; reprinted in *The Civilization of Christendom and Other Studies* (London, Swan Sonnenschein, 1893); *The Collected Works of Bernard Bosanquet*, 20 vols., edited by William Sweet (Bristol, Thoemmes Press, 1999), vol. 13, 160-207.

5   Bosanquet, 'The Communication of Moral Ideas,' 173.

6   Bosanquet, 'The Communication of Moral Ideas,' 179.

7   Dewey, 196.

8   Bosanquet, 'The Communication of Moral Ideas,' 179.

9   W. D. Lamont, *The Principles of Moral Judgement* (Oxford, Clarendon Press, 1946), 171.

10 See *The Philosophical Theory of the State*, new edition, edited by Gerald F. Gaus and William Sweet (Bristol, Thoemmes Press, 1999), chapter 1; cf also 207-11.

11 See Bosanquet's 'Review of Henry Sidgwick's *The Ethics of T. H. Green, Herbert Spencer, and James Martineau*' (originally in *Mind*, n.s. XII (1903): 381-90), in *The Collected Works of Bernard Bosanquet*, vol. 1, 41-52 at 46.

12 *The Philosophical Theory of the State*, 84.

13 See, for example, 'The Meaning of Teleology,' *Proceedings of the British Academy*, II (1905-1906): 235-45 and ch. IV of *The Principle of Individuality and Value. The Gifford Lectures for 1911 delivered in Edinburgh University* (London, Macmillan, 1912); *The Collected Works of Bernard Bosanquet*, vol. 6.

14 *The Philosophical Theory of the State*, 194.

15 'Review of Sidgwick's *The Ethics of T. H. Green*', 46.

16 See both sets of Gifford Lectures, *The Principle of Individuality and Value*, and *The Value and Destiny of the Individual, The Gifford Lectures for 1912* (London, Macmillan, 1913). See also 'The Absolute as Will,' (originally published in *Mind*, n.s. XXVIII (1919): 77-78) in *The Collected Works of Bernard Bosanquet*, vol. 1, 199-200.

17 'Life and Philosophy,' (originally in J. H. Muirhead, ed., *Contemporary British Philosophy* (London, Allen and Unwin, 1924), 51-74) in *The Collected Works of Bernard Bosanquet*, vol.1, xxxix-lx, at xlv.

18 *The Philosophical Theory of the State*, 36.

19 *The Philosophical Theory of the State*, 211.

20 See, for example, 'The Principles and Chief Dangers of the Administration of Charity' (originally published in *International Journal of Ethics*, III (1892-1893): 323-36) in *The Collected Works of Bernard Bosanquet*, vol. 14, 61-72, at 65.

21 See, for example, *The Philosophical Theory of the State*, 186-7.
22 See 'The Place of Leisure in Life', *International Journal of Ethics*, XXI (1910-1911): 153-65, and *The Principle of Individuality and Value*, 396-403.
23 *The Philosophical Theory of the State*, 25.
24 One will recall here Bosanquet's description of morality as 'being equal to the situation' (see 'Life and Philosophy,'. liv, as well as *Some Suggestions in Ethics*, 150 and *The Philosophical Theory of the State*, 39).
25 See *The Principle of Individuality and Value*, 396-403.
26 'Life and Philosophy', liv; cf. *The Philosophical Theory of the State*, 83.
27 *The Philosophical Theory of the State*, 84.
28 *The Philosophical Theory of the State*, 137.
29 Curiously, Bosanquet does not often use the term 'self realization' to describe the object of moral action, preferring in its place the term 'self transcendence.'
30 *The Philosophical Theory of the State*, 182.
31 *The Philosophical Theory of the State*, 183.
32 And, so, Bosanquet remarks that 'One might say that the socialist Individualist forgets that every social good must be spiritual, and the *laissez-faire* Individualist forgets that every spiritual good must be social.' See *The Social Criterion or How to Judge of Proposed Social Reforms. A Paper read before the Edinburgh Charity Organisation Society November 15, 1907* (originally published, Edinburgh and London, Blackwood, 1907) in *The Collected Works of Bernard Bosanquet*, vol.14, 213-228, at 217-218.
33 See *Some Suggestions in Ethics*, 2nd. ed., (London, Macmillan, 1919); *The Collected Works of Bernard Bosanquet*, vol. 16, ch. VII, 161; see also 'The History of Philosophy [in Germany in the Nineteenth Century]', (originally published in C. H. Herford (ed.), *Germany in the Nineteenth Century (Second Series)*. London, Manchester University Press with Longmans, 1912) in *The Collected Works of Bernard Bosanquet*, vol. 1, 491-518, at 495-6.
34 *Some Suggestions in Ethics*, 96.
35 Note his view that morality is 'individualistic' ('Life and Philosophy,' xlvi), and similarly critical comments about 'morality' in *The Philosophical Theory of the State*, chapter 10, 240ff. Still, it is important to recognise that here he understands 'morality' to be roughly the same as Kantian individualistic *Moralität*, not Hegel's *Sittlichkeit* or 'ethical life', which he would endorse.
36 See J. H. Muirhead, ed., *Bernard Bosanquet and His Friends. Letters Illustrating the Sources and the Development of his Philosophical Opinions* (London, Allen and Unwin, 1935); *The Collected Works of Bernard Bosanquet*, vol. 20, 37.
37 See Muirhead, *Friends*, 168.
38 London, Swan Sonnenschein, 1893 (*The Collected Works of Bernard Bosanquet*, vol. 13).
39 'On the Practical Value of Moral Philosophy. Inaugural Address Delivered October 21, 1903 [at the University of St. Andrews']; originally published (Edinburgh and London, Blackwood, 1903); reprinted in *Science and Philosophy and Other Essays by the Late Bernard Bosanquet*, edited by J. H. Muirhead and R. C. Bosanquet (London, Allen and Unwin, 1927). See *The Collected Works of Bernard Bosanquet*, vol. 19.
40 See *Some Suggestions in Ethics*, v.
41 'Life and Philosophy,' xliv-xlv.
42 See my ' "Absolute Idealism" and Finite Individuality,' in *Indian Philosophical Quarterly*, vol. XXIV, no. 4 (1997): 431-462. See also my 'F. H. Bradley and Bernard Bosanquet,'

in *Philosophy after F. H. Bradley*, ed. James Bradley (Bristol, Thoemmes Press, 1996), 31-56.

43 'Life and Philosophy,' xl; see 'The Place of Experts in Democracy. I. – Plato's Criticism of Democracy' (originally published in *Proceedings of the Aristotelian Society*, n.s. IX (1908-1909): 61-68) in *The Collected Works of Bernard Bosanquet*, vol. 1, 471-477, and 'The Motive of Public Assistance. A Practical Ideal' (originally published in *The Times*, September 20, 1920, 6; reprinted in *Charity Organisation Review*, n.s. XLVIII (1920): 145-48), in *The Collected Works of Bernard Bosanquet*, vol. 14, 319-322, as "Public Assistance: Neighbourly Kindness."

44 'Life and Philosophy,' xl.

45 See Bosanquet's 'Review of G. E. Moore, *Principia Ethica*' (originally in *Mind*, n.s. XIII (1904): 254-61) in *The Collected Works of Bernard Bosanquet*, vol. 1, 53-62, at 55; see also his 'Our Right to Regard Evil as a Mystery' (originally in *Mind*, o.s. VIII (1883): 419-21) in *The Collected Works of Bernard Bosanquet*, vol. 1, 11-14, at 13.

46 'Review of G. E. Moore, *Principia Ethica*,' 55.

47 *The Philosophical Theory of the State*, 166-7; see 'Will and Reason,' 58-9; see also 'The Organisation of Intelligence,' Lecture IV of Bosanquet's *Psychology of the Moral Self* (London, Macmillan, 1897); reprinted in *The Philosophical Theory of the State*, ed. Gaus and Sweet, 294-304.

48 'The Kingdom of God on Earth,' in *Essays and Addresses* (London, Swan Sonnenschein, 1889); *The Collected Works of Bernard Bosanquet*, vol.12, 108-30.

49 See, e.g., *The Philosophical Theory of the State*, 38-9 and n. 53 about conflicts of duties.

50 *Some Suggestions in Ethics*, 31.

51 The view that ethical life involves the existence of stations or positions and duties that are recognized by society is an important part of Bosanquet's account. Nevertheless, it is a view that T. H. Green traces back to Plato and Aristotle. See *Lectures on the Principles of Political Obligation* ed. Bernard Bosanquet (London, Macmillam, 1917); reprinted from *The Works of Thomas Hill Green*, ed. R. L. Nettleship, 2 vols. (London, 1885-1888), sec. 39. Green refers to the importance of fulfilling the 'duties of one's station' (*Prolegomena to Ethics*, 5th. ed., Oxford, 1906, sec. 183; see also secs. 313 and 338), though the notion is most frequently associated with F. H. Bradley. See *Ethical Studies* [1876], 2nd. edition (Oxford, Clarendon Press, 1927), 'Essay V'). It is unclear, however, whether this locution was first employed by Green or Bradley. See Jacob, 84-85.

52 *The Philosophical Theory of the State*, 38-9, n. 53.

53 *The Philosophical Theory of the State*, 38-9, n. 53.

54 *The Philosophical Theory of the State*, 38.

55 See Bosanquet's 'Review of Henry Sidgwick's *Practical Ethics*,' (originally in *International Journal of Ethics*, VII (1897-8): 390-94), in *The Collected Works of Bernard Bosanquet*, vol. 1, 75-9 at 75. See also his comment that 'All attempts at general guidance of this kind are and remain platitudes' ('The Communication of Moral Ideas,' 167).

56 'Will and Reason' (originally published in *Monist*, II (1891-1892): 18-30) in *The Collected Works of Bernard Bosanquet*, vol. 14, 49-60 at 50.

57 'The Communication of Moral Ideas,' 172.

58 'Need the ethical teacher himself have reflective ideas about morality? My own conviction would lead me to answer in the negative.' 'The Communication of Moral Ideas,' 202.

59 See Helen Bosanquet, *Bernard Bosanquet. A Short Account of his Life* (London, Macmillan, 1924), 44-5.

60 'On the Practical Value of Moral Philosophy,' (Edinburgh and London, Blackwood, 1903), 21-22.

61 Bosanquet's 'Review of Sidgwick's *Practical Ethics*,' 76. See 'The Communication of Moral Ideas', 175-6.

62 'Will and Reason', 58.

63 'The Communication of Moral Ideas,' 204.

64 'The Communication of Moral Ideas,' 195.

65 *The Philosophical Theory of the State*, 41.

66 See Jacob, 95. It is curious that Sidgwick's Presidential Address to the LES was titled, when published, 'My Station and its Duties' (*International Journal of Ethics*, IV (1893-94); reprinted as 'The Aims and Methods of an Ethical Society,' in *Practical Ethics: A Collection of Addresses and Essays* (London, Swan Sonnenschein, 1898).

67 It is indirectly discussed in Bosanquet's remarks on moral and artistic education. See, for example, 'Artistic Handiwork in Education', *The Hour Glass*, XI (1887): 281-83; *The Collected Works of Bernard Bosanquet*, vol. 1, 117-122); see also *Artistic Handiwork in Education. A Lecture Delivered in the Examination Schools at Oxford, before the Oxford Self-Help Society, December, 1887* (London, Cooperative Printing Society Ltd., 1888); reprinted in *Essays and Addresses* (London, Swan Sonnenschein, 1889), 71-91.

68 'On the Practical Value of Moral Philosophy,' 21.

69 In *The Collected Works of Bernard Bosanquet*, vol. 14, 149-60 at 151. Originally published in *The Charity Organisation Review*, n.s. III (1898): 122-33.

70 'On the Practical Value of Moral Philosophy,' 25.

71 'On the Practical Value of Moral Philosophy,' 26-7. Bosanquet continues, 'I will venture so far, for example, as to say that if the logical relation of individual and universal had been more familiar than it is to Herbert Spencer and his antagonists, we might have escaped, to the general advantage, something near a generation of irritating social controversy.'

72 'The Communication of Moral Ideas,' 196.

73 'Will and Reason,' 58.

74 'Will and Reason,' 53.

75 *The Philosophical Theory of the State*, 172.

76 *The Philosophical Theory of the State*, 167.

77 See Green's letter of 8 July 1876, in which Green wrote that while he 'thought some of Bradley's essays' on ethics were 'excellent,' there was 'no reason why [Bosanquet] should not write on the subject, too.' Included in *Collected Works of T. H. Green*, ed. Peter Nicholson, 5 vols. (Bristol, Thoemmes Press, 1997), vol. 5, 464-465.

78 See Muirhead, *Friends*, 139.

The Concept of Self-Transcendence in the Philosophy of Bernard Bosanquet[1]

STAMATOULA PANAGAKOU
University of York

INTRODUCTION

The purpose of this article is to show that the British Idealist philosopher Bernard Bosanquet (1848-1923) propounds a theory of individuality which is intrinsically related to the condition of self-transcendence that occupies a cardinal position in his metaphysics. My analysis attempts to clarify and systematise Bosanquet's views on the importance and meaning of the finite human individual as they are derived from his theorising on the ontological constitution of the finite being.[2] My claim is that Bosanquet's theory of self-transcendence and individuality does not annihilate the individual as many critics have contended. Throughout, I argue that the process of self-transcendence strengthens and completes the spiritual constitution of the finite self which should be seen as the central analytical category in Bosanquet's theorising on the essence of the finite human mind. Bosanquet's critics have failed to realise that his ontology is not referring to two different and distinct manifestations of being (the finite and the infinite being corresponding to the actual and the real being respectively). What Bosanquet actually does is to elaborate a complex narrative of different states or phases of being as they are hypostasised and ceaselessly surpassed in the changing yet concrete spiritual place of encounter which is identified with the boundaries of the finite self. The actual and the real or universal self are not separate or unrelated entities; they are intrinsically interrelated phases of the same entity (the finite human being) in its development towards completion and individuality. We can distinguish between the actual and the real self; though we cannot separate them, and we must always deal with them both, and both together. The attainment of the real self is the culmination of a complex spiritual process, the beginning and end of which are found in the microcosmic totality of the concrete universal, namely, the finite self. The transformation of the actual self into the real self does not mean the annihilation of the finite self because the process of transformation takes place in the context of the self-realising experience of the finite being. The "passage" from the actual to the real self is an event of crucial ontological importance. The "passage" from a particular and incomplete state of being that actuality implies to a more comprehensive and complete state of being that reality expresses is made possible because of the dynamics of self-transcendence that the finite self contains. In this sense, the human being[3] must be conceived of as the meeting-point of "universal determinations" stemming from the individual's participation in the life of ethical institutions (family, neighbourhood or district, civil society, the State and the community of States), and in the areas of human experience devoted to the realisation of Absolute Spirit (Art, Philosophy and Religion).

In Bernard Bosanquet's metaphysics, the condition of finiteness, the spiritual process of soul-making, the ontological formation of the self, and the assertion of individuality are structured around the dynamics of self-transcendence. The condition of self-transcendence is a fundamental requisite for the ontological completion of the finite human individual that leads to the crystallisation of the finite-infinite nature which characterises the essence of the human being's existence. For Bosanquet, the act of self-transcendence is not identified with the annihilation of the finite self – the latter being understood as the possible result of the multi-dimensional and erosive activity of factors exogenous and fatal to subjectivity. On the contrary, self-transcendence is a spiritual act signifying the re-assertion and emergence of the subject through a complex relational framework that has two main functions. First, to expand the spiritual limits of finiteness beyond the actuality of the immediate existence to the reality of the ideal or universal self which is a more comprehensive and inclusive unit than the sensitive self. Second, to enrich the content and meaning of the self by refusing to define the ultimate essence of the human being according to the restrictive criteria of isolation and exclusion and, thus, by including in the conceptualisation of the self the notion of otherness which is an integral part in the spiritual realisation of the finite human individual.

My analysis shows that Bosanquet's theorising on the condition of self-transcendence is formed through his philosophical discourse on three interrelated themes concerning the ontological dimension of his metaphysical project. These themes are: (a) the critique of the concept of pure ego; (b) the reaction to psychological individualism; and (c) teleology, finite consciousness, and individuality. The systemic element that synthesises in a coherent and constructive whole the analytical frameworks which correspond to the explication of those issues is the conceptualisation of the content of the process of self-transcendence as a spiritual act. The logic of the process of self-transcendence as a spiritual act revolves around the normative principle of transcending the transient actuality of finitude for the sake of reconstituting the ontological for-mation of the finite self.[4]

The finite self is the epicentre of the dialectic of the finite-infinite which substantiates the potentials of the double nature of the finite being through the operative spirit of self-transcendence. Both the dialectic of the finite-infinite and the condition of self-transcendence refer to the human being's spiritual struggle to acquire more complete states of self-realisation. Furthermore, they revolve around the complex structure of a vital nexus of trans-subjective and intra-subjective deter-minations that ceaselessly interweave and synthesise the constructive function of factors endogenous and exogenous to the microcosmic unit of the self-remoulding experience in their relation to the whole process of self-realisation.[5] The self, in its endeavour to attain fuller and more inclusive states of being, passes recurrently through the symbolic exper-iences of "death" and "rebirth" that correspond to the teleological dynamics of transforming or transmuting the essence of its finiteness.

THE CONCEPT OF PURE EGO

In his *Psychology of the Moral Self* (1904),[6] Bosanquet defends a concep-tion of the self that emphasises the inherent ontological complexity of the subject which, at once, knows and it is known in an inseparable apparent duality of a unifying purpose. The attributes of will and intelligence which characterise the self belong to a multi-relational spiritual unit whose limits are not fixed, and whose content is formed in a ceaseless self-restructuring process of expansion, fluctuation, momentary stabilisation, and transcendence of the given. At the moment of transcending the given, the self realises within its context the logic of negation. Negation is a fundamental spiritual activity of the finite self that makes the self, in order to be, not to be (Bosanquet, 1912: 232). The spirit of negation acts simultaneously at two interrelated and logically interdependent levels of the finite experience. First, at the level of the members of the whole being regarded as distinct from the totality of the whole and, second, at the level of the comprehensiveness of the whole being regarded as a spiritual unit crystallised, articulated, and re-emerged within the fluctuating limits of finite consciousness. The self negates a phase of its own constitution in order to incorporate within it a more comprehensive and inclusive content which is crystallised on the basis of the natural contextual relationality of its finite-infinite identity. The very idea of a self implies content or, using Bosanquet's words, the self is "a positive content to be realised, a certain set of ideas" (Bosanquet, 1904: 94). The content of the self is the product of a ceaseless reconstituting activity that takes place within a complex nexus of relations and fundamental connections characterising: (a) the self; (b) the environment of the self; and (c) the logic of the necessary relation of the self to its environment.

The complexity of the intra-subjective and trans-subjective nature of the above process is the result of the dialectic of the finite-infinite which conditions the finite consciousness and vindicates the spiritual membership of finite beings. The concept of the dialectic of the finite-infinite is central to our apprehending the condition of finiteness which means an ontological state of restless spiritual restructuring affecting the development of the individual. This spiritual restructuring is realised while the double process of transcending the boundaries of human finiteness and of returning to the initial, yet transformed, content of the finite self is taking place within finite consciousness and between consciousness and its environment (externality). Bosanquet asserts:

> This double being *is* the nature of the finite. It is the spirit of the whole, or of ultimate reality, working in and through a limited

external sphere. Its law is that of the real; its existence is the existence of an appearance (Bosanquet, 1913: 12).

It is the nature of the finite being to be a representative of universal determinations (Bosanquet, 1912: 140-141) that makes abstractions of the kind of "pure ego" or "abstract I" appear not only useless but unreal in our endeavour to capture the essence of the finite being. Any anatomy of finiteness based on the idea of pure ego[7] gives a defective and deceptive picture of the finite being because it disregards the fact that the "I" or self is necessarily accompanied by content (Bosanquet, 1904: 55) which is the product of a ceaseless dialectical association between the self and its environment, and is characterised by change, lack of stability, negation of the given, and affirmation of new states of ontological completion. The very essence of ego is the double nature of the finite-infinite being which sustains its continuity with the world that incorporates the manifestations of finite selfhood and, consequently, makes the world capable of finding meaningful expression and realisation in the spiritual realm of finite consciousness. As a result, the "pure ego" becomes what it was not supposed to be: a concrete universal which, from the standpoint of its inevitable yet enriched finiteness, defies abstraction, particularity, and unchangeable determinations. In other words, it becomes a microcosm the being of which is emerging through an inclusive multi-layered totality of tension, contradiction, conflict, suffering, absorption, satisfaction, and negation. The cardinal characteristics of the microcosmic nature of the finite being both demand and imply the concept of the "other," or the non-self, which is fundamentally related to the notion of the self and, subsequently to the self's conceptual crystallisation, comprehensive definition and logical completion. I now turn to Bosanquet's critique of psychological individualism, a subject-matter which is associated with his views on the apprehension of the "other."

THE REACTION TO PSYCHOLOGICAL INDIVIDUALISM

According to Bosanquet, the psychological individualism of Bentham, Spencer and Bain which is structured around the distinction between "self" and "others" generates a problematic and limited apprehension of both the content and inherent potentials of the self (Bosanquet, 1904: 92-96). Bosanquet's main objection to the philosophical discourse of psychological individualism is that it cannot account for the spiritual formation of the ideal or universal self which should not be conceived of as an entity distinct from the finite-infinite self, but as the ultimate realisation of the latter's ontological completion and concrete universality. The realisation of the ideal or universal self signifies a complicated spiritual moment that captures the self's reaching out and return to itself in the context of an infinite duration which makes possible the expansion of the transcending process that allows, as a consequence, the penetration of deeper and richer levels of experience which are or become part of the content of the finite individual. During the act of self-transcendence, the new content acquired is transformed into a constitutive element of the changing nature of the finite selfhood and, thus, the concreteness of immanence is effected by the spiritual dynamics of transcendence. The ideal or universal self is a spiritual formation and must be construed as the ultimate phase of the finite self in its double nature as a finite-infinite being. In Bosanquet's meta-physics, the act of self-transcendence does not annihilate the self; on the contrary, it strengthens its spiritual constitution by bringing about communion with the self of the others and with "all the great contents of developed human self – truth, beauty, religion, and social morality" (Bosanquet, 1904: 95). In Hegel's terms, the Subjective Spirit acquires completion and fulfils its potentials by participating in, and being ex-posed to the universal determinations of the Objective and the Absolute Spirit.

Both the hypostasisation and conceptualisation of the self require the "other," either as a human being or as a (spiritual) content which is regarded as the non-self from the standpoint of the finite self who experiences the inclusive reality of otherness deep inside the seemingly separate boundaries of its "atomistic" finitude. Bosanquet asserts that, contrary to the perspective of psychological individualism, the defini-tion of the self cannot start from the separate body as the separate self (Bosanquet, 1904: 92); this is an immediate impression that does not reveal the entire truth about the self because it is not permeated by the logical spirit – the spirit of the whole. Immediacy captures only one level of reality leaving aside the cluster of intertwined contents that account for the arduousness of reality despite its apparent systemic simplicity. Immediacy brings with it the danger of simplifying the complexity of experience by insisting on the first impression of finite consciousness. In other words, immediacy precedes the work of the "penetrative imagination" which systematises the material of experience and reveals the greatest possibilities inherent in the world of finite selfhood. The essence of finite selfhood is the ideal or universal self which: (a) is not an entity separate and distinct from the existence of the finite human being; but (b) is greater and more inclusive than the sensitive self, the self of our immediate perception. In fact, the basis of the universal self is the finite-infinite identity of human individuality that is generated from the reality of conflict and tension inherent in the finite human being's ontological structure. How does Bosanquet explain this being within the limits of the finite being, yet slightly different and more complete? What is the meaning of the spiritual transmutation of the fundamental structure of being that emerges through the ceaseless interplay of the intertwined elements of the finite-infinite conceptualisation of human nature?

The human individual does not originate in isolation, but "reflects some sort of community, so that from the first the self goes beyond the bodily unit" (Bosanquet, 1904: 87). The bodily unit, the material manifestation of separation, particularity and atomistic individuation, is a concrete yet partial representation of the substance of the finite human being whose deeper levels of the self encompass the content of a more comprehensive spiritual reality that is hypostasised through the complex interactive activity of the self with its environment. This interaction of the self with its environment is a spiritual activity which takes place in the realm of finite consciousness and is meaningfully related to the self-apprehending process of the finite mind. In his Gifford Lectures, Bosanquet provides us with the term that describes the character of the bodily unit: it is the word "appearance" (Bosanquet, 1913: 13). The word "appearance," however, must be strictly understood in the context of his metaphysics and not in relation to other irrelevant conceptual frameworks. Appearance is the material manifestation of the finite being, the limits of which are the visual limits of the bodily unit. The feature of appearance is attributed to something which stands out, produces itself in a specific manner and is clearly discerned. Appearance is the particular moment of finitude that captures the visible realisation of the separate microcosms which constitute the inclusive world of spiritual membership. As has already been noted, the discernible particular stands out as the meeting-point of a cluster of universal determinations which originate from "beneath" and "beyond" the apparent exclusive limitations of finite selfhood. The bodily unit presupposes a constellation of relations and connections that is partly created by the self itself and partly belongs to the contextual "genealogy" of selfhood, the existence of which does not depend on the limitations and perceptual capabilities of the individualised duration. As Bosanquet asserts, there is a substantial part of the individual's identity that is given and not created *ab initio* by the finite individual. In other words, the self and its environment relate substantially to each other and realise the state of structural and spiritual unity that underlies the condition of selfhood: "No one maintains that we ourselves made our positive qualities. Our language, our ancestors, our religion, our leading ideas, the country we live in, are given to us, not made by us" (Bosanquet, 1904: 125).

The spiritual reality of the ideal self that emerges through the ontological content of the bodily unit is the essential "moment" of recognising the ever-existing working of the whole inside the apparent particularity of the human individual. I use the term "apparent particularity"[8] in the sense of asserting that the intra-subjective reality of each particular and distinct finite being contains potentials and dimensions for development, growth, relationality, self-realisation and flourishing which enable it to overcome the limitations and restrictions embedded in the formal ontic normativity of finitude.[9] The notion of the ideal or universal self enables us to see the vital interrelation between the "self" and the "other" by having as our starting-point not the individual self in its (apparent) visible bodily isolation and separation, but the individual self in its whole (spiritual) manifestation that includes the human being's immediate experience. Bosanquet uses the word "immediate" in contrast to "real." The former refers to the material object of our first impression which can be perceived as the typical embodiment of a constellation of individualised universal determinations. The latter refers to the actual content of those determinations as it is crystallised and re-created under a variety of forms which tend: (a) to reconstitute both the content and context of any given state of being; (b) to enable the spiritual process of self-transcendence; and (c) to formulate new dimensions of development and perfection. The "real" is strictly associated with the recognition of the teleological perspective in our apprehension of human nature. In contrast to "immediacy" that captures only a particular phase of selfhood, "reality" deals with the life and spirit of human agency in their multiple manifestations of diversity, development and potentiality. As Bosanquet explains in his Gifford Lectures, to possess reality is not to identify the real with the immediately given, but to adopt an attitude to experience that discerns the spirit of totality in every particular manifestation:

> It tells us nothing to say that an experience is immediate; for there are countless immediates and there is nothing that cannot be immediate. But if we understand by immediate so far as may be the primary datum, the factual nucleus, the naïve apprehension, then it is the plain and unmistakable lesson of logic and of the world that the immediate cannot stand. You cannot anywhere, whether in life or in logic find rest and salvation by withdrawing from the intercourse and implications of life; no more in the world of individual property and self-maintenance than in the world of international politics and economics; no more in the world of logical apprehension than in that of moral service and religious devotion. Everywhere to possess reality is an arduous task; stability and solidity are not in the beginning, but, if anywhere, only in proportion as we enter the larger vistas of things (Bosanquet, 1912: 7).

The concept of the universal self encapsulates the non-self and arrests the moment of separation[10] that lies at the heart of psychological individualism. The "other" becomes "self" in the process of a fundamental spiritual transformation culminating in inclusiveness and completion. In this context, and speaking about the work of art – one of his favourite examples – Bosanquet states that "the spiritual view, or the spiritual being, is always that which has more in it, and never that which has less; it does not omit, it includes and transforms. The spiritual view of life, for instance, does not omit the affections, but transforms them; it takes them up into the whole of life" (Bosanquet, 1904: 127). Bosanquet's theorising on the metaphysics of the self revolves around a conceptual framework which emphasises the element of completion and comprehensiveness inherent in the teleology of the human individual. This remark leads us to some reflections on the issues of teleology and finite consciousness with respect to individuality which are the subject-matter of the third section of this article.

TELEOLOGY, FINITE CONSCIOUSNESS AND INDIVIDUALITY

Teleology is not the immediate translation into fact of fancies drawn from nowhere. It is the unity of a real individual, for whose parts, there is nothing undignified in framing and disciplining themselves to a definite conformity with the whole. When we think of Hegel's conception of the psychical, how, for him, the planetary, the terrestrial, and the climatic influences draw together and become organic to consciousness in the concrete soul-life of a race and an individual, we must recognise that to be something in particular, to be built up on a definite structure which has learned many detailed lessons of conformity to reality, is in principle what we should expect for the most central and concrete of all finite existences (Bosanquet, 1912: 178).

The dialectic of the finite-infinite which underlies Bosanquet's ontology is rooted in his teleological theory concerning human nature. Bosanquet echoes the Aristotelian standpoint in his assertion, first, that the "end" is the whole (Bosanquet, 1912: 181) and, second, that the core-meaning of the "end" refers to positive maturity (Bosanquet, 1912: 128-129). Teleology operates through the finite consciousness; the boundaries of finite mind, however, can neither limit nor restrict its nature and manifestations. Teleology must be understood as a normative principle which conditions finiteness but goes beyond the restrictive framework of its particular determinations because the essence of teleology is not identified with the realm of finite purpose (Bosanquet, 1912: 146). In Bosanquet's words: "Things are not teleological because

they are purposed, but are purposed because they are teleological"
(Bosanquet, 1912: 137). Teleology determines finiteness and opens to
it the potentiality of being submerged into a universal purpose but this
characteristic should not mislead us into believing that the above
function exhausts the meaning of teleology. In all respects, teleology
stands above finite consciousness. In fact, the finite consciousness
should not be regarded as the source of teleology, but as one of its
manifestations. The essence of teleology is the attainment of individuality which is defined as the union of comprehensiveness and coherence
the structure of which represents universal determinations (Bosanquet,
1912: 140-141).

Bosanquet's views on teleology are characterised by intrinsic notional
complexity. Although Bosanquet is not absolutely clear about it, he
seems to distinguish between two conceptions of the term teleology. By
"not clear about it," I mean that he does not clarify explicitly whether
both conceptions of the same general concept deserve the name
"teleology." It seems to me that the first conception refers to what we
commonly understand by this term, and the second conception contains the real meaning of the concept. In this context, it appears helpful
to distinguish between "teleology" and "Teleology," although Bosanquet
is not terribly consistent with this specific use of the terms. He
definitely uses "Teleology" when he refers to the "real" or "thick" conception of the notion, yet, sometimes, he means the same by "teleology";
the reverse situation never occurs. It needs to be emphasised, however,
that the aforementioned notional differentiation neither affects nor
distorts the gist of Bosanquet's argument. The remark has value with
respect to the crystallisation of the typical (formal) structure of his
synthesis, and not with respect to the systemic coherence of his argument. I now turn to the analysis of the two conceptions of teleology.

The first conception of teleology has a limited and particular reference. It signifies a plurality of purposes or pleasurable impulses with
which the finite consciousness satisfies its particular needs and attains
satisfaction. It refers to the "means and ends" discourse which is articulated in the context of the "world of claims" – a descriptive expression
used extensively by Bosanquet in his discussion of the particularity of
the finite self. However, the first conception of teleology can explain
neither teleology's universal functioning, nor its meaning beyond the

context of the individualised applications.[11] In this semantical framework, the meaning of teleology is narrow and restricted by the condition
of finiteness:

> It is vain to look to the bare fact of conscious purpose or impulse
> for the essence or significance of teleology. Purpose only means,
> *prima facie,* that, using consciousness in the very widest sense,
> some creature consciously wants something (Bosanquet, 1912:
> 136-137).

The second conception of the term teleology refers to its proper , or
real meaning. In this context, teleology relates the finite-infinite dimension of the human being with the universal spiritual totality which
includes yet transcends finite intelligences. The spirit of this conception
of teleology is the idea of completion that refers: (a) to the purposive
reality of the finite being apprehended as *entelechy*; and (b) to the
inclusive reality above finite consciousness. The boundaries of those
two "levels" of reality are not clear because the former is a manifestation
of the latter, and the latter is partially substantiated through the former.
The link between them is an almost mystical concept, the content of
which characterises the core-essence of finite consciousness: this concept is "the immanent individuality of the real" (Bosanquet, 1912:
152). By "the immanent individuality of the real," I understand the
spiritual reality that hypostasises the dialectic of the finite-infinite
which conditions human nature and, subsequently, substantiates the
universal purpose of completion inherent in the intra-subjective realm
of finite minds. It must be noted, that "completion" in this semantical
context does not mean "conclusion" in the sense of "the mere cessation
of growth" (Bosanquet, 1912: 128-129 & 135). Completion or completeness must be regarded as a kind of ontological necessity deeply
embedded in the nature of being. Completion is a process associated
with the realisation of individuality. Completion seems to have the
character of a timeless becoming, the phases of which unfold in two
dimensions: (a) deep into the inwardness of the real individual; and (b)
beyond the limitations of finite individuality in the territories of
thought, history, art, religion, society, and Nature, in which "mind
begins to transcend its finiteness" (Bosanquet, 1912: 133-134). The

spiritual symphony of the finite intelligences and their surrounding environment is performed throughout the content of finiteness and is expanded all over and throughout the levels of being. Where and how can one discern the foundations of teleology, in this complex unity of the finite-infinite determinations in their differentiation?

Bosanquet puts at the centre of his analysis the idea of Nature as the cradle of Teleology together with Art, Thought, and Religion. For him, the concept of Nature is a notion that is broader and more inclusive than the idea or the immediate impression of natural environment. In fact, Nature refers to the content of a comprehensive living structure within which the spirit itself finds its ultimate actualisation. Nature, Art, Thought and Religion are regarded as ceaselessly self-remoulding comprehensive totalities that refer to states of being which belong to the experiential horizon of the finite human mind for "mind is the meaning of externality" (Bosanquet, 1912: 220). Furthermore, Nature, Art, Thought and Religion are fundamentally associated with the spiritual realisation of the concrete universal, i.e. the finite self in its comprehensive hypostasisation. Bosanquet asserts, however, that the finite consciousnesses or minds are not the "sole vehicles of teleology" (Bosanquet, 1912: 135). It is important to understand Bosanquet's thesis without misinterpreting his views on this matter. The mis-interpretation of his position is the view that Bosanquet "sacrifices" the finite individual in the name of a "being" that is other than the human being. I argue that Bosanquet's conception of teleology vindicates the importance of the finite mind for the actualisation and unfolding of the continually reconstituting "universal project" that the real meaning of teleology implies. By the term "universal project," I mean what Bosanquet identifies as the eternal reality of the unconscious movement of the whole (Bosanquet, 1912: 153-155). The unconscious movement of the whole is concrete and immanent (in its particular historical manifestations) and transcendental (in its comprehensive transhistorical actualisation). Despite the fact that teleology is an unconscious move-ment in the sense that its operation through the world is not confined to the designs and purposes of finite consciousnesses, it does depend on the dynamics of a complex relational framework crystallised out of the action and reaction of the finite consciousnesses with each other and with their environment. After all, the very fact of conceptualising and apprehending teleology is inevitably related to the cognitive ability of the finite mind. It is not the finite mind that determines teleology, but it is the finite mind, being itself a manifestation of teleology, that meaningfully relates the expressions of teleology to a coherent whole in the context of immanence.

Teleology links together the unconscious with the conscious movement of the determinations of finite consciousness. It brings together "waves" of crystallising and substantiating the real which emerge through an unlimited spectrum of intra-subjective, trans-subjective and transhistorical constitutive elements of the totality of being. This vital process of creative unity leading both to the hypostasisation and transcendence of the real is actualised beneath and beyond the boundaries of the finite mind and opens up the human geography to the spiritual "deconstruction" of the limitations of finiteness and the rebirth of the self. Each separate mind participates in this universal drama of moulding and re-moulding the soul under the double nature of the finite-infinite identity of its being. The "finite" refers to the limitations of the individual. The "infinite" refers to the state of overcoming the limitations that characterises the condition of finitude which is based on a complex tripartite simultaneous action. The constitutive elements of this action are three. First, recognition of the self in the other and, thus, assertion of a spiritual relationality deeply embedded in the nature of being. Second, apprehension of Nature as an inclusive content, the apparent externality of which undergoes a fundamental spiritual transformation when it is meaningfully articulated through the notional contextuality of finite consciousness. Third, submergence of the finite self into the ultimate reality offered by Art, Philosophy or Thought, Religion, and Society or Ethical Life. Although Bosanquet does not always use these terms in the way and order with which I present them here, the pattern that consists of those fundamental categories of the real is a constantly recurrent pattern found in his theorising on the dialectic of the finite-infinite. As he explains, it is in "art, thought, society, history" that "mind begins to transcend its finiteness" (Bosanquet, 1912: 134). The dialectic of the finite-infinite is crystallised in the realm of the finite mind enabling it: (a) to actualise a continuous transfiguration of the immediate given; and (b) to assert the hypostasisation of the concrete universal in the life of the finite being. The dialectic of the finite-infinite, in spite of its realisation in the spiritual domain of the subject, has a trans-subjective or universal nature , namely, a character that relates the essence of the finite being to the unconscious movement of teleology whose foundations in the universe:

> . . . are far too deeply laid to be explained by, still more, to be restricted to, the intervention of finite consciousness. Everything goes to show that such consciousness should not be regarded as the source of teleology, but as itself a manifestation, falling within wider manifestations, of the immanent individuality of the real (Bosanquet, 1912: 152).

CONCLUSION

It has been argued that self-transcendence is central to Bosanquet's discourse on the metaphysics of the self. The concept of self-transcendence functions as a fundamental presupposition for the spiritual process of soul-making and the ontological completion of the finite human being. In fact, self-transcendence is the complementary aspect of the dialectic of the finite-infinite, i.e. of that complex and polymorphous intra-subjective and trans-subjective multi-dimensional activity which characterises the dynamics of structuring the individuality of the real. In the context of Bosanquet's metaphysics, I have constructively associated his thoughts on the idea of ideal or universal self[12] with an array of issues derived from the nature of his philosophical discourse and intrinsically related to his theorising on both the conceptualisation and apprehension of the finite human being in its finite-infinite identity. These issues are: (a) the concept of pure ego; (b) the reaction to psychological individualism; and (c) the relation between teleology, finite consciousness and individuality.

In assessing Bosanquet's views on the concept of pure ego, when this notion refers to an isolated and exclusive unit which is impervious to the influences of its surrounding environment, I have argued that he is right to regard it as an unreal and useless abstraction that is incapable of capturing the essence of the finite being. Bosanquet attacks the idea of pure ego by elaborating a powerful ontological theory that focuses on the intrinsic nature of the finite being to be considered as a representative of universal determinations. Furthermore, Bosanquet asserts that the self is realised not as an abstract but as a concrete universal which means that its content is characterised by change, "negation" or continuous overcoming of the given, affirmation of new states of ontological completion, and a ceaseless dialectical interaction with the inclusive reality that incorporates it. For Bosanquet, the self is a cosmos in itself representing diversity of impulses, conflict of determinations and plurality of structural ontic differentiations in both its external manifestation and inward affirmation. The essence of the self must be "captured" in the pulsing substance of a cluster of intertwined relations and determinations generated by the spiritual interconnectedness of the self with that ever-transforming totality which, for analytical reasons, I call the non-self. The self is part of this totality as it is permeated by its essence and, simultaneously, it permeates the totality's being with its own individual substance; there is an indispensable relation between the self and the non-self. The transfiguration of otherness into the self is a spiritual process of restructuring that operates within the boundaries of finitude without finally abolishing, though dramatically overcoming, the condition of finiteness.

In the part devoted to Bosanquet's critique of psychological individualism, I have claimed that Bosanquet develops a theory of being that conceives of the self in a fundamental interconnectedness with the other or the non-self. He opposes the ontological project of the atomistic individualists that focuses on distinguishing between "self" and "other" and he points out that this view expresses a limited and defective understanding of both the nature and essence of the finite being because it takes into account only the visible materiality of the appearance of the separate bodily existences. In systematising Bosanquet's insights concerning this subject, I have developed the idea of a "genealogy" of selfhood. The gist of this notion is that the sources of the self are found "beyond" and "beneath" the apparent exclusive limitations of finitude. This idea endeavours to capture the meaning of the ideal or universal self which refers to the essence of the finite human being in its spiritual totality. I have contended that the notion of the universal self is a cardinal analytical category sustaining Bosanquet's theorising on the metaphysics of the self. The universal self is neither a self separate from the finite self nor a projection into utopian states of the selfhood's realisation. On the contrary, it refers to the spiritual content of the finite self as it is ceaselessly substantiated and restructured within a complex framework of relations, interdependencies, and universal determinations.

Finally, in the third section, I have inquired into Bosanquet's views on teleology in relation to finite consciousness and individuality. Teleology operates within the boundaries of finite mind yet the inherent limitations of finitude cannot restrict its nature and manifestations. Teleology conditions finiteness without being identified with the realm of finite purposes; in its proper, real meaning, teleology stands above finite consciousness. Teleology is the impulse that sustains the spiritual process of the dialectic of the finite-infinite which takes place in the microcosmic universality of the finite mind and relates the particular finite consciousness to the universal determinations derived from the spiritual inclusivity of Nature, Art, Thought, and Religion. In this context, the spirit of teleology refers to the attainment of completion which is identified with individuality.

REFERENCES

Bosanquet, B. (1904) *Psychology of the Moral Self* (London, Macmillan and Co., Limited). Reprint of the 1897 First Edition.
Bosanquet, B. (1912) *The Principle of Individuality and Value* (London, Macmillan and Co., Limited).
Bosanquet, B. (1913) *The Value and Destiny of the Individual* (London, Macmillan and Co., Limited).

NOTES

1 This is a revised version of a paper presented at the Conference Bosanquet and the Legacy of British Idealism, Harris Manchester College, Oxford, 1st-2nd September 1999. I would like to thank the participants for their helpful comments. I am especially grateful to Peter P. Nicholson and David Boucher for their invaluable comments and suggestions for improvement. All remaining errors are mine. Finally, I wish to acknowledge the NATO Fellowships Programme of the Ministry of National Economy in Greece for its financial support.

2 My assessment of Bosanquet's reflections on the condition of self-transcendence in its relation to his ontology is based on the following books: *Psychology for the Moral Self* (1897), *The Principles of Individuality and Value* (1912), and *The Value and Destiny of the Individual* (1913). Bosanquet's insights on the condition of self-transcendence and the conceptualisation of individuality are also found in other books and articles. At present, and for the purposes of my inquiry, I have confined my analysis to those three contributions that I consider to be very important for the apprehension of his ontological theory. A comprehensive inquiry into Bosanquet's discourse on the metaphysics of the self will be the subject-matter of another study.

3 In Bosanquet's metaphysical project, the idea of the human being refers to the concrete universal which is capable of realising the real or universal or true self, despite the inherent limitations of its finitude.

4 The ontological formation of the finite self is a complex spiritual process which is characterised by the dialectical interweaving of the finite-infinite aspects of the human individual. In my analysis, I use the terms "dialectic" and "dialectical" in the sense of interconnection, interdependence, interrelation and spiritual exchange of ontological contents. In this context, the meaning of the term "dialectic" does not derive from the Marxist use of the word.

5 The psychical disposition and the strength of will of the human agent can be seen as endogenous factors. The activity of trans-subjective relations independent of the actual influence of the given subjectivity is an instance of an exogenous factor.

6 In this article I use the 1904 Edition of *Psychology of the Moral Self* which is a reprint of the 1897 first edition.

7 I refer to the idea of pure ego understood as a unit impervious to the influences of its surrounding environment and articulated in isolation.

8 By "apparent particularity," I do not mean that the human individual is not particular and distinct in its external, namely, somatic material manifestation; this is an inescapable state of being associated with the biological condition of finiteness.

9 In my analysis, "the formal ontic normativity of finitude" is a descriptive phrase referring to the conditions which determine the ontological constitution of finiteness.

10 The moment of separation is spiritually arrested. The self and the non-self are united in a transcendental oneness which, however, does not abolish the visible material particularity of the finite existence.

11 The limited explanatory power of the first conception of teleology stems from its inherent particularity.

12 The notion of the ideal or universal self refers to the reality of being behind the appearance of the finite existence. The ideal or universal self is the spiritual embodiment of the finite self's conscious or unconscious relationality which affects the ontological constitution of the self in its particular realisation. The ideal or universal or real self is characterised by a higher degree of comprehensiveness and completion in comparison with the actual self which is an incomplete phase of the finite selfhood.

COLLINGWOOD
CORNER

R. G. Collingwood's 'Christianity in Partibus'

JAMES CONNELLY AND PETER JOHNSON

INTRODUCTION

It is well-known that Collingwood's 'List of Work Done', amongst the Collingwood Papers in the Bodleian Library, Oxford,[1] refers to a number of items that have proved extremely difficult to trace. Amongst these is an entry reading: 'Christianity in Partibus, Challenge, 1918.' This raised questions. We know that Collingwood often made contributions to several ephemeral publications and that he regularly gave talks to various societies. But, in this case, did Collingwood's title refer to a lecture, a talk, a paper or an article? Was 'Challenge' a journal, a newspaper, a discussion society, or a religious group?

In attempting to track down Collingwood's reference, our first move was to work on the assumption that 'Challenge' was a printed work of some kind. The British Museum Library Catalogue does list a *Challenge*, but on enquiry this proved to be a series of religious Tracts, none of which were by Collingwood. However, the British Library helpfully offered the information that the British Newspaper Library at Colindale held copies of *The Challenge*, a weekly Christian review, 1914-1924, and this proved to be the breakthrough.

On inspection, it was found that *The Challenge* did contain Collingwood's essay (in issue No. 232, Vol 1X, 4 October, 1918, p.323, now reprinted in full here). Collingwood's choice of title – suggesting the difficulties besetting Christianity in the face of unbelief – reflects the essay's contents well. Similarly, *The Challenge* itself was a locus for the debates about the role of philosophy in restoring Christian spiritual life after the experiences of War: we know this thinking informed Collingwood's early writings on religion in such works as *Religion and Philosophy* (1916) and 'The Devil' in *Concerning Prayer* (1916). In fact, a number of the contributors to this latter volume also make regular appearances in the pages of *The Challenge*. There is considerable overlap between the discussions conducted or reported in the pages of *The Challenge* and the debates of the Cumnor Circle,[2] the religious group which Collingwood attended during the formative period of the development of his religious views. He regularly attended meetings of this group from 1912 until the mid-1930s. It was a discussion circle of theologians and philosophers who shared a liberal, modernist approach to theology. Members included A. E. J. Rawlinson, F. A. Cockin, B. H. Streeter and Lily Dougall: all of them frequent contributors to *The Challenge*. It is perhaps no surprise that both *Concerning Prayer* and *Religion and Philosophy* were reviewed favourably in *The Challenge*.

The Challenge is overwhelmingly liberal Anglican in tone and its mission, to provide the basis for spiritual reconstruction after the War, is reflected in Collingwood's own more philosophical writings at this time. In his essay Collingwood poses the question of how the non-religious can speak to the religious; this issue is central to any quest for spiritual renewal, namely, how can those who do not possess a common religious vocabulary (or, indeed, any religious vocabulary at all) share the same ethical beliefs? This is a matter which also goes to the heart of Collingwood's liberalism, thereby linking Collingwood's anxieties in 1918 with the fears and concerns he was to voice before the Second War.

This newly located text is, in our view, an important addition to the Collingwood oeuvre, one which should give students of Collingwood ample opportunity to indulge their appetite for philosophical reflection.

CHRISTIANITY IN PARTIBUS

By R.G. Collingwood, Author of "Religion and Philosophy".

There was a time, not very long ago, when a person who stood outside all definitely Christian communities and observed no forms of Christian worship was generally regarded as an enemy of society. The "irreligious" man, the man who rejected the Christian formulae and ceremonies, must necessarily (it was thought) be morally unsound; and if he showed ability in art or science, the fact was evidence of the viciousness of these pursuits rather than of a saving grace in the man.

Today the situation has changed. If anyone begins by reviewing his acquaintances and asking which of them are really serviceable to the world, which contribute something definite and indispensable to the progress of human life and thought, he will certainly find that many of these are not, in the sense laid down above, "religious". Some are merely indifferent to the claims of established Christianity; others hostile, if not to Christianity, at least to Christians. The religious temperament irritates them; they regard it as futile and misguided.

Now the importance of this opinion with regard to "religion" (still using the word in the sense of churchgoing, prayer, and acceptance of the creeds) is that those who hold it can no longer be looked upon as outcasts. They are doing the work of mankind; they are morally and intellectually sound and everyone recognises them to be so. Their opinion carries weight even with the most devoted Churchman. Thus religion is thrown on the defensive. Everyone sees that among his friends the best, most capable, most efficient, most honourable, are not necessarily religious; and everyone is naturally led to ask how religion can justify its claims if these qualities can be so brilliantly exemplified without its aid.

To adjust this difference between religion and the very serious body of "non-religious" opinion is one of the most important and difficult tasks of the present day. Most religious literature of late years takes the attitude of trying in a modest way to show to the non-religious man that religion is, after all, a thing worthy of consideration even by his superior intellect; and most of the large recent literature which treats religion from the standpoint of the "non-religious" man treats it decidedly *de haut en bas*, as a mental aberration deserving at best a kind of good-natured contempt. Both sides thus recognise the weight of the case against religion. Indeed, both sides are too ready to recognise this and to ignore the other. There is right on both sides, and it is a serious mistake to suppose that the religious temperament is the only one which stands in need of psychological analysis and corrective discipline.

But my immediate purpose is only concerned with one side – namely, with the non-religious man's case against religion; and indeed with only one aspect of that case. What is it at bottom that the non-religious man finds fault with in the religious? Sir Oliver Lodge tells us that the trouble consists in the religious man's preoccupation with the state of his soul. The modern man, he says, is not bothering about his sins; he has seen through the ideal of self-examination and penitence, and is occupied in getting things done, not in lamenting his failure to get other things done in the past.

Well, if the modern man is really not bothering about his sins, so much the worse for the modern man. A man must live, and in these days of competition he cannot afford to live slackly. He must criticise his living and try to improve it. Not to bother about one's sins is as sensible as not to bother about playing in tune if one is a violinist. The technique of living is quite as hard as the technique of playing the violin; and if each can be improved only by practice, practice can only be of use if based on and directed by a very vigorous and penetrating self-criticism.

But I think Sir Oliver Lodge's remark contains the root of the matter; if it is not true, it is at any rate the exact opposite of the truth – which is the next best thing. The modern man does care intensely about his own failings. In an age conspicuous for its self-consciousness we are all doing our best to analyse our own minds and to locate and reinforce their weak points. Self-criticism is rather a speciality of the modern man. And it is just this that makes him dissatisfied with "religion". For he thinks, rightly or wrongly, that the Christian ideal of self-criticism consists in a feverish search for sins that do not matter, and a total blindness to more disastrous failures and shortcomings. The religious man's self-examination errs (according to our modern man's opinion) not through excess but through defect. Religious ethics have, he thinks, concentrated their attention on a number of sins which are not really the most important ones; either because they have so long been fought against that they are now, comparatively speaking, stamped out; or because they were the most dangerous sins of the age when the religious ethic was codified, but now superseded by others; or because they are the least insidious and therefore the easiest to deal with; or for some other reason. Some people dislike the hymn tunes they hear in church, not because they are unmusical, but precisely because they are musical, and therefore dislike hearing the inferior products of an unmusical age; so our modern man dislikes the self-examination of the "religious" person just because he is an expert in self-examination and finds this form of it trivial and misguided. He wants people so to criticise themselves that they will become more alive, more active, more sensitive to important events around them; instead of that he finds their self-criticism making them progressively unsympathetic towards everything that matters most, progressively wrapped up in *minutiae* which are of no true service either to themselves or to the world.

Here again it would be a mistake to assume that the modern man is altogether in the right and the "religious" person entirely in the wrong. But there is some justification for the "non-religious" man's impatience. The morality of many professional Christians is deplorably petty and formalistic, apt to concentrate on details of external conduct and blind to the faults of character which most impede the world's progress.

But the really serious thing is that these faults are over and over again identified by outside observers with "religion", with Christianity, with the Churches. If Christianity means the following of Christ, it means having life, and having it more abundantly; being more, and not less, wide in outlook and discerning of the things that matter. If the self-criticism of Christians is formalistic, it is so exactly in proportion as they abandon the first rules of Christian morality. To pay less attention to mercy than to sacrifice, to devour widows' houses and to make long prayers, to substitute a morality of formalistic and ceremonial observance, prayer and obeisance, vestment and holy day, for the morality of a keen, living contact with the world – these are the faults of which the "non-religious" accuse the "religious". But they are the very faults against which the Christian ideal of life is most specifically directed. They are not Christianity, but anti-Christianity.

Thus the critic who says, "I stand for a life of fearless and untrammelled endeavour, and I despise the formalism and second-hand morality of these Christians," ought really to say, "I stand for the Christian morality, and I reject the paganism which I see around me usurping the name of Christianity". The spirit of prophetic Judaism was more faithfully served by the Jesus who was indicted for irreligion than by the priests who condemned Him; and there is a very real danger that the "non-religious" man may prove a more faithful trustee of the spirit of Christianity than many of those who call Jesus Lord.

The Challenge, Vol IX, No. 232, 4th October 1918, p. 323.

NOTES

1 See Ruth A. Burchnall, *Catalogue of the Papers of Robin George Collingwood, 1889-1943*, Dep. Collingwood 1-28, 1994, p.14, 22/2.
2 Sometimes in his unpublished manuscripts Collingwood referred to this simply as The Group.

Recent Publications

Compiled by
SUSAN DANIEL
Western Oregon University*

Belvedresi, Rosa. "Collingwood y el constructivismo historico." *Revista de Filosofia* 10 no. 7 (1997): 187-206.

Bevir, Mark. "Unreality and Particularity in the Philosophy of E. B. Bax and R. G. Collingwood." *History of the Human Sciences* 12 no. 3 (1999): 55-69.

Boucher, David, and Bruce Haddock, editors. *Collingwood Studies: Explorations.* Wales: Dinefwr Press, 1998.

Boucher, David. Review of *R. G. Collingwood,* by Peter Johnson *Collingwood Studies* V (1998): 70-74.

Brown, Phillip. "Was Collingwood a Relativist?" *Collingwood Studies* V (1998): 43-71.

Collini, Stefan. "When the Goose Cackled: The discovery of history and the world beyond the walls: how Collingwood wrote his last work." *Times Literary Supplement,* August 27, (1999): 3-6.

Collingwood, R. G. *The Principles of History: and Other Writings in Philosophy of History,* edited by William H. Dray and W. J. van der Dussen. Oxford: Oxford University Press, Inc., 1999.

_____. "Philosophy, History and Belief," introduced by James Connelly. *Collingwood Studies* V (1998): 136-51.

Connelly, James. "Bradley, Collingwood and the 'Other Metaphysics'." *Bradley Studies* 3 no. 2 (1997): 89-112.

* Notification of additional items would be welcome. Please send to Dr Susan Daniel, Philosophy and Religious Studies Department, Division of Humanities, Western Oregon University, Monmouth, OR 97361, USA, OR daniels@wou.edu

Dilworth, John. "Is Ridley Charitable to Collingwood?" *The Journal of Aesthetics and Art Criticism* 56 no. 4 (1998): 393-98.

Edwards, S. D. "The Art of Nursing." *Nursing Ethics* 5 no. 5 (1998): 393-400.

Eisenstein, Maurice. *Phenomenology of Civilization: Reason as a Regulative Principle in Collingwood and Husserl.* Lahnam, MD: University Press of America, 1999.

Gelder, Frederik van. Review of *History as Re-Enactment: R. G. Collingwood's Idea of History,* by William H. Dray. *Canadian Philosophical Reviews* 17 no.1 (1997): 25-27.

Gnosspelius, Janet. "Biographical Questions: Edward Collingwood 1824-1889 and Marie Imhoff 1826-1873." *Collingwood Studies* V (1998): 152-57.

Goldstein, Leon J. Review of *History as Re-Enactment: R. G. Collingwood's Idea of History,* by William H. Dray. *History and Theory* 37 no. 3 (1998): 409-21.

Hausman, Carl R. "Aaron Ridley's Defense of Collingwood Pursued." *The Journal of Aesthetics and Art Criticism* 56 no. 4 (1998): 391-93.

Holdcroft, David. "Bradley, Collingwood and the Presuppositions of Critical History." *Bradley Studies* 3 no. 1 (1997): 2-24.

Johnson, Peter. Review of *History as Re-Enactment: R. G. Collingwood's Idea of History,* by William H. Dray. *Philosophical Investigations* 21 no. 1 (1998): 88-91.

Lewis, Peter. "Collingwood and Wittgenstein: Struggling with Darkness." *Collingwood Studies* V (1998): 28-42.

Lund, James. "The Idea of the History of Philosophy: Beginnings." *Collingwood Studies* V (1998): 1-27.

Mann, Doug. "Reconstructing the Past: A Structural Idealist Approach." *Clio: A Journal of Literature, History, and the Philosophy of History* 27 no. 2 (1998): 221-49.

Martin, Rex. "Collingwood's Logic of Question and Answer, its Relation to Absolute Presuppositions: A Brief History." *Collingwood Studies* V (1998): 122-33.

_____. Review of *History as Re-Enactment: R. G. Collingwood's Idea of History,* by William H. Dray. *Collingwood Studies* V (1998): 174-80.

_____. "Collingwood's Essay on Metaphysics and the Three Conclusions to the Idea of Nature." *British Journal for the History of Philosophy* 7 no. 2 (1999): 333-51.

Panagakou, Stamatoula I. Review of *The First Mate's Log,* by R. G. Collingwood *Collingwood Studies* V (1998): 162-69.

Pompa, Leon. Review of *History as Re-Enactment: R. G. Collingwood's Idea of History,* by William H. Dray. *Philosophical Books* 38 no.3 (1997): 194-96.

Ridley, Aaron. *R. G. Collingwood.* In *The Great Philosophers Series* no. XXI, edited by Ray Monk and Frederic Raphael. London: Phoenix Press, 1998.

_____. "Not Ideal. Collingwood's Expression Theory." *The Journal of Aesthetics and Art Criticism* 55 no. 3 (1997): 263-72.

Saari, Heikki. "R. G. Collingwood's Emotivist Theory of Magic." *Collingwood Studies* V (1998): 90-108.

Schaub, Melissa. "The Role of the Reader in Collingwood's Philosophy of History." *Clio: A Journal of Literature, History, and the Philosophy of History* 27 no. 3 (1998): 363-85.

Simpson, Grace. "Collingwood's Latest Archaeology Misinterpreted by Bersu and Richmond." *Collingwood Studies* V (1998): 109-19.

Tucker, Aviezer. Review of *History as Re-Enactment: R. G. Collingwood's Idea of History,* by William H. Dray. *Philosophy of the Social Sciences* 27 no. 1, (1997): 102-29.

Vanheeswijck, Guido. "Collingwood's Metaphysics: not a Science of Pure Being, but Still a Science of Being." *International Philosophical Quarterly* 38 no. 2 (1998): 153-74.

Young, R. A. "R. G. Collingwood's Logic of Questions and Answers." *Bradley Studies* 3 no. 2 (1997): 151-75.

FURTHER LETTERS OF
R. G. COLLINGWOOD

Occasional Series No. 1

Collingwood's Exchange of Letters with R. d'E. Atkinson in the Oxford Magazine 1923

PETER JOHNSON

INTRODUCTION

In my book, *The Correspondence of R. G. Collingwood, An Illustrated Guide*, (R. G. Collingwood Society, 1998), I indicated, (p. x), that if more of Collingwood's letters were to come to light then they would be listed in *Collingwood Studies*. The following exchange between Collingwood and R. d'E. Atkinson was recently uncovered during a search I made of the *Oxford Magazine* for early unsigned Collingwood reviews.

Students of Collingwood are sure to find the new letters of great interest. They are among a very small group which show Collingwood engaging in public debate, in this instance on an educational issue, and explaining the philosophical thinking which lies behind his views. Collingwood's strictly philosophical concerns in these letters – the conceptual differences between philosophy and science; what philosophy can say to non-philosophy – reflect the preoccupations of the work he published in the period leading up to the appearance of *Speculum Mentis* in 1924. Collingwood's life-long determination not to allow philosophy to drift too far from life is well-known, but what these letters further reveal are the complexities involved in drawing practical conclusions from a general philosophical standpoint.

I have reprinted Collingwood's letters in full, and they are listed and described in the manner of the *Guide*. So as to give the complete flavour of the discussion, Atkinson's letters are also reprinted in their entirety. The subject of their exchange of views is the Proposal to establish a new Honour School of Philosophy and Science. To provide a context for this, the *Oxford Magazine* description of this Proposal is reprinted, followed by its report of the Debate on the Proposal which took place in Congregation on 13 February, 1923.

THE PROPOSED HONOUR SCHOOL
OF PHILOSOPHY AND SCIENCE

On February 13th, Congregation will be asked to vote upon a form of statute to establish a new final Honour School – the School of Philosophy and Science. As there seems to be a good deal of uncertainty in many quarters as to the scope of the proposed new school and the ideas underlying it, a brief general account may not be unwelcome to readers of the MAGAZINE.

Proposals to start some form of Honour School which should combine scientific and philosophical work have been mooted for some time back. A series of Committees, starting in 1910, was appointed to give shape to these ideas, and a tangible proposal was made in a report issued in 1914. However, owing to the war, no progress could be made in the matter at the time.

As soon as the war was over, the proposal was referred back to the various Boards concerned. Meanwhile, however, a number of historians and economists had begun to press for a similar scheme to include their subjects. A new committee was appointed, and eventually decided that a combination of Philosophy, Science and History was too large, and that to found a single school of Philosophy combined with two alternatives, of History and Science, would raise more difficulties than the establishment of two separate but analogous schools.

One of these two is now in existence as the Honour School of Philosophy, Politics and Economics, and will hold its first examination this summer. The complement of this is the new school now proposed. Owing, however, to the necessity found by the new committee of revising a number of details in the scheme, and to the then overcrowded condition of the Science Laboratories, which meant that it would be difficult for the existing staff to undertake the delivery of a new type of lecture, the scheme for a combination of Philosophy and Science, although the first in the field, has only now reached its definitive form.

The general ideas which have animated those who are anxious to see the proposed new School established may be briefly summarised as follows:

(1) There is at present a divorce between Philosophy and Natural Science. This is bad for Philosophy, which requires to be kept in constant relation with the progress of scientific thought if it is to have an adequate basis on which to build; it is also bad for Science, in which any tendency to narrowness and specialisation can best be checked by contact with the general ideas and the attempts at correlation and synthesis which Philosophy provides.

(2) It is at present practically impossible in Oxford for an undergraduate to obtain a general education into which Natural Science enters. In the Honour School of Natural Science, a man only reads one limited branch of science – Chemistry, Astronomy, Zoology, Physiology, etc. In other words, the Honour School of Natural Science is to all intents and purposes a professional School, taken almost exclusively by those who intend to continue working at the same type of subject in later life.

Even the scientific Preliminary Courses partake of this same character, a very large majority of those attending them doing so as a necessary prerequisite to entering for the Final Examination in the School of Natural Science.

In this respect our practice is wholly different from that, for instance, of the United States, where a certain modicum of Natural Science is looked upon as an essential part of higher education, and, indeed, in most Colleges and Universities is compulsory on all undergraduates. To put it bluntly, a really general education does not exist at present in Oxford, whether for those reading one of the "Humanities," or for those taking Science or Mathematics.

The advantages likely to accrue from such a School are therefore two-fold. (1) As regards the advancement of learning, Oxford would be one of the few Universities to undertake systematically this important task of correlating the facts and ideas of Science with each other and with other branches of study – a task becoming more difficult but correspondingly more important as the bulk and the specialisation of scientific research increases. (2) As regards the provision of a general education, the new School would make it possible for those desirous in after life of entering politics, the administrative services, business, journalism, etc., to have come into contact with the most important facts and ideas of Natural Science. At present, when such men and women take an Honour School, it has as a matter of fact till very recently been, in the great majority of cases, either Literae Humaniores or Modern History. English Literature and Modern Languages account for a few more, and the School of Philosophy, Politics and Economics will probably absorb an increasing number as time goes on.

The method adopted in the School of Literae Humaniores, of combining two distinct lines of study in a single Honours School, is a peculiar and successful product of Oxford. By the establishment of the School of Philosophy, Politics, and Economics, it has been recognised in principle that this same method can and should be applied in other fields. If the proposed School of Science and Philosophy is also set up, it will be the natural complement of Philosophy, Politics and Economics, and the two together will provide a real "Modern Greats."

[*Oxford Magazine*, February 8, 1923, p.198-9]

DEBATE ON THE PROPOSED NEW SCHOOL
OF PHILOSOPHY AND NATURAL SCIENCE

The proposal for a Final Honour School of Philosophy and Natural Science was defeated on Tuesday after a debate of nearly an hour and a half (66 to 38). Professor Webb, in an interesting speech, commended the Statute to the House as an attempt to end the divorce between two subjects which in earlier days were undivided, and explained the purpose and main principles of the proposal, and General Hartley, in support, explained the relations of the School to the existing Schools of Natural Science: he also pleaded that the time was opportune and justified the proposal of the "theoretic" study of Natural Science. The Warden of Wadham opposing the Statute laid stress on the wide range of subjects proposed and the difficulty of maintaining a standard in a School with few candidates. He spoke also of the difficulties of College teaching, especially in small Colleges, and asked the house to wait till the existing "Greats without Greek" had had longer trial. Professor Joachim made an earnest appeal on behalf of the new School which he believed would, if carried, be looked back upon forty years hence as a great landmark in philosophical study. Mr. Joseph, whose speech was the most remarkable in the debate, pointed out the serious difficulty in finding teachers and students for the new School, and suggested that the promoters were under an illusion in regard to the capacities of the hypothetical students. His speech was felt to be weighty and it carried votes. Professor Myres criticised the Warden of Wadham's view of Greats and gave a history of the inception of the scheme, which he warmly supported. The proposal was fairly and openly discussed and it was clear that the majority felt that the time was not yet ripe for the scheme.

[*Oxford Magazine*, February 15, 1923, p.212]

"SCIENCE GREATS"

(*To the Editor of the* OXFORD MAGAZINE)

SIR,

Behind much of the recent acrimony on the subject of "Science Greats" lies, among other things, a strong feeling that the philosophers have failed us. This may, of course, be due to a sheer misunderstanding on our part of their aim, and if so the obvious course is for us to state our ideas with enough fulness for the error to be pointed out. It seems to me then, that in the natural sciences questions which are definitely metaphysical are clamouring for answers, and the philosophers (as some of them admit, and others, less prudent, betray) are not in a position even to consider them. The question of Relativity provides an instructive example, and although to set it forth properly here is rather like trying to translate Aristotle into Latin, some sort of attempt must I feel be made.

It is found that algebraical equations can be used to describe the shape of geometrical curves. These equations take quite different forms according to the systems of co-ordinates employed; for example both in "Cartesian" and in "polar" co-ordinates we can readily obtain an equation which denotes an ellipse, and from either of these equations we can deduce the many important properties of that curve. In this case the two (principal) forms of the algebraical statement of the case are both of them tractable and productive. In the case, however, of the spirals, Cartesian co-ordinates produce equations which, though still necessarily correct, are quite useless; they contain an infinite number of terms and cannot be handled at all; neither form involves any difficulty of thought, but only the polar system is technically suitable. In the case of subjects treated by Relativity methods, we have the awkward situation that that system which is by far the most suitable technically (namely Relativity itself) involves considerable difficulties of thought. On the side of convenience it is comparable with the polar system as applied to the spirals; on the side of "conceivability" it is invariably greeted with a storm of protest at first, on *a priori* grounds. It is possible that everything could be adequately, though cumbrously, described in terms of a "stationary" three-dimensional ether and a "real" contraction in the direction of motion on the part of all matter moving through it, and a few other such assumptions which as a matter of fact are probably not difficult to justify on classical electromagnetic grounds; the result might be more "thinkable," but would it be more "true"? Would it even be *as* true ? May we follow the pragmatists and say that since neither destroys itself neither is wrong, or ought we to reject Relativity as far as picturing to ourselves what "really" occurs is concerned? The grounds of that rejection would be, I take it, that though the equations are convenient for description and prolific sources of correct prophecy, the assumptions behind them are "inconceivable." This is, of course, the lay view, and there is something to be said for it. Relativity states for example that there is no such thing as simultaneity, since two observers who have made every allowance for the velocity of light and so on may still differ as to the order in which they calculate that two events occurred; that an observer on a train of known length will find that a flash of light sent after the train from a stationary (or moving) source will take the same time to pass from the guard's van to the engine whether the train is stationary or moving at any speed, although an observer on the ground will disagree with him; that a bullet, fired forwards with a muzzle velocity equal (if that were possible) to that of light, from a pistol carried by a train moving also with the velocity of light, would travel over the stationary earth with a velocity still only that of light, and such apparently ridiculous notions. It is, however, no use stating off-hand that these ideas are unthinkable; they are borne out by every test that has been devised by a succession of furiously hostile critics, and these critics have subsequently been converted and have said that they can, more or less, and by the use of analogy, conceive of them if they must. But this is not absolutely satisfactory: if there were to be an alternative, and two systems of *description* could both be used, the question whether both are permissible as modes of physical thought about the "real" state of affairs appears to be one of metaphysics. All scientists take the pragmatic point of view; I understand that, in Oxford at least, that fact alone may be almost enough to convince most of the philosophers that their help is needed. To me, however, it even seems possible that if on the other hand no system but Relativity proves for a time adequate, it might be the privilege of metaphysics, having after real study decided that this was philosophically inadmissible, to stand out for the discovery of another; but this the metaphysicians are not entitled to do at present, because they cannot appreciate the difficulties; to use a hard word, they are not sufficiently educated for this purpose.

A second possible ground of complaint is that they were bound, if not to fail altogether, at least to fail us, in this and every important matter, from having attempted the impossible. Philosophical training starts with the prolonged study of Plato and Aristotle: these scientists lived in a time when it was fully conceivable that any man should be able to acquire the essential bases of all branches of knowledge, and should be able to evaluate and collate them. Modern philosophers are thus liable to assume that this is still broadly possible, but a fair case can be made out for doubting it. The following attitude is common: "Without an elaborate use of symbols the manifold development of mathematical principles would doubtless be impossible. But, if the principles themselves be not amenable to simple expression, we may fairly be excused for doubting their truth." Indeed, you may *not* so be excused; such an assumption is gratuitous, and distinctly unkind. It is also shallow, since specialists must be accepted. The symbols do in fact make possible a more simple expression of the *principles* than is otherwise obtainable, and even so they take years to become familiar with. Certainly they were not invented for fun, nor to outdistance the principles. The complexity of the universe is enormously greater than Aristotle ever contemplated, and the realms in which there may occur such a fundamental alteration of outlook as calls for a new metaphysic are widely spaced and difficult of entry.

The deduction from both these ideas seems to be that, if it were possible to provide a year's course which should give graduates in science or mathematics some elementary notions of metaphysics, science would certainly benefit, and even philosophy could not be made less useful. May we not hope shortly for some such development?

R. d'E. ATKINSON[1]

Hertford College.
March 5th, 1923.

[*Oxford Magazine*, March 8, 1923, p.278-9.]

1 Robert d'Escourt Atkinson, B.A., scholar of Hertford College, 1919-23.

O   *The Oxford Magazine*

0i   *To*: The Editor, *The Oxford Magazine*
Date: 9 March, 1923
Location: *The Oxford Magazine*
Reference: –
Subject-matter: Proposal to establish a Science "Greats"
Publication: *The Oxford Magazine*, 15 March, 1923, Vol 41, 1922-3, pp.301-2.

SCIENCE "GREATS"

(To the Editor of the OXFORD MAGAZINE)

SIR,

Mr. Atkinson's frank and courteous letter lifts the discussion of "Science Greats" to a level at which a reply is possible and indeed necessary. I therefore venture to attempt an answer, on my own behalf alone, in the same spirit in which he asks his questions. He calls upon philosophers to come over and help the scientists in such difficulties as that concerning Relativity. Can we accept such an invitation? Mr. Atkinson himself admits that we cannot. He says, and I agree, that we are not sufficiently educated; which means that we are not scientists. In philosophy he does us the honour to believe that we are educated, and I hope that we partly at least deserve his confidence. But this means that the problems of which he is thinking are scientific problems, and that only scientists can deal with them. This I believe to be true; for though he says they are philosophical problems I must confess that, so far as I have been able to grasp their meaning, they seem to me to be nothing of the kind. But whether they are called philosophical or scientific, the fact that scientists have raised them is proof that scientists can answer them. It is not, I submit, conceivable that one form of thought should raise problems which only another can solve, or that one kind of training should enable a man to ask questions which only another kind would enable him to answer. Any problem which arises out of the development of scientific thought must be soluble, if at all, only by a further development of the same kind of thinking; and a philosopher, with whatever admiration and interest he may watch the work of scientists, has no more right to forestall the result of their inquiries by an edict as to what is "philosophically admissible" than to tell the archaeologists what it is philosophically admissible for them to find in the inner chamber of Tutankhamen. Mr. Atkinson's invitation is based on his belief in the competence of philosophers in their own trade; and I, while thanking him from the bottom of my heart for so friendly and flattering a message, must answer that I decline his invitation because I reciprocate his opinions; because I have every confidence in the ability of scientists to solve their own problems far better than a consulting philosopher could do it for them.

This implies what I believe to be true, that science and philosophy are different things, and that each demands a specialised training which differs from that required by the other. I should go further than this, and say that in my opinion the chief need of philosophical thought to-day is to escape from an undue sense of the importance to itself of scientific methods. Philosophy has since the Renaissance done much to impede its own progress by aping science, as science did in the middle ages by aping philosophy. There is not much danger of philosophy's suffering from association with history, ancient or modern, for their methods and aims are not easily confused. But a young student learning science and philosophy at once would be trying to acquire simultaneously two techniques which have just enough in common to damage one another; he would learn enough philosophy to confuse his science, and enough science to confuse his philosophy. And this would, if I am right, do peculiar harm to philosophy at the present stage of its history. The two things, to be learnt well, must be learnt separately.

Though these considerations persuade me that an honour school of science and philosophy is undesirable, I have nothing but sympathy for Mr. Atkinson's wish for a post-graduate course in philosophy for any student of science who may want it; and I gladly pledge myself to assist such a scheme whenever it is put forward.

R. G. COLLINGWOOD

Pembroke College. March 9th, 1923

[*Oxford Magazine*, March 15, 1923, pp.301-2]

(*To the Editor of the* OXFORD MAGAZINE)

"SCIENCE GREATS"

SIR,

In reply to Mr. Collingwood's kind letter in your last number, and in pursuit of mutual understanding, I should like to ask for an elaboration of the thesis he puts forward there, that scientific and philosophic studies involve different forms of thought.

That statement, as it seems to me, is essentially scientific; it is as closely allied in nature to the conclusions of any one branch of "science" as those branches are to one another. Is it then essentially unphilosophical? Is it not rather the case that the majority of philosophical statements are and must be as scientific as this one?

In the abstract the scientific process is, of course, to make generalisations from selected phenomena, and to test those generalisations, or more often to test deductions from them, by reference as a rule to other phenomena or different aspects of the same phenomena, as far as seems necessary to "establish" them. As far as my acquaintance with philosophy goes, this is also the philosophic process. Perhaps the amount of deduction in philosophy is unusually large, so that the amount of necessary verification is unusually small; perhaps also the verifications are often so simple as to be performed almost unconsciously, – they may be capable of being seen by the mind as existent already in the experience stored by memory, so that the verification almost precedes the mind's assent to the proposition, – but the verification seems to me to be necessary; and this because, even assuming that the mind never makes a mistake in the process of deduction, there is no guarantee that either the preliminary observations, or the generalisation from them, are correct. A generalisation is, I imagine, always unwarrantable logically, and the amount of deduction that can be made from observations ungeneralised seems to me extremely small. Further the amount of deduction that can be performed without even observations appears to be absolutely nil. No one can dispute about the nature of thought, except on a basis of having thought, nor can one dispute about anything else without some experience of it, *i.e.* some observations, preferably "scientifically" made.

Philosophy appears to me then to differ from "science" in that it sets out to study a different field, and of course that it possesses, as each science does, its own technique to suit its own ends. I admit of course Mr. Collingwood's subordinate point, that the attempt to acquire simultaneously two slightly different techniques may be dangerous, but that is another matter. I fail to see how physics can be unable to raise a question which it is rather for philosophy to answer, when every day the astronomer raises questions for the physical chemist, the biologist and the pathologist for the organic chemist, the sociologist and the psychologist for them, and, I think I may fairly add, the theologian and the historian for them and for each other. These lines of study vary as to the extent to which they require quantitative methods, and in many other important respects, but in what way does philosophy stand aloof from them all? What is the vital distinction between "technique" and "form of thought"?

R. d' E. ATKINSON

Hertford College

[*Oxford Magazine*, May 3, 1923, p.320]

Oii To: The Editor, *The Oxford Magazine*
Date: 3-9 May, 1923
Location: *The Oxford Magazine*
Reference: –
Subject-matter: Elaboration of views on philosophy and science
Publication: *The Oxford Magazine*, 10 May, 1923, Vol 41, 1922-3, p.340.

"SCIENCE GREATS"

(*To the Editor of the* OXFORD MAGAZINE)

SIR,

Mr. Atkinson asks me to elaborate my statement that philosophy and science are different forms of thought and involve different techniques. A complete explanation would require a system of logic, but, if you will allow me the necessary space, I will try to state my meaning in a few words. I intended to imply that all the sciences exhibited in various ways one form of thought, and shared with modifications one technique; while philosophy was a different form of thought with a different technique, superficially similar in that science and philosophy both use the verbal form of the universal proposition, but profoundly dissimilar in the meaning that they attach to this verbal form and the process by which the meaning is reached. To say that science and philosophy are the same thing because they both *generalise* is, to my mind, as serious an equivocation as to say that fiction and history are the same thing because they both *narrate*.

Scientific thinking is (to use terms which are well established in modern logic) abstract thinking, and leads to the affirmation of an abstract universal: philosophical thinking is concrete thinking, and leads to a concrete universal. The process of selecting phenomena, framing generalisations which are "unwarrantable logically," and finally testing or verifying these generalisations – I quote Mr. Atkinson's account of scientific procedure – does not take place in philosophy at all. It is peculiar to science, and is the mark of the abstractness of scientific thought. The scientist treats a phenomenon as a case of a law, an example of a type, and ignores everything in it which does not belong to it in this capacity. The philosopher, at the risk of "biting off more than he can chew," refuses to simplify his task by this preliminary abstraction, but insists on seeing the object in its entirety or not at all. Hence, as has been generally recognised ever since the time of Plato, science is based on hypotheses or assumptions, and in any science there are certain assumptions which the scientist as such does not allow himself to question. This, in spite of Newton's "*hypotheses non fingo*," is the view of science generally accepted by both philosophers and scientists, and Mr. Atkinson implicitly adopts it in his first letter. But the business of philosophy is precisely to question all assumptions wherever it finds them. This too is a matter of general agreement. For Plato, philosophy is that which "destroys hypotheses," for Kant, in philosophy "anything like a hypothesis is contraband"; for Hegel, philosophy has "the singular duty of justifying its own starting-point," and so on. These radically divergent attitudes towards the question of hypotheses lead to a profound difference in the methods and structure of science and philosophy respectively. All the sciences work in one way, and are therefore connected by the possession of common methods and principles, and thus find, as Mr. Atkinson says, little difficulty in exchanging problems. For they all agree in making abstractions, and only differ in making different abstractions. A scientist is therefore apt to approach philosophy by assuming that it too makes a specific abstraction, or, as Mr. Atkinson puts it, has a specific "field." But philosophy makes no abstraction, has in that sense of the word no field: it is the attempt to overcome abstraction, to avoid the arbitrary cutting-up of reality into compartments.

Returning now to the original question, a problem raised by a physicist is philosophical only if it implies that the physicist is becoming critical not merely of the assumptions to which he has been accustomed, but of all assumptions whatever. The problem raised by Relativity which is so often taken for a philosophical problem concerns the proposed substitution of one set of assumptions for another. This is not a matter in which philosophers as such can very well help.

R. G. COLLINGWOOD

Pembroke College

[*Oxford Magazine*, May 10, 1923, p.340]

Review

by

SUSAN DANIEL

The Correspondence of R. G. Collingwood: An Illustrated Guide, by Peter Johnson. Swansea, Wales: The R. G. Collingwood Society, 1998, xvi + pp. 116.

While Collingwood made it clear that he did not want his private correspondence to be published a great deal of it is nonetheless now available to interested readers in the Bodleian Library, Oxford. In addition to these deposits, other letters are dispersed in a variety of locations – the hands of private individuals, other university libraries, and elsewhere – creating a bibliographical need for a guide to the correspondence. This volume is intended by Johnson to provide that guidance to scholars making it possible for them to locate the correspondence which may be relevant to their work.

The volume includes reference to over 360 letters and is organized alphabetically by the name of the person to whom the letters were written. The correspondents include many notable figures including Croce, de Ruggiero, Prichard, Ryle and Knox. Each entry lists the name of the correspondent, the date the letter was written, the current location of the letter, and a brief synopsis only of that portion of the content of the letter Johnson believes relevant to an understanding of Collingwood's work in philosophy and archaeology. He also includes biographical information about each correspondent and, in some cases, locates where Collingwood mentions them in his published work.

Johnson makes it clear in the introduction of his volume that while he believes the correspondence contains information important to the clarification of Collingwood's thought, and to the accurate dating of the composition of his published work, he also believes that Collingwood's fervent wish for privacy should be respected. As a result, Johnson nicely fulfills the bibliographic need of a guide to the correspondence while avoiding undue intrusion.

Adding to the interest of the volume is Johnson's own introduction where an insightful and useful overview of the correspondence is provided. Also of interest and making the volume unique indeed are a number of illustrations. These include a photograph of Collingwood as a fellow at Pembroke College, a self-portrait of W. G. Collingwood, a photograph of Barbara Crystal Collingwood – Collingwood's sister, Collingwood's sketches of Croce, a photograph taken of F. G. Simpson by Collingwood, and several others. The volume also contains a facsimile of a letter from R. G. Collingwood to V. E. Nash-Williams.

Obituary

by

MARTIN SHEPPARD

VERA COLLINGWOOD

Vera Collingwood was an outstanding photographer who made a distinctive contribution to British life. She was also a remarkable case of someone embarking late on a successful new career.

She was born Vera Fratoni in 1920, to a modest family from Lugnano, near Orvieto in Umbria, although she was brought up in Abruzzo, where her father served as an officer in the Carabinieri. Her brother became one of the most senior generals in the Italian army and was also a talented musician.

Vera went to university in Rome to study philosophy, where she was a brilliant student. During the German occupation of Italy, she carried letters for the Resistance. She also dived for the university. As a protégée of the philosophers Benedetto Croce and Guido de Ruggiero, she was introduced to Bill Collingwood, who had translated Croce into English. Bill was also the grandson of W. G. Collingwood, Ruskin's literary executor and first biographer. They married in Rome in 1947.

Bill had a highly successful career in British Airways and for almost 30 years Vera devoted herself to supporting her husband and to bringing up her son, while also pursuing her many interests, which included teaching evening classes at the City Lit. The tragedy of his early death in 1975 determined her to turn one of her interests into a career, to break out of the depression his death caused her. Although she had taken photographs to go with her lectures on Italian life, literature and history, she only took up photography seriously in her fifties.

Using simple, sometimes second-hand, equipment she became an outstanding photographer, with a good technical knowledge of her subject. She offered her services, free of charge other than expenses, to the National Trust, which had the sense to recognise her talent. For more than 20 years she produced a flow of high-quality work, setting herself rigorous standards.

Her meticulous and painstaking record, in black and white as well as in colour, of many National Trust and other houses, including Chastleton, Chiswick House, Cliveden, Fenton House, Hughenden, Osterley and Stowe, is a distinctive contribution to the historical building record. She had an ability to capture the essence of houses and gardens, using her natural eye for composition. Her sympathy for what she was photographing often enabled her to see a house or garden in a fresh perspective. Wherever she worked, her gift for friendship and generosity of spirit made her friends.

Her work proved highly popular and has been used not only in guidebooks, postcards, calendars but also to illustrate numerous books. An early one was *London Cemeteries* by Hugh Meller (1981). Late examples were *Mrs Coade's Stone* by Alison Kelly (1990), and *Country House Brewing in England* by Pamela Sambrook (1996), for which she photographed what remains of the private brewhouses that used to be a feature of the majority of country houses. Her passionate interest in gardens was reflected in the photographs she took for an exhibition on Fenton House garden in Hampstead, north London, where her pictures were paired with a set taken in the late 19th century.

Vera came to England, speaking little English, in 1947. She first lived in St Peter's Square, Hammersmith, which at that time housed a cosmopolitan array of artists and writers, including Julian Trevelyan and his wife Mary Fedden, A. P. Herbert, and Vera's near neighbour Alec Guinness, with whom she was soon very much at home. The son of other neighbours was William Bennett, the celebrated flautist, who became a close friend. In 1967 she moved to Strand on the Green, overlooking the Thames near Kew Bridge to a small 17th-century house that was the perfect setting for entertainment.

Hospitality to people of all ages was natural to Bill and Vera Collingwood. Vera was a wonderful cook who above all relished good ingredients cooked in the simplest way. She collaborated with Anna del Conte on her cookery books, which did much to popularise Italian cooking in Britain. After Bill's death Vera combined her new career with unfailing, even increased, hospitality to young and old alike. The power and warmth of her character allowed her to form friendships with a great variety of people, taking an interest in them and finding common ground. Her friendships were by no means restricted to people of her own age and class. She had an exceptional ability to encourage the young and diffident, treating them exactly as she would have treated the eminent.

Vera Collingwood had high standards in all she did. Her taste was impeccable. She was highly civilised herself and admired civilised people having a particularly high regard for those she saw (perhaps through rose-coloured glasses) as exemplifying a characteristic English mixture of intelligence and intellectual honesty. She loved literature, both English and Italian, and history, particularly Gibbon, whom she read late into the night and whose anti-clerical outlook she shared to the full. She was a good artist, whose paintings (mostly landscapes) were as idiosyncratic as her English. She had no television but was a passionate playgoer with an unerring taste for the unusual and the dramatic.

She also loved a debate. Vera was a true liberal by background and by temperament, something reinforced by her experiences under Fascism in Italy. She loved to think for herself and to express herself and for others to do the same. She liked to see two or more sides to a question. If people agreed with her she was quite capable of disagreeing with herself and her own previous opinion, both for the fun of it and to see where the argument would lead. This did not mean that her values and belief in high standards changed but that she was an original: she preferred to be with the minority. In politics, she was a Labour supporter (to the surprise of some of her neighbours). She was also from the earliest beginnings of moves towards a united Europe after the war, a committed pro-European.

Despite living in England for over 50 years, Vera always spoke her own inimitable and ever-surprising dialect of "improved" English, with its own unique vigour. Her friends treasured her latest coinages, which combined a mangling of grammar or idiom ("what are the news?" or I go upstair and comb my head") and a gift for mispronunciation ("sphincters" for "spinsters" and "dragoons" for "dragons"). While she became in some ways very English, she never stopped being Italian and above all never stopped being herself.

She was a true Italian mother in her devotion to her only son Robert. She was also immensely proud of her grandchildren, Elizabeth and Patrick, to whom she was an original and practical and hard-working grandmother, whether encouraging their drawing and writing or flying out to Prague (where Robert Collingwood has been working as a leading architect in the restoration of the city) with supplies of the baked beans and Jaffa cakes they had requested. Her reaction to her final illness was typically magnificent: totally unsentimental and unselfpitying.

Reprinted by permission from *The Independent* Obituaries, 19 September 1998.

LIFE MEMBERS OF THE
COLLINGWOOD SOCIETY

Dr Michael Beaney, David Blatchford, Professor David Boucher, Professor George Boyce, Dr Jonathan Bradbury, Professor R. Bradley, Lord Bragg, Rt. Hon. Lord Callaghan, Professor O. Caraiani, Anna Castriota, Mrs Mary Clapinson, Mr Bruce Coffin, Professor Janet Coleman, Rev. Jeremy Collingwood, Professor Conal Condren, Dr James Connelly, Dr Susan Daniel, Professor William Debbins, Mr Robin Denniston, Professor William Dray, Professor John Dunn, Professor David Eastwood, Dr Albert Fell, Professor Joe Femia, Mr Peter Foden, Rt. Hon. Michael Foot, Dr Elizabeth Frazer, Professor Frank Gilliard, Miss Janet Gnosspelius, Professor Leon Goldstein, David A. Griffiths, Dr Margit Hurup Grove, Professor Knud Haakonssen, Dr Bruce Haddock, Professor H. S. Harris, Dr Stein Helgeby, Professor Michael Hinz, Mr Sinclair Hood, John Horton, Dr John Hospers, Dr Marnie Hughes-Warrington, Sue Irving, Professor Wendy James, Professor Jeremy Jennings, Dr Douglas Johnson, Dr Peter Johnson, Susie Johnston, Professor William Johnston, Dr Norman Jones, Dr Maurice Keens-Soper, Professor Donald Kelley, Dr Paul Kelly, Professor Kenneth Ketner, Professor Michael Krausz, Julian Lethbridge, Peter Lewis, George Livadas, Florin Lobont, Professor Alasdair MacIntyre, Dr Maria Markoczy, Professor Rex Martin, Neville Masterman, Wayne Mastin, Donald Matthews, Dr C. Behan McCullagh, Dr Graham McFee, Ken McIntyre, Hugh McLean, Iain Miller, Professor Kenneth Minogue, Dr Ivan Molloy, Timothy Morgan, Professor Myra Moss, Professor Terry Nardin, Professor Jay Newman, Peter Nicholson, Dr Francis O'Gorman, Dr Robert Orr, Elizabeth Pakis, Professor Carole Pateman, Roy Pateman, Dr Zbigniew Pelczynski, Dr Rik Peters, Lord Professor Raymond Plant, Professor Clementina Gily Reda, Dr Angela Requate, Dr Dwaine Richins, William Rieckmann, Peri Roberts, Professor Lionel Rubinoff, Professor Alan Ryan, Mrs Brigit Sanders, Herman Simissen, Dr Grace Simpson, Professor Quentin Skinner, Mrs Teresa Smith, Professor Robert Stevens, Guy Stock, Peter Strong, Dr Hidemi Suganami, Sherwood Sugden, Dr Peter Sutch, Professor Donald S. Taylor, Professor Richard Taylor, Leo Ten Hag, Rt. Hon. The Baroness Thatcher, Dr Julian Thomas, Dr Martyn P. Thompson, Professor Jan van der Dussen, Jeanne van der Stappen-Haeyvaert, Naomi van Loo, Professor Guido Vanheeswijck, Professor Donald Verene, Professor Andrew Vincent, Dr Kallistes Ware, Professor Lawrence Wilde, Professor Howard Williams, Andrew Wilson, Dr Adrian Wilson, Dr Ian Winchester, Professor David Wood, Dr Elizabeth Wright.

NEW LITERARY HISTORY

A Journal of Theory and Interpretation

RALPH COHEN, EDITOR

Prepayment is required.
Annual subscriptions:
$31.00, individuals;
$107.00, institutions.
Foreign postage:
$5.00, Canada & Mexico;
$11.50, outside North America.
Single-issue price:
$9.00, individuals;
$32.00, institutions.

Payment must be drawn on a U.S. bank in U.S. dollars or made by international money order. MD residents add 5% sales tax. For orders shipped to Canada add 7% GST (#124004946RT).

Send orders to: The Johns Hopkins University Press, P.O. Box 19966, Baltimore, MD 21211-0966,U.S.A.

To place an order using Visa or MasterCard, **call toll-free 1-800-548-1784, FAX** us at **(410) 516-6968,** or email to:
jlorder@jhupress.jhu.edu

New Literary History focuses on theory and interpretation—the reasons for literary change, the definitions of periods, and the evolution of styles, conventions, and genres. *NLH* has always resisted short-lived trends and subsuming ideologies. By delving into the theoretical basis of practical criticism, the journal reexamines the relation between past works and present critical and theoretical needs. A major international forum for scholarly interchange, *NLH* has brought into English many of today's foremost theorists whose works had never before been translated. Under Ralph Cohen's continuous editorship, *NLH* has become what he envisioned thiry years ago: "a journal that is a challenge to the profession of letters." Recognized by the Council of Editors of Learned Journals (CELJ) for publishing one of the Best Special Issues of 1996.

Published quarterly in February, May, August, and November.

J_h *Published by* THE JOHNS HOPKINS UNIVERSITY PRESS
www.press.jhu.edu/press/journals/nlh

EX2K